THE GIFT OF MUSIC & SONG

THE GIFT OF MUSIC & SONG

INTERVIEWS WITH JAMAICAN WOMEN WRITERS

JACQUELINE BISHOP

PEEPAL TREE

First published in 2021 by
Peepal Tree Press Ltd
17 King's Avenue
Leeds LS6 1QS
England

ISBN13: 97818452324768

Supported using public funding by
ARTS COUNCIL
ENGLAND

CONTENTS

ACKNOWLEDGEMENTS

The first thanks go to the writers interviewed in this book. There simply would be no book without your wide-ranging responses to to the questions. I thank Sharon Leach, the Bookends editor at the *Jamaica Observer*, for allowing for the publication of most of these interviews. Sharon, I acknowledge and thank you not only for making space for these interviews in Bookends but for editing and copy-editing these interviews TO EXCELLENCE. Loretta Collins Klobah, Timothy J. Reiss and Geoffrey Philp have together formed a core reading group of these interviews over the years. It feels good to make public something that has been private and intimate – our reading group and the avid interest of these three people in these interviews. I especially want to thank Loretta for sharing these interviews widely on social media, and to Geoffrey Philp for calling for publication of these interviews time and time again. Who knows if Jeremy Poynting of Peepal Tree Press saw Geoffrey's exhortations about publication, but I am so happy that Peepal Tree Press approached me about publishing them. Finally, I want to acknowledge and thank Marcia Douglas for volunteering to put together the "Ixora Chain" which forms the afterword of this book. Your enthusiasm, Marcia, encapsulates all the love, grit, determination and beauty that has gone into and resulted from the process of making this book.

This book is dedicated to Hazel Campbell, vibrant and alive in these interviews, but who, unfortunately, we lost prior to publication. The loss of Hazel highlights the necessity of doing this kind of work.

Thanks to the *Jamaica Observer* for permission to reprint:

"The Gift of Music and Song: An Interview with Hazel Campbell". *Bookends Magazine*. *The Jamaica Observer*. Kingston: Jamaica. July 12th, 2015.
"Explaining Ourselves to Ourselves: An Interview with Writer Marcia Douglas". *Bookends Magazine*. *The Jamaica Observer*. Kingston: Jamaica. July 19th, 2015.
"Yemoja sits on my head: An interview with Opal Palmer Adisa". *Bookends Magazine*. *The Jamaica Observer*. Kingston: Jamaica. April 12, 2015.
"Making the maximum impact while we are here: An interview with poet Keisha-Gaye Anderson". *Bookends Magazine*. *The Jamaica Observer*. Kingston: Jamaica. April 19th, 2015.
"'White Caribbean': An interview with biographer Michela Calderaro on the life and work of Jamaican poet Eliot Bliss". *Bookends Magazine*.

The Jamaica Observer, Kingston, Jamaica. April 26th, 2015.

"The blessing and burden of being a poet: An interview with Millicent AA Graham". *Bookends Magazine, The Jamaica Observer*, Kingston, Jamaica. May 3rd, 2015.

"Mountains, land, sea and sand: An interview with poet Tanya Shirley", *Bookends Magazine, The Jamaica Observer*, Kingston, Jamaica, August 9th and 16th, 2015.

"Journeying Towards Integration: Novelist Patricia Powell Tackles Healing in Her Most Recent Novel", *Bookends Magazine, The Jamaica Observer*, Kingston, Jamaica, August 23rd, 2015.

"Holding A Mirror Up To Society: An Interview with Sharon Leach", *Bookends Magazine, The Jamaica Observer*, Kingston, Jamaica. April 3rd, 2016.

"Writing Helps Me Maintain My Sanity: An Interview With Poet Ann-Margaret Lim", *Bookends Magazine, The Jamaica Observer*, Kingston, Jamaica, April 15th 2018.

"In Pamela Mordecai's Work Issues of Belonging and Identity Emerge", *Bookends Magazine, The Jamaica Observer*, Kingston, Jamaica, April 1 & 8th 2018.

"Novelist Jean D'Costa Believes in Feeding the Cultural Imagination", *Bookends Magazine, The Jamaica Observer*, Kingston, Jamaica, March 25th, 2018.

"Christine Craig Makes the Case for Inclusiveness", *Bookends Magazine, The Jamaica Observer*, Kingston, Jamaica, March 11th, 2018.

"Velma Pollard's tribute poems – intertextual dialogue between poets", *Bookends Magazine, The Jamaica Observer*, Kingston, Jamaica, March 4th, 2018.

"The Muse of Memory is the Muse of Poetry: An Interview with Poet Laureate Lorna Goodison", *Bookends Magazine, The Jamaica Observer*. Kingston, Jamaica, March 31, 2019.

"Kerry Young's Historical Novels Shed Light on a Vibrant Chinese Community in Jamaica", *The Jamaica Observer*, Kingston, Jamaica, March 31, 2019.

"Of Hearts Revealed: An Interview with Olive Senior", by Jacqueline Bishop & Dolace McLean appeared in *Calabash: A Journal of Caribbean Arts and Letters*, September 8, 2013, The Department of Spanish & Portuguese, New York University.

ONE NATION, MANY VOICES

ALL OUR JAMAICAS: A FOREWORD

INTERVIEWER: SHARON LEACH

SL: First things first, Jacqueline, I must say thanks for the commitment you have shown in conducting these interviews over the many years. What I want to know is this: when I asked you to do them, I was achingly aware that a newspaper in some metropolis would be able to commission you and financially compensate you for such a project. Why in heaven's name did you agree to do this remarkable public service for the *Observer*?

JB: I guess there are several answers and not only one answer to this question. To begin with, I think one of the things I am always engaged with is writing my way back to the Caribbean, to Jamaica, and doing these interviews helps me to do just that. You see, one of the main things that these interviews have in common is all our engagements with the island of Jamaica, no matter where we are writing from. I am really fascinated to see how so many writers see this one place, even when we are spread out all over the world. So that is one reason to do this. A second reason, of course, is to engage with a Jamaican audience. I guess as someone who has lived longer outside Jamaica than I have lived on the island, I don't want the two Jamaicas that exist for me to diverge too sharply: the Jamaica that I have in my head and the Jamaica that is there today. These interviews help me to keep the two (and more) Jamaicas in place. But more than that, I love the feeling that the work I do is appreciated, and you and the audience for these Bookends interviews have always let me know that these interviews were appreciated, and I was so happy about that. So that is another incentive. There is something to be said, too, for building an archive of interviews within Jamaica instead of outside the region. Finally, to be honest about it, I do not know too many publications here in the United States that would dedicate the kind of space to the far-reaching, wide-ranging interviews that Bookends does. You oftentimes dedicate the entire magazine to an interview. So those are some of the reasons why I do this.

SL: I find that you have grown into a formidable interviewer, dare I suggest one of the preeminent ones from the region. A Jacqueline Bishop interview, these days, has a certain cachet. What is it about the genre that you obviously love so much?

JB: My love of interviewing grows out of a love of reading and listening to a good interview and my training as well as an oral historian, which I did years back at Columbia University's famed Oral History Program. I think when I am interviewing a writer I am always trying to understand a couple of things: to understand what went into the making of a body of work (and I always try to limit my interviews to a few pieces of work), even though, if you notice, I almost never interview someone who, as a writer, has published only one work. I have been around long enough to see so many people flame out so easily that I wait oftentimes to see what is going on first. That said, in an interview, I am trying to engage with and understand something about a work that I have in front of me. Consequently, I give the work a very close reading to come up with my questions. Next, I am trying to understanding something about the creator of that work and what they might be trying to say with this work. As a writer and visual artist myself, I know that a work can take you to all sorts of strange and surprising places, and it is those places that I am trying to get to in an interview and why I love the genre so much. Because it reveals the work and its creator.

SL: Following up on that question, I've read lots of interviews before, but there's a quality about how you deal with your subjects that makes them so accessible, so human, and that seems to be the point of divergence from other interviews that range from pedestrian to unnecessarily academic. What in your opinion are the hallmarks of a great interview?

JB: I think it is all about what you see as the role of the interview, the purpose and audience for which you are conducting the interview. I see the role of the interview as both illuminating the author's thoughts and shedding light on the author's work. Saying that does not mean that this is an easy process, because some authors are resistant, sometimes unnecessarily so, and then there are a very few interviewees, a very few that I have met, who simply do not want to engage with the ideas in their work. But, overall, a great interview gives us insight into the author and the work that they have created. Now we need to pay careful attention here, because so many interlocutors see the interview as their chance to call attention to themselves. Yes, as I tell the students in my oral history class, an interview IS a conversation, but it is one in which you are trying to get the person you have chosen to interview to share THEIR ideas. If they ask you your opinion, I tell the students, feel free to go ahead and share your opinion; this is a conversation after all. But your interview is really in trouble if there is more of you in it than the person you are purporting to interview.

The other thing that I would say is this: An interview needs to adhere to all the forms of storytelling like a poem, a song, or anything else. There has to be a narrative arc in an interview. A clear beginning, middle, and an end, which people – ordinary people – can follow. Sometimes I am reading an interview and I get confused in it. I am reading one right now. Don't know if I am up or down. No. You need a clear narrative arc. Finally, I want to say something about the language used in an interview. On the one hand, you cannot talk down to your subject, as if they are a simpleton or something. The very pedestrian language you are talking about and which often comes with the very pedestrian questions implicit in the questioning. What is your favourite colour? That kind of thing. I cannot begin to tell you how many times the women here have said about my interview questions, *My goodness, I feel like this is the first time someone has taken me and my writing seriously*. The other end of this is unnecessarily complex questions, what you call "academic" questions, which, in the final analysis, are really about the interviewer and their own anxieties. Anyway, I think I was lucky that my interviews were going to be published in a newspaper, and going to be read by a large swath of the public. That meant that I had to strike a balance: neither talking down to my subjects (and their audience) nor making things unnecessarily complex.

SL: You're the definition of a multi-hyphenate. You're a writer, a visual artist and academic. You seem able to effectively straddle the various genres, but, I'm wondering, is there a favourite? I have always told you your productivity is enviable. How do you find time to evenly distribute your time between your various interests?

JB: I often say that if someone were to wake me up at night and shake me loose, that poet would fall out first, followed by writer, and then visual artist, but I think those are only the art forms that I have practised longer and am consequently more comfortable in. At this point, there are no favourites, though some are more demanding than others. It is still the case that I can sit down at the computer and decide to write a fictional piece, and pretty much do it; while a poem is still something that I have to wait for. She shows up in her good time, Poetry, but the good thing is, when she does show up, Miss Poetry, she tends to hang around for a while so I never just get one poem, but several all at once; a bouquet. With the visual arts, I have to plan for that, or work through something, to figure out where I am going. That, incidentally, is something that all my art forms have in common: I never know from start to finish where they will end up. Time is often a consideration, and so I always relish the long school holidays, particularly the summer holidays, in getting things done. Interestingly enough, while I often devote large swaths of time to one project – I can get fixated on something for days or weeks at a time – I think it serves my interest to have multiple interests and preoccupations because I am fastidious and believe I would pick and pick one thing to death. So it is good to have several projects and things to move around.

SL: Growing up, did you envisage a career path in letters? If so, why? If not, what did you see yourself becoming?

JB: No, I did not envision a career at all in letters. Poetry, in fact, was going to be this thing that took care of me and would fill up these notebooks and it would be all mine. I was going to be a medical doctor… my big important and "serious" job in the world. Mind you, I could not do the sciences, and, frankly, had little to no interest in them. But I was going to be a medical doctor. You'd be surprised how long I carried on that charade. I just spent a day at the beach with a friend of mine from high school, and we got to talking about why our high school, which is one of the more prominent Catholic girls' schools in Kingston, has not produced as many writers and visual artists as, say, St. Hugh's High School (where I know you went to school, Sharon) did. One of the things that really stands out in these interviews is how many writers St. Hugh's produced! I think the answer to why St. Hugh's produced so many fine women writers, yourself among them, Sharon, with Lorna Goodison, Jean D'Costa and several others, is that fine library that Jean talks about in her interview and the emphasis placed on creative writing there.

But back to my friend and our day at the beach. As we were sitting and chatting in Far Rockaway, she told me how she was discouraged from becoming a teacher by the guidance counsellor, then discouraged from her second choice of career, which was a veterinarian; and then she said, OK, then, I want to be a medical doctor, and that pleased the guidance counsellor enormously and she was tracked as such. In my case, I was pushed to be a medical doctor and kept doing advanced maths, physics, chemistry and all sorts of things that I failed miserably at. Honestly, I should have been taking literature, art, needlework, all the things I loved. Plus, all those things would have been far more beneficial to my life these days, and I would have felt less like a failure. If you look at the school where I went to, Holy Childhood High School, we have been very good, excellent actually, in turning out women in the medical profession, women in business, law and education. We truly excel in those areas. But much less so in the arts, and I think it is where the focus and the emphasis is put. At Holy Childhood, at least when I was there several decades ago, those who ran the school then believed in you so much, and wanted so much for you and from you, that they made sure to let you know, arts and letters, and all the things considered traditionally "female", were not going to limit you in any way shape or form. So much so that they weren't even going to prepare you for any such thing in the first place. I think in this book of interviews, only Marcia Douglas and I, as writers, actually went to and graduated from Holy Childhood High.

SL: You were born in Jamaica. What was a young Jacqueline Bishop's childhood in Jamaica like?

JB: I was born in Jamaica and lived on the island until my late teenage years. What stands out about my life on the island is some sharp contrasts and contradictions. Since we were renters, my family moved around a lot. As a child, I did not see much of my mother at all and was raised in large part by my grandmother. I have whole stretches of my life where I cannot recall my mother at all, but can always recall my grandmother. We lived in rented houses in many of the places considered garrison areas these days, and it was me, my grandmother, my older brother, and my aunts and uncles. My mother was a presence that would flit in and out. She, my mother, lived "uptown" and had another family, with my younger brother and his father. My father was a postman based at the Cross Roads Post Office and he would come and visit me when we lived on Penrith Road and he would always throw me up in the air and catch me. My father delighted in me and I delighted in him. The few times I saw her, I thought my mother was the most beautiful woman in the world because she was very dark-skinned and had a huge "souls" Afro.

My father, on the other hand, I still think of as the most handsome man, ever. Everyone falls in love with my father. My grandmother loved him to her dying day. Nights when my grandmother was washing I would lean into her side as she washed, and I believed myself to be one with my grandmother. In fact, my grandmother had two daughters who lived with us – Milva, who was slightly older than me, and Venice, who was a year or so younger than me – and I remember plotting how to get rid of these two girls so I could have my grandmother all to myself!

We lived for a long time, all of us, in an apartment on Penrith Road, where there was a school called Grantham College. Lord, the escapades that we children had at that place! But certain things come to mind so strongly. There was a tree that had blossoms that Venice and I would pick and comb the hair of those blossoms (the woman's tongue tree); there was a large Lignum Vitae tree in that yard; and all around there seemed to be bush land. Large guinep and mango trees, and such. One time my brother, who seemed afraid of absolutely nothing in life, climbed the large guinep tree and the branch broke and he fell to the ground and was knocked unconscious. My grandmother ran around with him, sick with worry. I remember two white rabbits that we somehow had as pets, and a cherry tree in the neighbours' yard that was full of ripe, red cherries, and I let my infernal brother talk me into going over the barbed-wire fence to pick de people's cherries. De Chinese people next door where the cherry tree was based had large dogs and my brother started saying, de people coming, de dogs coming, and in hurrying to get back through the barbed-wire fence I tore up my leg and started crying. My older aunt Milva and my brother of course begged me to stop my crying and not say anything to Granny, but they were worried about the rust on the fence, and knew they had to do something about my leg. The solution they came up with was to open up and throw salt into the wound. Of course, Granny found out about the escapade, what with all the cow-bawling! Then there was the time my brother tricked me into eating bird peppers, saying that they were so pretty they must be sweet, and Granny chased him around the house to give him a good whipping! And on and on.

I remember going to several basic schools before I started out at John Mills All-Age School, and I must say I loved John Mills All-Age. I went there up until grade four or five when, on my first try, I sat and passed the Common Entrance examination for Holy Childhood High School. Two things stand out for me about John Mills: in the middle of the school yard, there were two elaborate gardens. One, a flower garden and the other a vegetable garden where I saw eggplants being grown for the first time. No one ate the big purple things, but they always appeared and seemed rather mysterious to me. There were jungle gyms and swings at that school, and the only thing I hated about John Mills were the bathrooms which were always filthy. I was very, very bright at John Mills. Very bright. Always did well in school there. Two teachers, Mrs. Brown and Mrs. Trowers, stand out in my mind. Mrs. Brown in particular, because I would finish reading all my school books so early that she would always give me additional books to read. I was ahead of everyone else. If I grew up to become a teacher, it is in large part because of those two women.

SL: You've lived most of your life in the United States, but you still think of yourself as Jamaican. Correct? Indeed, your writing, and even your painting, tends to reflect what I think is a sort of emotional and psychological conundrum about where, exactly, home is for you. The Italian critic Michela Calderaro noted of your recent *By the Rivers of Babylon* exhibition that your works "reflect the dichotomy of artists who live at a distance, both physical and psychological, from their birthplace". Would you say that you are any closer to resolving that tension?

JB: Yes and no. I have lived long enough in New York that New York feels like home to me. My apartment where I have lived forever in Harlem is certainly home. I love it, and hate to be away from it. It is where I am always trying to get back to – even from Jamaica these days, because everything I want is there including my much-beloved cat, Dali. But you and I are close friends, Sharon, and when I talk to you – or my father – and you are in Jamaica, and I am away from Jamaica, I get nostalgic. The different fruit seasons are particularly hard on me. These days I find myself wondering if my nostalgia would be lessened if I lived somewhere like Florida, where so much of the fruits and the flowers and the landscape are the same as in Jamaica. I am forever and always, it seems, plotting my return to Jamaica, even though when I am there, there is so much colour/ class/ racial politics to drive me insane. And there are simple day-to-day inconveniences that I cannot see myself living with on a daily basis. A friend of mine, who is not exactly poor, was telling me about the recent shortage of medications for chemotherapy and for high blood pressure and diabetes on the island. My father, who lived through that unforgettable 1980 general election, finds the crime and murder rate on the island incomprehensible these days, and only escalating. To me, the level of crime and insecurity on the island is a public health crisis. I don't know if I can take on all of that right now, by moving back "home". So I will continue in my tenuous state.

SL: Of that same exhibition, the artist Margaret Evangeline had this to say: "Bishop's performative-writing paintings are many things, among them luminous visual texts and personal reflections, especially about exile and memory (collective and personal), but they are, above all, political paintings on different levels." Some artists shirk from that 'political' tag. Do you think of yourself as an artist, and for that matter, a writer, who is political? Is it possible to be an artist who isn't?

JB: I think the underlying premise of your question is that it is not possible to NOT be a political writer and with this I agree. I see myself as a political writer. Politics imbues everything we do. Those moments when we say that we are not being political are when, I think, we are at our most political. I do think, though, that it is also true that our works, our creative works, can almost become didactic in their politics and the work can become more about the politics than about the craft, so I think we have to watch out for that, too. It is a delicate dance. Perhaps the politics functions best in a work when it emerges *within* the work than when it is foisted *upon* the work. What do I mean by this? It seems fashionable these days to say, *I write the books I want to read.* But I much prefer saying, *I write the books that choose me to bring them into the world.* The ones where the characters are, like, *Hey, you, I choose you to bring me into the world.* And I'm oftentimes, like, *Go away, I want to sleep! I want to paint! I have other things to do!* And the character is sitting on the bed, studying her nails, and looking back at me from time to time, and you know that no one is going to bed tonight, until you start listening to what this woman has to say. And still another way to look at it is this: In one of my workshops with Paule Marshall when I was in grad school, we were workshopping a story, and after we had all spoken, Marshall said, "But what about this fish tank in the story?" And we all were, like, the fish tank? Who cares about the fish tank? And she said, "Well, look at the fish tank and, when the man puts his hand in the fish tank to catch the fish, how big and distorted his hand gets. Isn't it like the relationship this woman has found herself in with this man! Those big distorted hands in that fish tank? I think it's all about the fish tank!" And suddenly we all saw it. The fish tank was the main image, the political image, in the story, but not even the writer had seen it. The politics was there, imbued within an image in the story, but it was organic to the story instead of foisted into the story.

SL: I know this will be difficult, but I have to ask anyway. One of the hugest influences on your life was your talismanic grandmother, who died about three years ago. Anyone who has read your work knows she was the great love of your life. Tell me, what has the adjustment been like, living and working in a space where your beloved granny isn't there physically and psychologically to inspire and motivate you in your various mediums of endeavour?

JB: Why you want to make me cry, Sharon Leach? Why you want to do this to me? Have me talk about my grandmother? Losing my grandmother is by far the hardest thing that I have ever gone through in my life thus far. You know, a part of me still does not believe it. That she is gone. Not my grandmother! She is/was so larger than life for me. I get called on the fact, all the time, that I still speak of her in the present tense, and I still jump up out of my sleep at night thinking someone is coming to tell me that my grandmother has died. The way I describe my grandmother is that she was a woman who never saw a mountain she could not climb. My grandmother was a woman who would strip herself naked in a fight. She would give me the most amazing straightforward advice. I guess the long and short of the answer to your question is that I don't believe she is gone. That is, of course, until I go to Nonsuch and I get to her house and it is empty. Or I have to drive past the cemetery, and I turn my head and look the other way, because the whole thing is too unbearable. I interviewed her before she died, so I have her voice recorded, but I just find it really hard to believe such a presence can ever be stilled.

SL: You're a beloved professor, a master interlocutor, a formidable writer; you seem to have it all. What frontier is left for you to cross now? Why does teaching thrill you so much?

JB: Of course, I can think of all the ways I do not have it all. But why bore the reader with that? I doubt there's anyone who ever feels that they have it all. Money in the bank would certainly help, that's for sure! I have a dream of seeing some of my short stories made into films. That is certainly a frontier, a dream of mine. Regarding the question about teaching, I think what I love so much about teaching is how much you get to engage, over and over again, and touch the future. That is perhaps the best part about teaching. I teach undergraduates, who are often teenagers and young people coming from all parts of the world, and I think, oh wow, I get to see what the future will look like in ten or fifteen years. That really excites and thrills me. Another thing that really thrills me about teaching is how much I learn from my students. I think teaching is a two-way street: you learn at least as much from your students as your students learn from you. I have been teaching at NYU for decades now, and I am lucky in so far as I have students literally coming from all parts of the world to study at NYU, and so I get to see and understand and glean, if imperfectly, some of the forces at play in different parts of the world.

SL: Why did you choose to use the framing of "Creating a Cultural Imagination"; "Explaining Ourselves to Ourselves" and "Writing a New Jamaican Story" that you used in putting together this book of interviews?

JB: I think the framing came from the women in the book and the interviews themselves much more so than they came from me. I think, more than anything else, I was just lucky enough to spot the framing among the interviews. While the framing device did help in organising the interviews – in so far as I think that where I placed the women is how I see them operating within their writing – the borders among the framing devices are quite porous, and, in fact, what I first did in organising the book was to arrange women based on when they started publishing. The device of arranging interviews based on when the authors started publishing fell, oftentimes, in line with the themes that came up in the interviews, which again, I emphasise, is porous. But what I started to notice, as well, is that some interviews just seemed to be in conversation with other interviews. For example, based on when she started publishing, Opal Palmer Adisa, should be in the section "Creating a Cultural Imagination", but what her interview was largely about – speaking clearly and directly about menstruation and female sexuality – was more in keeping with the work of Tanya Shirley and your work, Sharon Leach, and so she ended up in the section "Writing A New Jamaican Story". Similarly, the ways in which Marcia Douglas utilises non-linear narrative in her work, I could see her in the section on "Writing a New Jamaican Story", but in her interview, she spoke so powerfully about the Asian women's experience that her interview fed right into Ann-Margaret Lim's interview, so I ended up placing them next to each other. Similarly, Kerry Young's interview could be placed in the section "Writing A New Jamaican Story", but because of her detailed explorations of the Chinese-Jamaican story, I felt it spoke quite well to issues in Ann-Margaret Lim's and Marcia Douglas's interview and so it was placed in the section "Explaining Ourselves to Ourselves." More than anything, I placed the interviews in order of how they seemed to be speaking to each other. So, the sections of this book are very porous, questionable and tenuous.

SL: Why the focus on female Jamaican writers?

JB: Well, why not the focus on Jamaican female writers? Why not hear what we/they have to say? Especially in the age of #MeToo. Though I have been conducting these interviews long before the #MeToo stories started coming out. I think oftentimes people forget how submerged women's voices actually are in Caribbean literature. If we go back to the so-called "Golden Age" of Caribbean literature it is almost all male, and we seem now to be in another age where the main voices given space in Caribbean and Jamaican literature are male voices. There are complicated reasons for this, but they all in one way or another revolve around sexism and misogyny and the undermining of female voices and female creativity, and oftentimes other women are complicit in this. Class, as well, plays a powerful role in this. What women produce/ed is oftentimes more easily discarded and seen as "less than". In addition, a man and a woman can produce the exact same thing or a woman can produce this thing and it is overlooked and a man takes it, runs with it and wins a gazillion awards and is celebrated. Of course, there are enthusiasms and outbursts, where attention, and particularly lip-service, is paid to women's creativity but it never seems to be in any sustained way. The serious producers, it seems to always be asserted, are the male producers. So much needs to be deconstructed and looked at. When will women's writing and women's work and women's worth be "serious" enough? "Hard-hitting" and "enduring" enough? As much as those new masculinist traditions of today themselves are rife with anxieties! In this regard, the interviews of Christine Craig and the biographer of Eliot Bliss, Michela Calderaro, speak very eloquently to these questions. As Craig points out in her interview, so many men are quick to give empty lip service, but not much more, to women writers. Calderaro unpacks the various ways that Bliss was thwarted, over and over again, in seeking to get published and how she died leaving behind boxes and boxes of unpublished work. I am not so sure it is that much different for many Jamaican, and other Caribbean women writers today, than it was for Eliot Bliss, back when she was writing, so that is why the focus on female Jamaican writers.

SL: Where would you say that Jamaican writing is moving to these days? What were some of the interesting things and takeaways you found out in doing these interviews?

JB: Taking the second question first, I was surprised that Jamaica had an openly lesbian writer born on the island in 1903 and that she was white creole and that she wrote and published and lived her life fully as a lesbian. That was absolutely stunning to me. She knew Jean Rhys and influenced Rhys's *Wide Sargasso Sea*. That is just a big W.O.W! Welcome home and welcome to your tribe and to this book, Eliot Bliss. Thank you, Michela Calderaro, for doing so much in returning her to us. I hope there will be reprintings of *Luminous Isle*, *Saraband*, and all the other works that Michela found. I hope that Michela's biography of Bliss, which I had a chance to read in manuscript form and which is totally amazing, will, as well, find a publisher.

Sometimes small things open up into larger moments. For example, there was a small food store when I lived in the Bronx that had a section that sold Caribbean literature, and in this section I found books by Hazel Campbell, which I bought. I remember buying, for example, *Tillie Bummie & Other Stories* for my younger sister who at the time was a little chubby. Years later, I met Hazel Campbell and I was a little overwhelmed, because Hazel had lived so long in my mind as a writer. These days, I would say Hazel and I are friends and I adore that woman. Still, in her interview, it was surprising to know how much she loved music and song.

I think where I see Jamaican literature moving, as expressed in these interviews, is deeper and deeper engagement with various aspects of Jamaican history and culture. The women are staking out moments and places in Jamaican history and they are really examining those moments and those places quite forcefully. The interviews by the Jamaican women in the first part of the book, along with that of Pamela Mordecai are breathtaking in this regard. Pamela Mordecai, for example, rewriting atrocities in Thomas Thistlewood's diaries. Ann-Margaret Lim engaging with the Jamaican Tainos. Millicent Graham talking to the great Grandy Nanny. Keisha-Gaye Anderson advancing alternatives to Christianity about a very Christian country! And all along Olive Senior and Lorna Goodison have been making of Jamaican history and culture, a muse, and introducing us to all kinds of fascinating Jamaican characters and historical moments and cultural practices.

For the women mainly in the last section of the book, there is a fresh new engagement with the female body and with a more urban Jamaica. These are women who are listening to sound systems and who enjoy going to dancehalls. They enjoy the pleasures of the body. Indeed, some of Tanya Shirley's poems crack me up with laughter and outright self-identification. Tanya Shirley (like Opal Palmer Adisa and like you, Sharon Leach) is not at all afraid of sexual pleasure, and seems to relish it. Not in any kind of prurient or even self-conscious way, but as a fact of life. With you three, people live in apartments, some of these women are involved with other women's husbands, they are using public restrooms and reading what other women write on these restroom walls, they are identifying with what these women have to say, all the while praying for rain because the place is so hot and there is a shortage of water! In the case of Patricia Powell, they have completely changed their gender in their writing and assumed a male identity, and they have assumed the responsibility of male damage, due to sexual abuse, onto themselves in their writing. For her part, Shara McCallum unapologetically celebrates women and revels in Jamaican patwa. The scope is hopeful, boundary-breaking and breathtaking.

I will end by saying, as a writer myself, doing these interviews, has been such a rewarding experience. Totally fulfilling. These interviews are not at all the end or even the sum total of Jamaican women writing these days. I see this as but a selection of Jamaican women writers writing today. When her interview was published in Bookends, Velma Pollard sent me a note that said, Jacqueline, these interviews are all like an ixora chain following behind each other. Velma will never know how much she made me cry when I read what she said that day as I thought, yes, Velma, these interviews are individual blossoms in a great big bunch of ixora flowers. Now, all because of Velma Pollard's words, I will always see these interviews, each of them as individual chains in a great big bunch of ixora. I hope our readers will become part of our bright red ixora flowers.

FEEDING THE CULTURAL IMAGINATION

NOVELIST JEAN D'COSTA BELIEVES IN FEEDING THE CULTURAL IMAGINATION

Jean D'Costa is a Jamaican children's novelist, linguist, and professor emeritus. Her novels for children aged eleven to thirteen have been praised for their use of both Jamaican Creole and Standard English and have been well received in her home country and the Caribbean. Her two most popular novels, *Sprat Morrison* (1972) and *Escape to Last Man Peak* (1976), have been used in schools throughout Jamaica and the Caribbean region. For her outstanding contributions to children's literature and linguistics, D'Costa has won several accolades. She was awarded the Jamaica Reading Association's Children's Writers Award in 1976. She also attained The Hamilton College Gertrude Flesh Bristol award in 1984 and the Institute of Jamaica's Silver Musgrave Medal in 1994. There is also a literary award named in her honour in Jamaica and *Escape to Last Man Peak* has been optioned to be made into a movie.

❧

JB: Jean D'Costa, it feels particularly wonderful for me, since I read and absolutely loved your books as a student in high school, to have this chance to interview you. For this interview, I want to focus on your two novels for young adults, *Escape to Last Man Peak* and *Sprat Morrison*. But before I do, I want to find out something about the writer of these books: Can you tell us about your childhood?

JDC: I was born on Jan 13th, 1937, at 20 Carpenter Road, Half-Way-Tree (now Kingston 10), in my grandmother's vast four-poster bed: I was the last of three children for my schoolteacher parents. My aunt Lilla (Uncle Bob's wife) and my grandmother Mumah (Mrs George Creary) were in attendance. I arrived squalling and quarrelling. Uncle Bob, my dad's older brother, registered my birth: I was probably the sixth or seventh Creary baby born on Carpenter Road, and the last but one of some 25 grandchildren.

The small-farmer Crearys had moved to Kingston from Glengoffe in the St Catherine hills, in the 1920s; Uncle Bob, a sanitary inspector, and Aunt Lilla lived next door to Pupah and Mumah, who had a two-room cottage built by Pupah, a skilled carpenter/cabinetmaker. George Creary Sr died about two years before my time, but I have always felt close to him because every wooden thing in that cottage had been made by him: his work was exact, symmetrical, careful, and everyone remembered him as a kind and affectionate man.

I was not a wonderful baby: I cried and cried, ate very little, and visited doctors, but no one knew what was wrong.

My mother was an Anglican, so I was christened by Canon H.G. Lovell (Dad's friend) at St Andrew Parish church in March 1937, and not at the Methodist church in which my father, George Lemuel Creary, had been raised. My given names were Jean Constance, and my godmothers were Mrs Edith Dalton James, my mother's sister, and Mrs Espeut, Mamma's friend from Shortwood College days; my godfather was a nephew of Mrs James, because this christening marked a major reconciliation with Aunt Edith and the James family: "Jean was the olive branch," said my father in later years. He probably said it at the time, too.

By three months, I was stronger and less fretful, so Mamma took me home to Vaughansfield in St James, where Dad was principal of an elementary school run by the Anglican Church (and held in the church itself). My mother had taught there (1927-30), before she was married to Dad, so Vaughansfield has great importance in our family lore. They had returned there in December 1936 after four years in the rainy Saint Andrew hills, Mount James, where I was conceived and where I have always longed to live, so rich and romantic were the stories told me of the place we had come from, just before "my" time. There was no teachers' cottage at Vaughansfield, so my family lived in the old rectory up the hill from the church. My father got us out of that house in about December 1938, because he considered it too dangerous: fierce thunderstorms were common, and he feared a lightning strike.

My first and deepest memories are of Vaughansfield, a place where government roads ended and the Cockpit Country began. These memories have never left me, even though I have changed, and the place changed, so that going back there did not recreate those first and glorious times.

My memory is cinematic and sensory: I see scenes that are completely lifelike, and sometimes the memories include the feel of the air, the wind, the light, textures of walls, windows, the flooring under my feet and hands, water in a bathtub, washing my face, sheets and scratchy blankets in bed, and a few smells, like the jasmine bush and its perfume at night. I especially remember things out of reach: doorknobs, towels on racks, tables, desks, shelves. Everything was so fascinating but so high up and far away, hard to reach. So were people.

My first memory is of sitting on the floor in a pool of golden afternoon light, wearing only a cloth diaper, and noticing that something clear and crystalline was flowing out from me and streaming away down the floor. It was the same temperature as me. Miraculous! I worked out that this mystery came from inside me, but how? Why? I couldn't stand or walk, so I sat and admired, and wondered, until huge disapproving noises miles above my head stopped all thought, and a pair of hands as big as buckets picked me up. For years, I told no one about this memory, believing that everybody remembers such commonplace things! When I was in Kingston, aged about nine, I told Dad about it and he identified the house and the likely date (September 1937), and told me that very few people remember so far back in their lives.

I have other memories of crawling on the rectory verandah, going down its stone steps on hands and bottom, or of being pushed around on a tricycle by the Big Two (my sister Pansy and my brother Bobby), and not being able to reach things on tables, and studying big people's feet, shoes, stockings, socks, toes, skirts, trousers, and listening to these people make regulated noises above my head that they said were praying and Bible reading, quite different from just talking.

When we moved over to Mr Sinclair's house nearby (but lower down, safer), I could walk and run, but everything was still high over my head: the dining table, guinea grass down the hillside, most beds. I remember climbing over the rails of my crib bed one afternoon because I did not want to waste time sleeping when Life was going on. The floor was very far away, but I made it safely. Mamma was upset; Dad laughed.

Some vivid memories include Dad opening a newspaper full of huge black letters and saying, "They've gone and done it now." That was September 1939: WWII.

The smell of Vicks Vaporub recalls black rainy nights when our nurse-maid, Zenie, plastered it on my face to make me stop talking and go to sleep. And there was the two-day stay at MoBay hospital, never to be forgotten.

I loved the hills, roads, and fields of Vaughansfield, its changeable weather, the voices of people, the life around the school.

There are a great many vivid Vaughansfield memories: my suddenly refusing to sit beside my brother, because he had "whiteskin", avoiding him for a week, and then suddenly switching, and refusing to sit beside my sister's best friend, Patsy, because she was "black skin". I was not punished: instead everyone seemed to be avoiding me, which was worse. It was like an illness that I could not stop, and then it went away by itself. The remarks about colour went on around me all the time: "A who him? Him a white man or him a backra?" "She favour coolie royal."

"You come from my country?" This last from a Chinese shopkeeper to my sister. Unknown to our parents, we three used to introduce ourselves to strangers as "sister-brother-sister, same-father-same-mother", for people expected to account for our non-resemblances, and we did indeed have the same two parents, unlike many people we knew.

As for all the gossip, the duppy stories, the tales of disasters near and far, the rumours of war: all settled on me like dye into cloth. And stayed along with the choral voices singing in the school, the first church goings and prayer meetings, and voices calling by night from the hills, with drums.

We stayed at Vaughansfield until December 1940, when we moved to Somerton, St James. World War II had begun to affect our lives, first through news of disasters such as Dunkirk, and then in threats to Jamaica itself. Dad and my mother talked to us, explained things, told stories of all kinds, loved jokes, and made sure we understood whatever happened to us or around us.

In both places I was surrounded by talk and storytelling. I heard and re-heard accounts of my parents' and grandparents' lives, all kinds of family gossip and family history. These stories were so vivid that they became in some cases part of my memory, as if I were the little boy who ran all the way to the Chinese shop in January 1907, to find all the goods thrown on the floor, and everybody terrified of the earthquake. Some of my parents' childhood stories have entered my fiction as part of the characters' adventures.

I felt as if I had been alive since 1900!

The place also influenced me. Vaughansfield marked the end of government roads, and the beginning of trails into the Cockpit country. At Vaughansfield people talked about Maroons and rebels, and plotting uprisings, and though I did not know the names, the fever and passion of Jamaica 100 years before still lingered in the air. At Christmas, I heard children far and wide crying out, "Chrismus come but once a year! Hooray!" I did not know that this was the echo of the slaves' only holiday, but I felt a poignancy and urgency in the re-echoing voices, and they have never left.

At Somerton occurred some of the most important literary/linguistic events of my life. We were read to constantly, and I was able to read by the age of four. I sat my first exam (a Sunday school exam at the Presbyterian church) in 1941, and passed. It was a lovely challenge. Words and stories simply stuck in my mind, burrowing deep and turning up when least expected. My conversation with adults was precocious and sometimes highly embarrassing for everyone except me. I asked questions nonstop. I studied people's faces, bodies, dress, mannerisms, and behaviour. I remembered a great deal. My mother lived in terror of my remarks, questions and suppositions. She always answered my questions clearly and fully. I trusted her and told her everything.

The next great event came in about 1942, when I woke one morning with an acute toothache and a high fever. There was no doctor or dentist: I must wait two days to be taken to Montego Bay on the bus.

I sat at the dining table, weeping, with my swollen face, when my father came and sat in front of me. "Would you like me to tell you a story?"

I agreed, miserably.

He then began to recite. The rhythm and words were music, and soon the drama, tragedy and romance of Walter Scott's famous *The Lady of the Lake* filled every space around us, blotting out the immediate world and lifting me far, far away into a fight for a homeland, into loyalties and betrayals, with fiery beacons raised on mountain tops, murder and revenge in a land of wild mountains and lakes, lonely glens, waterfalls and ruined castles, and Scots pursuing Scots across time and space. I was bewitched. Some 10,000 lines later, his voice relaxed, and ceased. I came slowly to myself. The sun now shone through the opposite, western window. It was no longer morning but early afternoon. The fever was gone; the pain was gone; my face was not swollen. I was not ill. I was well. It was like coming back from a long, vivid journey and seeing the everyday world again, with dazed surprise. The words had hypnotised me; transformed me; transported me. I was no longer quite the same person as before.

My father had a deep love of history and literature; his college books and his college memories were treasure troves. My mother also loved books: romances, adventures, tales about animals, family life, strange journeys. Both parents loved dramas, and they composed many school plays, pageants and rallies. Bible stories were everywhere.

Pilgrim's Progress was a standard source of drama. I was surrounded with people making up scenery and costumes from whatever lay at hand. The Presbyterian Sunday school (1941-44) was a wonderful place for recitals, plays, and children's activities. Nothing in Kingston ever met that standard!

My mother read us many novels, of which the most important, for me, was Victor Hugo's *Les Miserables*. I now realise that this tale was so real to us that it became branded on my memory, as if I had been an invisible witness to all of its doings, and the ethical world it held up to us became the ethics of my family, and of my own self.

By December 1944, I felt completely formed as a mind and as a personality; all that remained was for me to go on learning.

So when people ask me, "Where did you grow up?" and I say, "St James," it is true. Many very important events lay ahead of me, and I had lots to learn, but the main framework of my tastes, my mind, my ethics, my views of people and of myself were in place by the time I left St James in December 1944.

This sense was hammered home in December 1943, when my aunt Edith James tried to adopt me. She offered to take me over, send me to St Andrew Prep School (an expensive privilege!), and have me live with her at Lyndhurst Road in Kingston. My three cousins (all older than me by some ten to fifteen years) would be my home companions.

My mother was dead set against this. She recalled her unhappy time with the Jameses, but much had happened since 1927. My father laughed and said, "Let Jean decide."

My sister was starting as a boarder at St Hugh's High School in Jan 1944, so it was decided that Mamma, Pansy and I would all go to Aunt Edith's in Kingston. Mamma settled Pansy at St Hugh's and left for home. I had a week on my own in which to make up my mind.

The Jameses tried to make me happy. They wanted me to have Shirley Temple curls, but I despised Shirley Temple and curls. My hair needed plaits, not stupid curls! I rejected the fussy dresses they got me as foolish. I was not allowed to use the books in the bookcase. I could not go back into the bedroom once I was up and dressed. Adults were not to be approached unless in an emergency. There was no one to talk to except one boy next door, and he did not know very much. In those days, I preferred adults to children, because adults knew stuff, and children knew very little.

Aunt Edith was interesting but hardly ever at home. She took me to a bookstore downtown, and told me that I could have all the books I wanted off the shelf by the front entrance. I thought her magnificent! After chatting to the manager at the back, she came back to find that I had piled about fifty books on the floor: the shelves were quite bare. With some coughing she explained that she could afford only ONE book, and I should choose. I understood very well about money and the shortage thereof, so I put everything back except a lovely novel, *Princess Charming*, the first novel I ever owned, and one that I have read again and again through the decades.

At the end of the week I told Aunt Edith that she was too busy to have me around, for I had many questions and she had no time (I did not mention curls and Shirley Temple – I had some manners by then). We parted as good friends. A kind lady let me sit beside her on the country bus back to St James. I returned in triumph.

During these years, other important experiences changed me. My first movie (in 1941, I think) was the musical *Rose Marie*. The operatic music thrilled me even more than the romantic ballads like *Indian Love Call*. I fell in love with the stage, with opera and ballet, although I lacked the words for them, and no one else at home was interested.

I was also reading *The Gleaner* avidly, noting movies, movie stars, local news and most of all, war news and international news. The names of places and people rang music in my mind. Great horrible battles went on at Stalingrad, at Singapore, in Okinawa, at Kursk. One name was prominent: Field Marshal Timoshenko. I took that name, and so did many other Jamaicans, but I think I am the only female who did so. He was one of my heroes for years. The map of the whole world became depicted in my mind: for my mother loved maps and geography, my father loved history and ideas, and they were always ready to talk about such things. They talked to friends and people who came to see them on school and church business. Universal adult suffrage was a high point; everyone would vote in 1944. We knew all of the party songs. We even had a pet goat named Census. Country life was full of visiting, talk, and getting along with people.

My elementary schooling was as significant as secondary school. In January 1944, I began life in what is now grade four, where I stayed for two terms and then moved up to grade five. It was highly enjoyable. I loved my teachers but found most of my classmates boring. That changed.

In December 1944, we made the great move to Kingston, and I started at Whitfield Town elementary school (where my parents taught) in grade five. Then my first major educational disaster happened. Schools had exams at different times then, and at Whitfield we sat the annual exam in March. Alas, I passed. I was sent up to Grade 6 although I knew I couldn't do the maths, and begged and begged to stay in Grade 5. No dice. My grasp of decimals and other mathematical concepts never fully recovered. The result would be long-lasting anxiety and many failures in maths at the secondary level. Apparently, I had come first, but that doesn't mean that any of us children had really understood what we were being taught. If it was bad for me, what about the others? At that time, a faint sense of anxiety for the welfare of other children seeped into my mind, and never left. I did not have many friends among classmates, because they bored me. Children knew so little, and a lot of it was nonsense, so I went after books and adults. Yet it was these children who befriended me, who warned me, firmly and clearly, about the dangers of life in Kingston. The black-'eart man; the rich man in the flashy car, offering sweets; the big ole man offering anything. They explained what the strange limp rubber things were that sometimes appeared in the school after a weekend; they explained what these "rubbers" were for; they drew a cordon around the dangerous world of adults, and our world. I have been everlastingly grateful to them.

Thanks to all of these elementary school mates, I became conscious of people's difficulties: of not being able to read properly; of being "passed up" through grade after grade; of not having the books, or the writing materials, or a new uniform, or good shoes that fitted; of sometimes not having enough to eat; of not going to the doctor for an illness; of putting up with trouble. And with all of this, they loved jokes, tales, games and plain mischief, in which I found myself able to assist. I discovered the heady joy of making children laugh.

In 1948, my best friend took me to the most private and serious place at school (behind the girls' toilets) and said solemnly, "Jean Creary, you are the headmaster's daughter and you are the WORST child at Whitfield School!" It was the nicest thing anyone had ever said to me.

It is in these days that my love of entertaining children began to grow. I told stories and listened to stories; I read to others; I made up games; I played tricks; I made people laugh; we all acted in plays; we shared novels; we went to special movie shows for schools (Pearl Buck's *Dragon Seed* – it terrified me and stayed in my mind for years – Lassie movies; my heroine was Margaret O'Brien, tomboy, adventurer).

We went to hear Paul Robeson sing; we went aboard a British warship in Kingston harbour; we walked in military file to the Carib cinema and to Ward Theatre, and because these movies and shows were so rare, they blossomed in our minds.

The Children's Library at Half-Way-Tree reconciled me to living in Kingston. By 1949, I had read the entire collection (a couple thousand?), some several times, and could recall the titles and authors' names for several years to come. I now had favourite authors; favourite series; and always the hope for more. Anything in print simply begged me to read it. This was also the period in which I discovered the joy of study for its own sake, and I gladly read my parents' college texts (except for mathematics); devoured (many times) the 12 volumes of *Newnes Pictorial Knowledge* (edited by Enid Blyton and others, designed for Grades 6 to 10); books about words and their origins; anatomy texts; and any other books I could lay hands on.

During the run-up to my second attempt at an island scholarship, Dad let me stay home for six weeks to study. This period was one of the best in my life, finishing worksheet after worksheet and rewarding myself with any of the textbooks lying around the house. I was alone at home (I paid no attention to either my grandmother or to our helper) and I read all day, and took breaks going fast on the swing on the guinep tree. My brother and sister (the only people I really enjoyed) were off at boarding school, but I missed no one: the books were more than enough.

Unknown to the parents, I borrowed pulp westerns from the 20-year-old fellow next door, and hid them under the mattress. They taught me melodrama, the uses of landscape, and dynamics of character. In summer 1947, I read my sister's Senior Cambridge texts: Lord Macaulay's *Lays of Ancient Rome* and Conrad's *Youth* and *Gaspar Ruiz*. Once more I was altered by the experience. I did not mean to learn *Horatius* by heart: it simply happened, as if reading it was like being injected with a magical substance. Once heard in my mind, it could not be erased. The summer holiday took on strange and glorious echoes; I felt sort of drunk. The effect of *Youth* was similar, but different. I was ten, but the saga of the old ship on her last voyage, her strange and glorious death in brilliant fire, a flaming jewel in the Indian Ocean – all this passed into me and changed me. But *Gaspar Ruiz*, with its focus on mature married love and divided loyalties terrified me. Set in vast mountains, amidst violent revolution burns the violent love of hero and heroine. I was scared. And I was spending holidays roaming wild at Orange Valley estate in Trelawny, dreaming of finding Arawak or Spanish remains among ruined old sugar factories.

JB: Now, can you talk about your educational and early professional experiences? Where did you attend for your secondary and tertiary education? What were those experiences like? What did you study?

JDC: In January 1949, I left home for St Hilda's DHS, a boarder at what was said to be the best academic school for girls in Jamaica (but St Andrew High School and Wolmer's High School might differ). St Hilda's came as a horrible shock. Brown's Town was lovely, but St Hilda's was a prison. Because I was bright, I entered a form with girls 18 months older than me, girls who had already done two years of geometry, algebra, Latin and French. I was supposed to catch up – without assistance. The kindly French teacher assigned me a "French sister", for which (and to whom) I am eternally grateful. I discovered I could take geography instead of Latin, an easy option for me; but there was no solution to my ignorance in mathematics.

For the next three years, I suffered the anxiety and humiliation of constant failure in those subjects, knowing that failure in mathematics would deprive me of a School Certificate, no matter how good my other subjects might be. I could not let down my family, so from then on I studied during every single vacation.

I now had the lasting benefit of discovering what it means to fail. And what it means to get up each time and try again. From then, I began to spend every holiday studying. My sister was good at maths and helped me a little; my father was too busy and worn-out in those days to help. I worked alone, mostly. My mother encouraged me, and helped me with French vocabulary. It pained me to realise that I was getting an education far beyond hers. I felt I had to make up to her for things she had never had. She was very distressed at my unhappiness at St Hilda's, and lent me her *Jane Eyre*. I read it every holiday from 1949 to 1953: the romance lacked conviction, the mad wife was no Jamaican imaginable, the missionary suitor was a cold jerk, but the school was very, very real, and Helen Burns was my ideal. Lowood was St Hilda's.

St Hilda's was snobbish, racist (although I did not understand or realise this aspect for many years), and full of cliques, "teacher's pets", and designated outsiders. In my first term, I realised that one of my dormitory mates, JM, was always alone during afternoon recess because she did not belong socially with the little white/light upper-class 10-year-olds in third form. I offered to read to her during recess: at her wish, I began with *Julius Caesar*. We got to Act 3 in about four days. The head mistress summoned me to her study, a terrifying matter.

Miss Norman was a shy, reserved English lady with a damaged throat: her speech was difficult and scratchy. She told me that St Hilda's girls never had friendships save with members of their own forms, and that JM and I must not spend time together. I became coldly and bitterly angry with the injustice, especially for what it would do to JM's isolation and loneliness.

We were expected to sit or walk in twos and threes during free time and recess: I made sure to sit and walk alone thereafter. I felt eyes watching me, and I was glad. I became known as a most peculiar person who used long, strange words and was conceited. I had no real friends, but in my form I was the designated lookout for danger (teachers and Nurse) if the form decided that it needed privacy. I trusted very few people at St Hilda's.

I also was astonished to hear the deputy headmistress informing some sixth-formers that "domestic work is soul-destroying: therefore, we have menials to perform such tasks". They sat there and believed her, not noticing that the head parlour maid was standing right beside them, also listening. I guess that she read my face, for slowly, thereafter, that parlour maid went out of her way, discreetly, silently, to do small but very kind favours for me for the rest of my days at St Hilda's. Later on, this included making sure that we sixth-formers ate up the last of the mistresses' Sunday supper: cake, Jell-O with tinned fruit, sandwiches. Elvira had my back! Twenty years later when I visited the school, she was head of domestic staff, full of dignity and know-how. I will never forget the hug we exchanged. Meanwhile, my troubles mounted. One term I earned 2% on the geometry final. Mercifully, my first maths teacher won a scholarship and left for London. She was replaced by one of Jamaica's best: Marjorie Thomas, later head of St Hugh's High School, and a brilliant teacher. Miss Thomas had no pets; she made no jokes; she spoke very little; she explained superbly. She counselled each of us as to how to manage our skills in the subject, and our time of study, and in the exam itself.

From the teachers at St Hilda's came my baked-in philosophy as a teacher: doing by and large the opposite of what they did.

Above all, respect the subject. It matters more than you or me. It will be alive when we are dead.

Have no favourites.

Never insult a student in front of others. Insults may be delivered in private, to best effect.

Surprise people with kindness. It works better and longer than rage.

Measure the energy and strength of each student and engage at that level, for best results.

Allow students to redo, rethink because that is when the subject truly takes root in them. Give sudden, unexpected extensions.

Remember that each one will see the material in a unique way, so listen to each viewpoint.

The subject matter is greater and of more value than any of us: we are conduits.

I got a respectable but not brilliant pass in Senior Cambridge at the age of fourteen. Thanks to being so young, I spent the next three years in sixth form at St Hilda's; became a prefect; became Head Girl (I was really shocked at that); helped run the school during the polio epidemic of 1954; and survived the shock of my mother's death in 1952 (I was fifteen) by reading all of Tennyson.

Those three years of leisurely study were fabulous. I took English literature; history; French; and art. I had three sets of classmates over three years, and I studied three different exam syllabi: 18th century British history; 19th century European history; the lives of Mazzini; of Garibaldi; of Napoleon. In English, ten Shakespeare plays and four of Chaucer's Tales, as well as the General Prologue to the *Canterbury Tales*. In French – oh joy – the poetry of Hugo, Baudelaire, Verlaine, and others, with Molière, Corneille and Racine to balance things. I discovered Mallarmé and the Symbolist poets.

In afternoon recess, those days, I went with another sixth-former to St Mark's church so that she could practise on the pipe organ; she played Bach and Handel while I read *War and Peace*. I was fairly drunk with words and books those days, even managing to read *Anna Karenina* in French, because I couldn't find it in English. I even started Latin and enjoyed it immensely for one term, until the return of the deputy head from a term's leave led to Miss Norman writing to tell my dad that students could not take subjects at the Senior Cambridge level if they were also sitting Higher Schools. Dad and I believed Miss Norman, and the classes stopped. In 1963 when I began teaching at the University of the West Indies, I happened to go to the offices of the Cambridge Overseas Examinations Unit and idly asked if this rule still held.

It had never existed.

Miss Johnson, angry because I took geography instead of Latin, and angrier because I did not become one of her satellites, had her revenge. I did not even know.

In December 1954, I left St Hilda's, the Lowood of my life. After Christmas I discovered that I could return to school for a year and try for the Jamaica Scholarship. I was confident of being good at history and French, but unsure of English literature, even though I had always seemed to do best in English. St Hilda's deputy headmistress had succeeded in making me unsure of English as my subject, even though my marks were as follows: English Literature (A+); history (A-); French (B+); art (A).

I chose to go to St Hugh's, one of the most important choices of my life.

As a boarder in a small boarding house near the school, I found myself with two other sixth-formers in charge of about twelve younger girls. Our landlady matron had little idea of what to do, other than feed us and keep the place clean and tidy. So all of the discipline, advising, helping and caretaking fell to me, Hope M, and Daisy M. It was here that I became closest to and fondest of children as children. *Escape to Last Man Peak* may have been formed here, as a social unit. We looked after each other; the oldest of us checked on the health of the others; we were all friends. It was the opposite of St Hilda's.

At school, it was wonderful. The teachers actually liked the children. Also, St Hugh's had the best school library in Jamaica; here were all the Russian novelists, just waiting. St Hugh's also followed a somewhat different curriculum. In English and European history I now studied the 16th and 17th centuries, a great boon ever after. The English literature teacher was a young, brilliant Englishwoman who lent us all sorts of novels. I read *For Whom the Bell Tolls*, and never recovered. I also read in astonishment *The Secret Life of Salvador Dali*, understanding nothing of orgasms or intrauterine memories, but finding him a vivid, drunken mind.

St Hugh's gave me, in addition, a significant and lasting gift. I was due to take the University scholarship-entrance examination in March 1955. The headmistress, Mrs Landale, sent for me before she signed the form. She was very puzzled and troubled because I had listed French and history as my exam subjects, excluding English totally. When she asked me why, I said truthfully that I thought I was better at those subjects than I was in English. There was a long silence.

"But you got an A+ in English; your other subjects are good but that is stellar."

I tried to argue, but she just kept looking steadily at me. I did not fully realise that it was the negative influence of Miss Iris Johnson of St Hilda's at work.

Mrs Landale said, after a long pause, that she would sign the form as it stood, but if I were to win a scholarship, would I make her a promise? I agreed happily: anything.

She said, "Please sign up for the English honours course. Promise me."

I agreed. Ten chances to one I wouldn't win anything.

The exam was delicious; the French was great fun and the history even better. I came first in the West Indies and had my picture in the *Gleaner*, to my dad's delight. In October, I registered for English honours with history as second subject, and changed that to French later in the term.

And lived happily (for the most part) ever after.

My three years at Oxford, pursuing a degree in Jacobean drama, were of course very important in my life, as was my appointment (seemingly by chance) to the position of Assistant Lecturer in Anglo-Saxon and linguistics in the Department of English, University College West Indies, in October 1962.

JB: I am curious to know why you started writing for children and what the milieu was like for you when you started. Several writers I know went away and did correspondence courses, was that your case as well? Did you belong to writers' groups on the island?

JDC: Stories surrounded me all my life, oral and written. The idea of a course never once occurred to me: I was living the real thing. There were no writers' groups that I ever heard of, but at University College West Indies many, many students were passionate writers: Derek Walcott, Slade Hopkinson, Velma Pollard, Garth St Omer, Edward Baugh, Mervyn Morris. These are my generation, the friends with whom I explored life at University College, West Indies. The Scribblers' Group reviewed plays, poems, and short fiction every two weeks or so, an almost all-night session of great tension and hilarity. In those days, I wrote bad poetry, which Eddie Baugh was kind enough to read for me.

After a few years, I decided that if one had nothing to say, one should stop writing, and shut up. So ended my poetics, for the most part. Stories kept on running through my head as a form of personal, private entertainment. Even though I have taught creative writing for several years, I distrust many of the tenets of this trade. Writers need to listen, to read, to listen even more, to read copiously, to immerse themselves in the universe of language and imagination. Some "exercises" do help; keeping notes and journals also helps, but may hinder some imaginations.

JB: You have an award for children's literature named in your honour. What would you say is the state of children's literature being written in Jamaica today? Did you play any role in having the award named in your honour?

JDC: The entries have been fewer than I would like to see. I think the possible writers are lurking in schools and colleges, thinking it's too stuffy and formal to enter a competition. Language remains an inhibition. We don't have the means of encouraging more writing.

I had no role at all in the creation of the competition and the award. It all came as a surprise and a delight.

JB: *Sprat Morrison* for a first book is remarkably accomplished. What went into writing it? Did you, for example, know someone like Sprat? How long did it take you to write the book? What was the process like, and how did you go about getting it published?

JDC: My father and I used to talk a lot about children's needs and delights, and the difficulties of having so little for Jamaicans to read in school. Ideas for this audience were constantly bubbling in my mind, especially when I visited a school and spent time with the children. Just being among them stirred stories in the depths of my mind. *Sprat Morrison* came as a surprise to me, however.

The character of Sprat is based on my friends from elementary school. I got the idea quite suddenly in December 1967, when I went to buy a Christmas gift for a bright nine-year-old girl. The bookstore was disappointing: nothing spoke to a Jamaican child of the time. It was all the very same stuff that I saw on King Street in 1947. These books were now so remote from the world of 1967 that I went home in a rage and put a sheet of paper in the typewriter, and began. I could see, hear, and feel Sprat in my mind: he belongs in the Jamaica of 1967.

Sprat was alive in my mind, and all his world was mine to describe. I wrote Chapter One in a single sitting and had to change very little of it afterwards. Once I realised that Sprat was around and we were going to do a lot together, the story kept dragging me back to the typewriter. However, my work in schools and my exposure to Ministry of Education policies cautioned me. If this story was to reach my target audience safely, it would have to be specially shaped.

I made certain deliberate choices, for I wanted all children to enjoy the story. Girls will read about boys, but boys won't read about girls, so the main character is a boy. Next, I wanted children to enjoy the story for themselves, without adult intervention if possible. So each chapter is a separate adventure, inviting both the fast reader and the slow to take in Sprat's world. The focus is on Sprat and his friends, with adults on the margins of their world.

Diction formed the greatest problem. No one would allow a novel tainted with patois anywhere near the schools, and I wanted children in school to have at least one book that would cheer them up, amuse them, and show them their world. The action had to be set out such that a lot of speech comes through the narrator and not as dialogue. Such dialogue as occurs had to be limited by topic and situation so that Standard Jamaican English or Standard English would be normal usage for my audience. Dropping in a few key words that have double meanings in patois and Standard English ("rude bwoy", for example) made direct links to my readers.

Then I wanted Sprat to appeal to all Jamaican children, town and country, so he lives on the edge of urban life with country connections. Hence Papine, and the goats (which were there when I was a student at Mona; I knew them well). Sprat is an only child, with a few friends. The choice of situation and action keeps his dialogue limited and allows for reported speech. These conditions allowed the use of Standard English, as most Jamaicans were (and are) prejudiced against the use of Jamaican Creole in writing.

And I tested Sprat in several schools, paying close attention to children's findings and advice. It is the basis of my work as a writer to go first to the audience and have them tell me if the work is working, and if not, what is wrong. Children never mislead a storyteller/writer.

Timing was on my side. The Ministry of Education was then desperately searching for children's books that could be used in secondary schools. Vic Reid and I attended a meeting at the ministry. We were told that we would have to surrender our copyright to the ministry and receive a one-time cash payment. Vic refused; I accepted. *Sprat Morrison* then became ministry property until 1983. Annoying as it was to lose my copyright, the arrangement ensured that my book was widely distributed in Jamaica (and only in Jamaica). Its success, however, enabled me to make a direct arrangement with Longman for my later children's books. I have been very fortunate.

JB: One of the things that stand out in both books is the sheer knowledge of the landscape, which is quite impressive. How did you come to have such an in-depth knowledge of the landscape and Jamaican plants and flowers?

JDC: I am a country girl. Observing nature has always been a passion, a necessity. I hate cities. I love bush-bush, long stays in the mountains, anywhere rural. All of my lifelong friends love nature and plants; botany was a favourite subject at St Hilda's. My parents had similar tastes and interests, my sister to a lesser extent, and so did many of my cousins. The children's books of my own childhood presented me with landscapes and the plant and animal life that enriched them. It would never occur to me to omit the setting which is part of the characters' world and consciousness, even if ignored much of the time and taken for granted.

JB: There are hints throughout *Sprat Morrison* as to what Sprat's friends grew up to be as adults, but not so with Sprat. Why is that so and do you want to hazard a guess as to what Sprat grew up to become?

JDC: Many children have asked this question, and I have no good answer. Sprat's friends will become certain kinds of professionals because their basic personalities shape that destiny. This concept applies most of all to Blossom Wright: she is already a teacher. The boys are more varied in their skills and fortunes. Sprat seems to be the average good-natured person who will work at whatever chance brings his way. He is Every-boy: he has no special skill beyond good nature, good sense, imagination, and some backbone. He will make good, no matter what. I think that is why I cannot see him confined in any particular job or profession.

JB: Now turning to *Escape to Last Man Peak*, the first thing that jumps out at me is that more Jamaican patois is used in this book than in *Sprat Morrison*. Why did you make the decision to do this?

JDC: *Escape to Last Man Peak* came about in a totally different fashion. Call it an unintended pregnancy! On the night of Dec 31, 1971, I saw the whole adventure in a dream. I was an invisible witness, from Spanish Town to Trelawny hills. Just as the children cross the last stream to climb the last hill, I become visible to the last of them, Sylvia, who brushes her hair out of her eyes, looks at me directly and says, "This is our story. Please write it." Then she turns and walks off up the hill. I started writing like a mad person the next day, and kept it up for two months, marking no essays, preparing no lectures, teaching out of memory and old notes. The story dragged me to the typewriter each day.

I had to write what I heard them saying, and they are Jamaicans. It was especially important to get their speech as correct as possible: correct in Jamaican terms. The same prohibitions still held, but this time I wasn't going to knuckle under to prejudice. Instead, I once more used the narrative voice to cover stretches of speech-acts; dialogue was often conditioned by topic, so that the dialogue could emerge in Standard Jamaican English, or Jamaican Dialect (modified to match Standard), or in Jamaican creole (patois). Once more I could use terms with different meanings in both languages to signal my Jamaican readers: "turn out", as meaning "develop infection" is one such usage.

JB: Another thing that comes across very clearly for me in this book, and marks it, actually, as being written by a woman, is the many references to sewing, embroidery making, crochet and quilts that are referenced throughout this work. Can you articulate whether these are/were art forms that you remember being actively done on the island?

JDC: Needlework was much practised all over Jamaica in the 1940s, but began to die in the latter 1950s with the arrival of cheaper manufactured goods. Up till then, most people used to make their own doilies, napkins, runners, tablecloths, bedspreads – not to mention baby clothes and special items for weddings and burials! Embroidered handkerchiefs were a popular gift. My mother sewed exquisitely, but all her work was either for things people ordered, or for the church (altar linen). My sister was pretty good, and so were some cousins. Every household seemed to have some woman who could do embroidery as well as make pillowcases and children's clothes, and darn socks. Sewing was a money-saving skill.

The joke is that I am a terrible needlewoman. Even so, I went to sewing class and saw the beautiful work done by other girls, of which the most exquisite was that of a Chinese girl. Her work is celebrated in "Escape", for it is what Nellie finds in the abandoned house. This touch honours my schoolmate from 1950, whom I have not seen since 1954.

JB: *Escape to Last Man Peak* has a lot of adult themes. Children are abandoned and have to fend for themselves and, in the process, meet terrible insecurity, hunger and violence. As I read I kept wondering, what makes this a book, after all, a book for children? What distinguishes children's literature, specifically young adult literature, from adult literature?

JDC: Children are not stupid. They know instinctively how precarious their lives are, and how dangerous the world can be. Tales of survival are essential to growing up as strong and confident persons; such adventure tales form the mainstay of folklore as well as of popular children's fiction, movies, and games. Many adults have so forgotten their own past that they believe children's fiction to be some sort of simplistic, sugary entertainment.

The difference between a worthwhile children's book and a good adult novel lies mainly in viewpoint, not in plot or characters. Viewpoint determines how much is revealed, as well as how it is revealed. Viewpoint selects not only detail but tone, which is the all-important relationship between speaker and audience. With the right tone, one may describe horrors like a clinician, and not scare the reader.

The child viewpoint speaks with the intellectual clarity of the child; the adult viewpoint looks at details and consequences. A child can describe a crime in simple, innocent language while the adult cannot fail to give darker, more analytic and sinister aspects. This difference does not mean that the child viewpoint is shallow or stupid, rather, its very innocence can let it present tragic situations that adults see only as horrific.

By and large, adult fiction commands a vast schema, interlocking characters, plot, setting, history and culture so as to argue for a particular worldview. The viewpoint and tone permit the work to take on any complexity it needs, be it military history, or abnormal psychology, or the nature of mass migrations, or futuristic science.

Children's fiction may use any of these platforms, but the viewpoint will selectively present experience and information distilled by a child's level of awareness. Often this level of innocence may create wonderful ironies (sometimes tragic, sometimes comic) between what the child viewpoint sees and reports, and what an adult reader knows to be the case. One sees this pattern in Holocaust literature for children, where the adult reader will know the full horror of pursuit and war, while the child character will feel the threat deeply but not parse its details, and lead the child reader to want to know more, and to never forget.

JB: I also found myself wondering, because of the very vivid descriptions, if indeed there had been an epidemic in Jamaica. If so, what more can you tell us about it? What preparations did you engage in, in writing this book?

JDC: Alas, I never expected "Escape" to last so long! It is a sci-fi futuristic work, conceived in the early 1970s, for events in the 1990s. Twenty years seemed a long time in those days. I imagined an epidemic differing from the ones I'd heard about: 19th century blasts of cholera and smallpox, sometimes of typhoid fever. My sci-fi reading (and my reading in the sciences) suggested that a virus was likely to be the next major plague because antibiotics had controlled the old bacterial diseases. It seemed likely to be a pandemic, thanks to global travel and trade, so the virus reaches Jamaica from overseas, where it has killed millions. I discussed this aspect of the work with friends in the Faculty of Medicine, University of the West Indies, and they said that a virus was just the thing for the end of the 20th century and yes, it could selectively attack healthy adults and skip children and the old.

It also seemed likely to me (in 1970-73) that the soaring bauxite industry in Jamaica might be doomed, and I wondered what those empty factories would be like. I did not dream that acts of Jamaica's Government would begin to shrink that industry in the mid-1970s.

JB: None of the books referenced in *Escape to Last Man's Peak* are Jamaican texts, which, given when the book was written, is understandable. So, were you then consciously creating a Jamaican literary tradition when you set out to write your books? If yes, why was that so urgent and important to you?

JDC: I was not consciously setting out to create "a Jamaican literary tradition". I set out consciously to give Jamaican children some fun, some encouragement, some words and sentences to play with, in their own world. They deserve to have books designed for their unique pleasure. Their world enables me to write, and without those children, I have nothing to say.

If one lives close to other people, one will never be lacking in stories, characters, and plots. Creative writing classes may help in mechanics, but cannot make a story alive. One has to listen; observe; recall; listen some more; watch; think; think again; play the stories around in one's mind; laugh; run; watch. I guess one might call the process "feeding one's cultural imagination".

JB: Finally, what is Jean D'Costa working on these days?

JDC: I am trying to keep two promises. The first was made to the late Leeta Hearne, and that is to write my memoirs. Mrs Hearne typed out the first copy of *Sprat Morrison* for me in 1970 when I submitted it to the Ministry of Education for consideration. She was one of the principal readers of my fiction over the years, and a very close friend.

The second was made to the late M. P. Patterson, once publications Officer for the Ministry of Education. This request is harder, for Patsy wants me to write all of the stories (true and imagined) that I have told her over the years. These include duppy stories; life in racist England; oddities at St Hilda's; dreams.

Oh, well. Must keep trying!

THE GIFT OF MUSIC & SONG: AN INTERVIEW WITH HAZEL CAMPBELL

Hazel Campbell was born in Jamaica in 1940, and passed away on 12 December 2018. One of Jamaica's leading short story writers, her writing career spanned fifty years. She attended Merl Grove High School and obtained a BA in English & Spanish at UWI, Mona, followed by Diplomas in Mass Communications and Management Studies. Before her retirement she worked as a teacher, as a public relations worker, editor, features writer and video producer for the Jamaican Information Service, the Ministry of Foreign Affairs and the Creative Production and Training Centre; later she worked as a freelance Communications Consultant.

Her first publication was *The Rag Doll & Other Stories* (Savacou, 1978), followed by *Women's Tongue* (Savacou, 1985) and then *Singerman* (Peepal Tree, 1991). Her stories have also been published in *West Indian Stories*, 1981; *Caribanthology I*, 1981; *Focus 1983*; and *Facing the Sea*, 1986. Her publications for children include *Tilly Bummie, Ramgoat Dashalong, Juice Box and Scandal, Follow the Peacock* and others. In 2019, her collected stories, *Jamaica on My Mind*, was published by Peepal Tree Press.

❧

JB: Hazel, I want to start off by thanking you for the work you do. It was immensely important to me to have your work, your voice, as an example of how to approach writing from a Jamaican female perspective. I devoured your work as a beginning writer. So I guess my first question to you is: How, exactly, did you decide to become a writer? What told you it was possible for you?

HC: Thanks, Jackie. I treasure that statement. It's great to know that my writing helped your vision.

I really don't know some of the reasons why I chose to become a writer. I had great literature teachers when I attended both Merle Grove High School and Excelsior High School. Still, I would say I was basically adrift on trying to figure out how to become a writer. In my early teens I sent away for a short story course at an English college, but that correspondence course was not very helpful to me. Furthermore, school magazines were few and far between when I was coming up … I did not have any sense of direction and I did not know what to do.

Later, when I was at the University of the West Indies, where I did my bachelor's degree in English and Spanish literature, there still was not much guidance here on writing and how to become a writer. But what happened was that at UWI we were getting seriously interested in Caribbean writing. We were reading John Hearne, George Lamming, Edgar Mittelholzer, Orlando Patterson, Andrew Salkey, Roger Mais and others, either because they were recommended reading, or people were saying (excitedly) "Have you read this!!!" Inspiration soared. Then I became an English Language teacher and I began to teach myself how to write. So I guess at the end of the day, it's probably really, sort of, I write because I must.

JB: In your statement "Why I Write", you said, "In a way, the adventures of the people" in the books in Britain that you were reading "were more real than my own existence". Can you explain what you mean by this and the impact that this had on you? As well, further on in your statement, you talk about discovering the first generation of West Indian writers while in high school. Can you explain how the works that you started reading in the sixth form of high school were different and what impact these works had on you?

HC: You have to remember that books were extremely important. Anything in print was treated with great reverence (more so when they originated in the 'mother' country). So books and the people in them – their lives and adventures – were far more important than my mundane existence. Even the squalor in some of Charles Dickens's books. They stretched my imagination. I think the writing in the books I read must also have been good enough to effortlessly transport me into their world and that is the essence of good writing, wherever it originates.

The West Indian books were exciting because the people I knew, things I knew – things which I might have thought of as 'ordinary' – were now in books. They had become LITERATURE. I could look at life around me in a different light. Roger Mais – Wow! I think perhaps one can understand that only if one grew up in the colonial era.

JB: You have said your mother was a great storyteller. Can you tell me more about this woman and what made her such a great storyteller?

HC: My mother was from deep rural Jamaica and she had a fount of stories. Especially Anancy stories which, following the rural tradition, she would tell the children in the yard at night. In my early days, there was no radio or television, so this was entertainment, especially during the holidays. After a day spent playing, storytelling was very welcome. I regret that I can't remember some of her stories, which I think must have been unique as I haven't heard any like those anywhere else. Probably that's where the desire to write started. I celebrated some of her stories in my children's book *Tilly Bummie*. I think she must have thought me quite strange to want to be a writer, but she was supportive, so she forked out the first payment on a correspondence writing course I took, which I didn't complete.

JB: Here in the US, having a child, or children, is often seen to be detrimental to the career of women artists in particular. I notice, from your dedications in your books, that you take great pride in being a mother and even a grandmother. So I wonder: what impact did being a mother and even a grandmother have on your writing?

HC: I got married at an early age. Being married and having children was something one did as a woman. That I juggled teaching, having babies (in quick succession), university and starting a writing career is a tribute to my husband, who was only 23 years old when we got married. Now, I think we were quite crazy and if my mother did not help us with the babies, I don't know what we would have done! This is why I advised my girls to finish their education before getting into all that, because it was very difficult.

I actually started writing for children because I was so busy I had no time to tell my children about my childhood, and my mother's stories. My children are my mainstay, at this point of my life, and my grands, my joy. I write stories for my granddaughter, using her name. She recently warned me NOT to write anymore stories about her. But we are good friends. She illustrated the cover of *Mr King's Daughter*.

JB: You recently published two collections of stories for adults, *When Times Are Strange* and *My Darling You*. What prompted you to publish these books in e-format? In these collections you revisited some of the stories from older collections, how, if at all, did you change those older stories?

HC: I guess, by this, I have enough experience to know when the stories are 'ready' to be published and e-publishing is quick and easy. The stories in *When Times are Strange*, with one exception, were published by Savacou and have been out of print for a long time. When I looked at them again I thought they were still relevant and, indeed, that some of them recorded an important part of the Jamaican experience in the 1970s. I made only very minor changes to these stories and since it was a self-published e-book, I was able to add some introductory comments, which I am sure a traditional publisher would not allow.

JB: Your two new collections bring to five the total number of collections of stories for adults that you have published. Why specifically the short story format for you, with regard to writing for adults? Any possibility of a novel for adults? Is there any possibility of you putting out a collection incorporating all your stories for adults so far?[1]

HC: I like the short story form. It is versatile, allows for experimentation and gets to the point quickly. I have three half-written novels, which I keep promising to settle down to complete. But although I know where I want to go with them, I keep putting off writing. I haven't thought about a comprehensive collection.

JB: There is a poem by you at the beginning of *My Darling You* and it made me wonder how much poetry you've written and is there any chance of seeing more poems from you?

HC: I don't really write poetry. For some reason, a poem will come to me whole, and fit into something else that I am writing, then I will write it down, but I don't think I am very good at this.

JB: There are some overarching themes in the two new collections – colour, class, gender issues – do you think these are still pervasive problems in Jamaican society? I am thinking now of the story "See Me in Me Benz an T'ing" and the fact that, over 40 years later, that story still seems as relevant to me today as perhaps when it was first written.

HC: I don't think one can truthfully write about a Jamaican situation without being conscious of these touchy issues. I didn't consciously pick these as themes. They arise from the characters and their interaction with one another. Our prejudices come out in all sorts of ways. I like to think that I merely record, I don't judge. The woman in "See Me in Me Benz..." and Mrs Telfer in "Supermarket Blues" had serious lessons to learn from their confrontation with those from a lower socio-economic group, but it is suggested rather than laboured. A lot has changed, however; women are far more visible in business, public life, etc. But we are still struggling with our image – skin bleaching, for example.

JB: Another theme in your work is the sense that women are acted upon, instead of being actors in their own right. Whether it is Miss Girlie or Melissa or most of the other characters in both collections. There are significant societal pressures placed on women in almost all of these stories. You've just answered my next question: in what ways, if any, have you seen the position of women in Jamaican society change, if at all, in the years since you have started writing and publishing your works? Perhaps you can elaborate on this.

HC: Many of our women, mainly through education and upward mobility, now have much greater recognition and control over their lives, nationally, I think. But we still have the Miss Girlies and Melissas. The thing is, though, that Miss Girlie wasn't weak. She chose to stay with the man even though he was pushing her into prostitution. She had worked out a way to satisfy his need for more money and keep her integrity. What I like about that story is that in the end, when she is watching him walk away, he becomes almost literally 'a little man'.

> She watched him walking away and the strangest thing happened. He seemed to get smaller and smaller, so that by the time he turned the corner he looked like a very little man she had once seen in a reading book. It must be the light, she thought, through her unshed tears.

I liked that. "The Thursday Wife" seems meek, but she also had worked out how to become independent of, and survive her cheating husband. Walking away is probably not the only strength a woman has.

JB: The focus of this interview is on your two recent collections of stories for adults, but I also read and loved *Mr King's Daughter*, which is a young adult novella. And here, the woman actually was able to break out of the strict pressures imposed on her by class and by her father. But I could not help wondering, without giving away too much about the story, why the father did not pursue the daughter when she left with the housekeeper? That question has nagged at me for several days now and I just need an answer!

HC: That story kept threatening to become much longer, and to move away from being a folktale. I had to keep pulling it back. It could have had a scene in which she told off the father before she left, perhaps, but he was a foolish man and he was no longer important to the story, so I dropped him.

JB: Finally, song lyrics are incredibly important to you. Not only the often hilarious lyrics you make up in your stories, but also church songs and so many lyrics and songs running through your work. Indeed, one book is dedicated to the late singer Whitney Houston. Why are songs so important to you?

HC: I am a seriously thwarted musician/songwriter/singer. I can't sing more than an octave, (lower G to G). I can't remember the words of songs, even those I like. (I often make up my own words.) There's a story behind all that. I just recently worked out what happened in my early life that created some of this confusion. But, I grew up in the Church of God, and for me the music was the best part of the service – always. I don't really listen to much of today's pop. I like gospel but not much of the modern styles. I love our folk music.

After Whitney Houston died, I found her story so riveting that I immersed myself in her music. Thanks to YouTube, I listened to her recorded songs and followed her concert tours and really I am in awe at her talent. When the stories in *My Darling You* were ready, I still had no title, and then Whitney died and everybody was playing I Will Always Love You, and her many different ways of singing "My darling you" caught my attention. But notice, I added the subtitle "love stories, sort of" because the stories are about love relationships but there is no physical touching in most of them – that's the "sort of" part.

I don't know if I believe in reincarnation, but I have asked the Lord that if I am coming back please, please, please give me the gifts of music and song.

Endnote:
1. This indeed happened a few years after this interview, when Peepal Tree Press published a collection of Hazel Campbell's adult short stories, *Jamaica on My Mind* (2019). It brought together most of the stories from the Savacou collections, *The Rag Doll* (1978) and *Woman's Tongue* (1985), all of *Singerman* (1991) and most of the stories Hazel wrote after that. Sadly, whilst Hazel never saw the printed book, she was able to suggest the title, discuss the contents, respond to suggested edits and approve the cover image.

VELMA POLLAR'S TRIBUTE POEMS –
AN INTERTEXTUAL DIALOGUE BETWEEN POETS

Born in Jamaica in 1937, **Velma Pollard** was educated at Excelsior High School in Kingston and at the University College of the West Indies. She received an MA in Education from McGill University and an MA in the teaching of English from Columbia University. She taught in high schools and universities in Jamaica, Trinidad, Guyana and the USA ,and is retired from the University of the West Indies where she was Dean of the Faculty of Education.

She has always written, but none of her work went beyond her desk until 1975 when encouraged by her sister Erna Brodber and others, notably Jean D'Costa who sent one of her stories to *Jamaica Journal*, she started sending pieces to journals in the region. Her first short story and fable collection, *Considering Woman* was published in 1989. Her novella *Karl* won the Casa de las Americas in 1992 and *Homestretch*, also written for children, was published in 1994. Her monograph, *Dread Talk – the Language of the Rastafari* was published in 1994 by Canoe Press. She has also edited several anthologies of writing for schools.

Peepal Tree Press have published four collections of Velma Pollard's poetry, *Crown Point* (1988), *Shame Trees Don't Grow Here* (1993), *Leaving Traces* (2008) and *And Caret Bay Again: New and Selected Poems* (2013), which also contains poems from her collection *The Best Philosophers I Know Can't Read and Write* (Mango Press, 2001) and a collection of short stories, fables and memoir, *Considering Woman I & II* (2010), which contains the earlier Women's Press collection as well as new stories.

❦

JB: Velma, I want to start off by asking you to tell us where you grew up in Jamaica and what your childhood was like.

VP: I grew up in Woodside, Pear Tree Grove PO, St Mary, not to be confused with Woodside, Clarendon or anywhere else. When I was three years old my parents relocated there from Blackstonedge, St Ann, where generations of Brodbers – my father's family – have lived. Woodside is deep rural, forty miles from Kingston, five miles from Highgate, the nearest town. Port Maria, the parish capital, is twelve and a half miles away. Hospital, Court House, the Mayor's Office are there. All important business is conducted there.

JB: What was a childhood like in a village like Woodside in the Forties?

VP: Life revolved around home, school, church. Let me begin with church, which was Anglican, part of the Highgate cure, which meant that the rector (priest) in charge of St Cyprian's, Highgate, would visit Woodside once per month: on "Parson Sunday". The other Sundays the service was conducted by a series of lay preachers headed by whoever was the current principal (known then as the headmaster) of the elementary (now primary) school. Parson Sunday was important. The priest arrived by car with his assistant and the ritual included Holy Communion, which was not a part of the service on other Sundays. My family attended church every Sunday at 11:00am. My mother was the church organist. My family played an important part in the functioning of the church. My father's sister was the church secretary and treasurer. Her husband was the people's warden. Sunday School, which took place in the afternoon after Sunday dinner and a little rest, was led by my mother. On a Saturday afternoon there was choir practice and the dressing of the church by a "girls group". This involved reaping ferns to adorn the area above the altar in a fan formation. Next morning, bright hibiscus blooms would be added to the pattern.

Monday to Friday the church became school, with pews becoming benches with desks set out in front of them. Blackboards and a corridor separated classes. The actual Woodside School house was built long after I left for high school. School started at 9:00 am and went till 4:00 pm with a recess break and a lunch break in which we went home for lunch, except on Inspection Day, which I will describe later. I have come to understand that I was privileged in terms of the experience I had in school there, particularly in the earlier years. City people, those bold enough to expose their thoughts, sometimes ask what could make people like my sister and me, brought up in Jamaican "bush", emerge so literate and actually become writers. I think I should spend some time talking about the cultural aspect of school in a district like Woodside.

When I started school the principal was Mr E.G. Roper, who would later become known as principal of St Elizabeth and Kingston Technical schools. The emphasis was on the three Rs (reading, writing, arithmetic), but a considerable amount of time was spent on aesthetic enterprises like elocution, singing and drama. So, for example, we had a school choir. I remember being made to stand on a stool to be tall enough to conduct the choir which was practising under a large tree near the tombs in the churchyard. The group was set out in different rows representing treble, alto, tenor, bass, in that order. I still remember the tunes and even the words of some of the songs. One was a Brahms lullaby to words beginning: "Lullaby and good night with roses bedight."

We sang solos and duets, as well. We wrote poems and drew pictures for competitions. There was an annual Eisteddfod where our artistic efforts were displayed. My siblings all know that I won a first prize for singing "Annie Laurie" ('Maxwelton braes are bonnie/where early fa's the dew/And it's there that Annie Laurie/Gied me her promise true"). So I do not understand how now I can hardly turn a tune!

On Inspection Day a senior official, sent from the Ministry of Education, came to check the school records and to assess our prowess by asking random questions of students from any class. He might ask that someone spell a word or recite a poem. That day we ate with our mother at the headmaster's cottage.

Home reinforced the cultural experience. There was a pedal organ at home just like the one at school/church. After school and on weekends my mother played chiefly from the Community Song Book. I suspect it was an American publication. It was full of Irish and Scottish nostalgic songs like, "I'll Take You Home Again, Kathleen", "Molly Malone", "Flow Gently, Sweet Afton", and "Loch Lomond", but it also had Negro spirituals like "Old Black Joe", whose lyrics I would contest much later in life. There was no TV and very limited radio, but I do not remember feeling deprived or complaining of boredom the way later children did. We sang and we read. On a Friday, my mother's package of books from the Port Maria Public Library arrived at the post office and she mailed back the last week's loan. Our parents played games like checkers and cards with us. Cards were elevating – games like "Concentration" and "Thanks":

"May I have your Jacks, please?"

"Thanks."

Community spirit was strong in my district. There was club hall, which was the centre of secular life. It was a shop, a gift to the community from my aunt's family, restructured to be a hall where meetings were held several evenings per month: Jamaica Agricultural Society, All Island Banana Growers' Association. Some evenings men played dominoes there. As children, we accompanied our parents and fell asleep on the benches while they went over the "minutes of the last monthly meeting", or we slept in my aunt's house across the street until they lifted us, sleeping, home. Then there was 4H Club (Head, Hands, Heart, Health), really associated with the school. Here we learned skills including cattle judging, which had the added excitement of our going to the Agricultural Station at Orange River near Highgate to compete with other schools.

Eventually, the wooden club hall building was replaced with a concrete structure constructed largely by community hands. I remember moonlight nights when the community turned out to carry stones from the church premises to the site to construct the foundation of the building.

JB: I note that you were encouraged to publish your early work by your sister, Erna Brodber, as well as by the writer Jean D'Costa, two of your contemporaries. All three of you have laid a solid foundation for Jamaican literature while continuing to write really important works. These days I find myself wondering, without MFA programmes and such, how did you and your contemporaries receive feedback on your work? Were there writers' groups, for example, that you were part of when you started writing seriously?

VP: This is an interesting question and I know that in the generation of Jamaican writers after mine, all (or most) mention Mervyn Morris and Edward Baugh as people who provided guidance and feedback for them. I lived outside of Jamaica for 15 years of my adult life and had no access to that kind of interaction, except for writing to my sister who commented when she read the first few pages of *Karl*, my novella, "You can write." I returned to Jamaica in 1975 and showed the short story "My Mother" to Jean D'Costa, who sent it to *Jamaica Journal*. I was, however, aware of the notion of fledgling writers sharing material with their peers. As an undergraduate at Mona in the Fifties, a "scribblers' group" met at the Students' Union from time to time for just that kind of sharing. Perhaps my habit of excessive revision is the result of the absence of a reader so I had to be my own, what Morris calls "crap detector". When I returned to Jamaica, however, Kamau Brathwaite would read whatever I asked him to and make short insightful comments. My sister continued to read what I wrote and friends who were interested – Cecile Carrington, for example – read and gave advice. I would have the ear of Olive Senior, too, whenever she was around.

JB: Though the focus here will be on your book *And Caret Bay Again, New and Selected Poems*, I know you have published fiction and non-fiction works as well. How do you understand yourself genre-wise as a writer? Primarily a fiction writer, poet, some combination thereof, and why?

VP: I have always described myself as a teacher who writes. My writing has had to exist in the shadow of my career as a lecturer in Language Education and before that as a teacher of languages and literature. Within the creative arena, however, I see myself equally as a writer of short fiction, as of poetry. Material comes into my head already tagged, the decision already made as to which genre I will use. There is one particular instance, however, where having written a poem, the title poem of my third collection *The Best Philosophers I Know Can't Read and Write*, I felt I needed to revisit the piece and elaborate on it. The short story which does that is "A Night's Tale" in *Karl and Other Stories*.

JB: *And Caret Bay Again* consists of new and selected poems from four previous collections. How did you make the decision as to which poems from those other collections to include and what to leave out?

VP: A number of considerations came into play. I knew, for example, that I had to leave space for new poems and that there were some I had to include especially from *Crown Point*, my earliest collection, which many readers may not have seen. I still wonder how some poems came to be left out. When, at a reading from that collection, someone in the audience requested a poem she particularly wanted to hear, I wondered how it had been excluded. But that is inevitable.

JB: The thing that stands out for me most in this collection of poems is the narrator's engagement with the sea. More than anything else there is a love of the ocean in these poems. But what is particularly interesting to me about this engagement is that the narrator always seems to have her back to the land looking out at the ocean. What do you think accounts for this looking away from the island out to the horizon?

VP: This one is easy and the remark is only true for the collections after *Crown Point*. I fell in love with the sea in 1987 when I spent a semester at the University of the (US) Virgin Islands. I was on a Fulbright Fellowship researching indirectness in black people's speech. I chose Los Angeles, Gainesville and Charlotte Amalie, carefully avoiding cold locations. In Charlotte Amalie, St Thomas, United States Virgin Islands, I found a small apartment on Mandahl Peak which looks out on the sea, straight onto an island close by and several as far as eye can see. I grew up twelve and a half miles from the sea. From Mandahl Peak I saw it as soon as I looked outside my window. During that period, I also learned to get on a ferry and experience other wonders of the world like the Baths in Virgin Gorda, British Virgin Islands. Now I wonder how I omitted from *New and Selected* three poems about the Baths written on different visits between 1988 and 1998. When I saw the Baths I wanted to know how/why I had seen the Coliseum in Rome before I saw this natural wonder. Those poems are in *Leaving Traces*. So, it is less that my back was to the land than that my face was to the sea.

In Charlotte Amalie I met a Jamaican girl I had known from the USA. She was not in love with St Thomas. She missed the Jamaican landscape and the variety of flowers. I, on the other hand, discovered the beauty of the sea visible from every hillside and appreciated the external beauty I had come to recognise.

JB: Another thing that stood out quite firmly for me in this collection is that most of these poems do not take place in Jamaica. The poems are narrated through a Jamaican consciousness, but for the most part are not situated on the island. A two-part question: Do you consider yourself a Jamaican poet or a poet from Jamaica? Secondly, what do you think accounts for the almost ephemeral quality of the attachment to the Jamaican landscape in the collection?

VP: First, let me say I never thought of that distinction. I know I am a Jamaican by birth, by citizenship, by culture, but I also am a poet from Jamaica. I lived outside of Jamaica in four different countries for fifteen years of my adult life and since my return I have spent many semesters in other places. I am not sure about the ephemeral quality of my attachment to Jamaica. What I know is that Jamaica has always been with me wherever I have lived. I remember my children saying, when we finally came to live here, that they thought I would stop praising the beauty of the island once I came home, but that I kept on remarking on it ad nauseam. I did not know they had noticed, but I can tell you that every morning that I drove up the Queen's Way to work on the Mona campus, the mesmerising beauty of what I saw struck me. That is the case with other special views in Jamaica like the view from Spur Tree that looks down on Appleton Estate.

There was a time when I wanted to learn to paint so I could record the beauty of the island and how much the mountains meant to me even when I was away. I made plans but then I bought a George Rodney painting that I thought expressed my feelings and figured I could settle for that, and wrote a poem instead. It is "Long Mountain" in the collection.

JB: I must say I was a little surprised that there was so little patois and dread talk used in so many of these poems and wondered about the reason/s behind this decision?

VP: I think you see more conscious intent in my poetry than I am aware of. There was no decision to include or not to include patwa (Jamaican Creole). I think you find it wherever it comes naturally. Since I saw your question I compared my poetry with my fiction in that regard. And indeed, my fiction has a lot more patwa than my poems but it is always in the mouths of the characters who would use it in their day-to-day interaction. In my poems I am, most of the time, the speaker and the Jamaican that I speak naturally is closer to English than to Patwa. Jamaica Creole and Dread Talk have indeed been the subjects of most of my academic research and that is perhaps what led you to expect them to be present in my poetry. I do remember at least one "I-man" in the collection: in the poem "Confessions of a Son" though I seldom use Dread Talk in my own speech.

JB: One of the things I really enjoyed in the collection is the many moving moments when you seemed to be having a dialogue with several poets – Lorna Goodison, Nancy Morejón, Olive Senior, Mervyn Morris, Eddie Baugh, Derek Walcott, just to name a few. I am astonished at the ways that the tribute poems function as a kind of intertextual dialogue among and between so many poets in your collections. This makes me wonder what point or even example you were offering up in doing this so readily and often in your work?

VP: Again, there is the notion of intent, which I think is *not* a significant part of my creative process when it comes to poems. I mostly observe and write. I am not here offering any point or example. All the tributes are chosen because of some relationship between the subject matter and the person named. By the way, Walcott is not among them though I know exactly which poem I thought of naming for him.

"View Up Through Her Window", for Olive Senior, describes a view through a window to Senior's garden in Toronto. It is as literal as that. The lines "gardening /no longer in the tropics" gives it away. *Gardening in the Tropics* is perhaps her most well-known poetry collection certainly in the Caribbean. It has been on the compulsory list for the Caribbean Examinations Council in the region for many years. Eddie Baugh's "The Warner Woman" was already famous when mine was written, so I dedicated that poem to him. The circumstances which made me write "Words" are similar to those preventing Baugh, in a very moving poem, from sharing with his mother, who liked words, "Metastases" which is what the X-ray she was carrying described. A poem dedicated to Goodison begins like a response to one of hers in the "Heartease" series. The poem to Morris did not set out to copy his style, but when I found I had written such a concise and tight poem I had to acknowledge his effect on my subconscious. Nancy Morejón fell while running in the rain to greet me at a conference where women from all the countries in that poem ("Name") were interacting. I like your notion of "intertextual dialogue". I like to think it indicates the extent to which we are aware of each other's writing. After all, we are from a small society. Of course, there are many tributes which have nothing to do with poetry. Several, unfortunately, have to do with death or dying and apply particularly to the person named or to his/her family.

JB: I now know that Caret Bay is an actual place in the Virgin Islands. But returning to it again and again across several collections as you do in your writing begins to mythologise the place, as well. So, I ask you, what does Caret Bay mean to you both as an actual and a symbolic place?

VP: Since your opening sentence, I went on the web to find Caret Bay and noticed that the formation I write about is not represented; that it is featured as a place to rent an apartment if you are a tourist. Truth is, I never even noticed those apartments. Caret Bay has a beach with a spectacular rock formation (reproduced on the jacket of the collection). The beach is at the bottom of a steep red-dirt incline. I found there an intense calm in the midst of all the visible natural wonder reproduced in "Caret Bay 1".

Stone cabbages
fullformed from rockface...

stone flakes in layers
near overhanging cliffs
make silkscreens
everywhere

so little sand here...

I did not see the commercial area which lies perhaps before and after the red dirt path that leads to the beach. I was silent most of the time that first evening I was taken there: "this evening needs no syllables..." I am not surprised that the smoke from the Rasta man's hidden home is compared to incense which I associate with the Anglican church service. And so, I kept returning to it each time I was on St Thomas to recreate that peace. There was one visit where I ended up there early morning before getting on a 10:00 am flight because that is when it could be fitted in. I have written as much about the Baths at Virgin Gorda, three poems from three visits in a ten-year period, the last one with disgust at what tourists were doing to it. At my last visit, Caret Bay was still untouched, perhaps because the beach itself is not that great. The strange geographical features and the overall ambience continue to hold me.

JB: Throughout the collection there is often an unnamed male lover accompanying or being thought of by the female narrator in many of these poems. Yet the poems refuse to be explicit about who this lover is and retreats into metaphor when issues of sexuality are raised. Can you spend some time telling us why, time and time again, this happens in poems such as "Heavens Cherubim High Horsed Or The Meeting Of The Two Sevens (May 1977)"?

VP: Yes, there are many male companions in the poems but some of them have nothing to do with me. The problem with writing in the first person is that the reader might "take it personally", translate it literally. My prose has suffered that way as well. I was once invited to subscribe to a collection about writers and their mothers. The story "My Mother" has nothing at all to do with my own mother. The poem you chose is an excellent example of the first person working its show. It describes an interaction in which I was a mere onlooker. I was in an academic/literary group over a period of a week visiting and speaking at several universities in the USA. The particular couple I wrote about had not met before but over the week spent time discussing unlikely interests. Each was excited as he/she discovered more and more mutual passions. The excitement was palpable. This encounter could not become a love affair. There was nothing physical about it. In any case they lived on different continents in age and geography. By the time I wrote the first draft of the poem I was in an airport waiting on my plane sitting near one of them. The group had disbanded; each was on the way to his/her own country.

I have seen this happen to another poet at a recent reading. She read a poem and the MC who was her friend remarked that she was surprised that the poem was about an experience she thought she alone had had. The reader laughed and admitted that it was the friend's experience she had heard her recount and wrote it as if it had been hers. The moral of that story is: "Never trust a poet!" I am sure you can agree.

JB: I noticed that the narrator's path throughout the Caribbean in the collection takes her to some of the places not as frequently chronicled in Caribbean literature – the Virgin Islands, Virgin Gorda, Tortola, Montserrat. Why are you, the writer, so fascinated with these places and are you making a subtle argument about their placement and inclusion within the canon of Caribbean literature?

VP: Sorry, but I am not conscious of making any argument! A reviewer once described me as a woman who travels to many places and writes about them. In the context in which he wrote it sounded like a put-down, but perhaps it is a simple truth. The US and British Virgin Islands are part of what got added to my experience as a result of that Fulbright in 1986-87. Much of my writing for the next 10 years is affected by my encounter with those 1,000 islands and their fascinating histories. With regard to Montserrat, I was at a conference in Antigua a few years after the eruption of the volcano and took the opportunity to go there by ferry to see what the volcano had left of the island. If, however, my writing seems like a "subtle argument" for their inclusion in the canon, then I am happy!

JB: One of the strongest poems in the collection is "While TV Towers Burn (Fall, 2001)", in which the images and message of the poem coalesce into one of the utmost urgency. There are lines, for example such as "tell them but they won't hear/ tell them but they don't care" … "terror is terror anywhere." Can you take the time to explain why you wrote this poem and what it is that you would like a reader to understand about the arguments being made within it?

VP: I was in Richmond, Virginia on a semester's teaching assignment when 9/11 happened. My telephone rang and my friend, Daryl Dance, trying to keep her voice calm said, "Turn on your TV." Orange flames and grey smoke were alternating on the screen. I think I kept the TV on all through the days that followed. At the university there were special programmes to help students cope with their emotions. Some of them were from areas close to the flames and were understandably confused. Formal classes did not resume till administration felt that the students were able to concentrate on anything beside what had happened. I couldn't possibly not write. And I could not possibly make no comment as events unfolded.

I suppose I exploited the event and its aftermath to trot out some of my cynical attitudes to the US of A and its attitude to the Other. I was struck by the local outflow of hate and its unthinking responses resulting in the death of ordinary people: a turbaned old man, a white man who had a "nigger" friend. Then I pointed to other instances of terror all over the world throughout history. I was not saying anything new, just putting it all together. I hoped that readers would have read Tennyson's "The Charge of the Light Brigade" referred to in "ring the brigade bell/toll for three hundred dead" and would know what the Hydra was. I could only frame my reaction in terms of other horrors that came to me. Unfortunately, the collection accidentally omits section five which goes on to the Anthrax scare that paralysed the system immediately after and the war on Iraq that was soon to come.

JB: The poem "After 'Furious Flower' 2004" could be a primer for Hurricanes Irma and Maria that swept through the Caribbean in 2017 causing incalculable damage in some places. One of the things that immediately became noticeable to me in the aftermath of the two destructive hurricanes was that it was so many people outside of the region (including people like myself from the region) who were most loudly saying what should now happen within the region. As someone who lives in the region, given that some of the places you clearly love have been levelled by these hurricanes, what are some of the priorities, especially where writing and the literary arts are concerned, that you would like to see emphasised in rebuilding the places impacted by the hurricanes?

VP: Frankly, I think that writing is one of the few things the hurricanes would not have touched. I am pretty sure the writers have been treating them already. In fact, the first assurances I had that a friend in Puerto Rico is alive and well was a poem she had sent to a mutual friend describing her experience. I myself have several poems about earlier hurricanes that devastated some islands. I was particularly moved by shots of Dominica after, since my "David" was a reaction to the 1979 destruction there. I already have been notified by the *Caribbean Writer* that after a short hurricane-induced delay we can expect the next issue soon. I have been buoyed up by these two facts and see them as symbols of what writers and writing are about. So I would not expect any thought to be given to facilitating writing. There are hospitals and schools to rebuild. In a way, the restoration of schools already facilitates the budding poets there with the continuation of their craft.

JB: In the poem "After Lamour (for Eddie Baugh)" you write about a Warner Woman with "yellow pencils shooting from her head". I read this fortune teller as the female equivalent of one of your other really strong poems "Sugar Sweet", in which you talk about the ways in which sugar, the backbone of slave society, has now fallen out of favour in many places around the world. Both poems made me wonder if there remained a place for both sugar and the warner woman in today's Jamaican society.

VP: I don't think I have an answer for that one. I never thought of putting those two poems together but now you ask: well, the warner woman may have gone but we still have tea-leaf and palm readers and we still have significant dreams and their meanings. And those dreams are still consulted for betting on horses and buying Lotto tickets. That takes care of the predictive aspect. In the case of sugar, some doctors are now suggesting that the body does better with brown sugar than with the supplements which I also mention in the poem. In terms of the economics of sugar production there is a very big question there which people with knowledge about the situation are trying to answer, certainly in Jamaica.

JB: Finally, my absolute favourite poem of yours in the collection is "Su Su". I love the imagery and I especially love the word play and the playfulness in that poem. Of course, susu is gossip as well as an informal banking system which has sustained and maintained generations of Jamaicans. Can you tell us a little bit about the making of that poem, what you were trying to get across in it, and how do you see this poem in retrospect?

VP: First off, "Su Su" is a very Jamaican poem so we have to discount the meaning connected to the "informal banking system". Su Su is its name in Trinidad and some other islands; in Jamaica it is "Partner". Su Su as gossip, however, is very Jamaican ("as you turn you back them susu pon you" are lines from a song whose title I do not remember). The story behind that poem is a little complicated. The year was 1986. The Vice-Chancellor of the University had gone off on university business and ended up having surgery in New York. He died there. He was buried in a place where nobody had been buried before: in the Japanese Garden, just behind the University Chapel (hence the line "im shouldn bury there"). There are several poui trees round there so "Su Su" is also the sound of the wind through the leaves of those trees.

The notion is that The Vice Chancellor's spirit would come back to get other members of the University community: "im a go come back fi dem have no fear". After all, he could not preside over meetings beyond the grave if his constituency was absent. Three months after his burial, Doris Brathwaite, wife of the poet/historian Kamau Brathwaite died very soon after being diagnosed with cancer. After her funeral, Neville Hall, from the Department of History and at that time Dean of Humanities, said in my presence, "The grim reaper reapeth."

A mere two or three weeks after that, a minibus overtaking another minibus slammed into Hall's car. He was taken to hospital where he died after a week in intensive care. Obviously, the Vice-Chancellor's spirit was taking members of the community one by one. Nobody knew who would be next. Of course, as with every other situation there is a suitable Jamaican proverb:

"tiday fi mi

tumaro fi yu"

I think I just wanted to put folk intuition and fact together in a very unlikely situation. I, as the educated ignorant unbeliever, am in there as well. I, too, like the play on words which characterises the poem. Unfortunately, it takes me back to a very sad time. Leaves as symbol of the temporary nature of life turn up in many of my poems, for example in "Fall Leaves" in a totally other geographical location where "leaves must fall/and branches weep… and say again next Fall /with tears 'don't leave'", or in my farewell poem to Dr Marjorie Denbow, where the leaves of the coconut tree turn beautiful yellow as they die.

I agree with you, however, that "Su Su" is special.

CHRISTINE CRAIG MAKES THE CASE FOR
INCLUSIVENESS

Christine Craig is a short story writer and poet who also writes children's fiction. Her short stories and poems have been published in Caribbean, British and American anthologies and journals. In 1989 she was awarded a Fellowship to the International Writer's Program at the University of Iowa.

Her first publications, *Emanuel and His Parrot* (1970) and *Emanuel Goes to Market* (1971), written for children, were a collaboration with her then husband, Jamaican artist Karl 'Jerry' Craig. These were the first full colour children's books to feature a Jamaican child. She has written and directed a series of Jamaican history vignettes for children's television, and in 1990, Heinemann Caribbean published *Bird Gang*, a novella for children.

Her first collection of poetry, *Quadrille for Tigers*, was published by Mina Press in 1984. This was followed by *Mint Tea and Other Stories* (1993). In 2010, Peepal Tree published *All Things Bright & Quadrille for Tigers*.

Craig was instrumental in setting up the Women's Bureau in the 1980s, for governmental and non-governmental protection of women's rights in Jamaica. Along with Denis Watson, she co-authored *Guyana at the Cross-roads*, 1992. Also in 1992, she co-edited Jamaica's National Report to the World Conference on the Environment, Rio de Janeiro. She tutored English Literature at the University of the West Indies in the 1990s and was Adjunct Professor of Fiction and Commercial Writing at Barry University, Miami, Florida. From 1990 to 1998, she was Miami Editor of *The Jamaica Gleaner* in Miami, Florida, responsible for news and features.

She lives in Fort Lauderdale, Florida.

❧

JB: Christine, I want to start by asking you to recall a little of your childhood. I know you were born in Kingston, but spent most of your childhood growing up in St Elizabeth. What was growing up there like?

CC: We, my twin sister Penny and I, were sent to live with our grandparents in Nain, St Elizabeth, as tiny babies. Grandfather was a retired agricultural inspector; Grandma, a retired teacher. They lived on a small farm and we could have invented the term "farm to table". They had already brought up four children, all exceptional adults, and by the time we came along they were mellow experts! My earliest memories are of a world of red earth, blue skies, green trees, flowers, yellow birds, the sound of cows lowing and the smell of wet earth. I think these early sensual imprints leached into my DNA so that I would later and forever be seduced, moved, stirred up by certain combinations of those early sights, sounds, smells.

The autobiographical poem in *Quadrille*, "Prelude to Another Life", started off as a riff on Wordsworth's "Prelude" and Walcott's "Another Life" – I know, what ambition! – but took on a life of its own. So, while some of this sounds idealised, it's the truth from a child's experience.

JB: Later you would go on to attend Hampton, in St Elizabeth. So how did that wonderful poem "Butterfly Season at St Hugh's" come about? Can you talk about what went into the writing of this poem?

CC: My daughters, Rachael and Rebecca went to St Hugh's. There is a four-year gap between them, so that was many years of school drop-offs and pick-ups. I must have seen that cycle of caterpillar and butterfly many times over, but one day, the colours, the movement, the life cycle on two different levels all coalesced. It's one of my poems that start with an outer image and move into an interior space, so I was happy with it and yet surprised that so many readers who had no experience of this particular school could relate to it.

JB: This interview will focus on your book *Christine Craig: Poems* which encompasses two collections of your poems, *All Things Bright* and *Quadrille for Tigers* published by Peepal Tree Press in the UK. Usually in a situation where there is more than one volume in a work, the older work is placed ahead of the newer works to get a sense of the writer's development. Why did you make the decision to do otherwise?

CC: Honestly, there was no big decision process. I sent Peepal Tree *All Things Bright* and they decided to add the work from *Quadrille*. It made sense to me and I'm a grateful fan of Peepal Tree Press. But for them, many of us would have manuscripts mouldering away in dusty desk drawers.

JB: A strong feminist ethic pervades many of these poems, as well as an insistence on breaking silences throughout the collection, almost as if to say there is a need to hear female voices in and from Jamaican society. Indeed, the powerful poem "Elsa's Version" is quite strident in this regard. Can you explain the meaning behind the title and why this feminist insistence in this poem and in your writing in general?

CC: I had read a book in which there were three key characters, two men and a woman. In one section, the writer effectively used the technique of using the point of view of each of the men to advance the story.

The female character was Elsa, but she never had her point of view explored. The poem is not a "diss" of that book; the woman's name could be any other. The poem is my manifesto. I hate the hollow, hypocritical tributes some men make about Jamaican women while they practise all sorts of sexist behaviour, in the workplace, in politics, in the home. Women have been making their own way forward from way back in slavery days, so we don't need empty platitudes that mask roadblocks to our progress and subtle and not-so-subtle violence against us.

JB: And yet the poem "The Stranger" is a deeply moving and sympathetic portrayal of what undergirds masculinity in Jamaican society and the many ways in which societal norms become obstacles to even the men who purportedly benefit from patriarchy. Why did you write this poem and what are some of the arguments that you are making in it?

CC: Often, people assume that feminists are women who have had bad experiences with men. This is a stereotype that is often not true and certainly was not in my case. My mother left us, her three very young daughters, with my father and she went back to England. We were brought up by our father who was progressive and open-minded while being fairly firm with us on key issues. So I have had good relationships with the men in my life and come to feminism not out of some basic animosity but out of my deep-rooted desire for fairness in the way people treat each other. "The Stranger" is a difficult poem to talk about. I was looking at relationships from various viewpoints, without laying blame or attaching labels. The female persona is a composite of many women searchers who, even when they come to hostile, unknown territory, are seeking to find love, comfort, meaning in a relationship with a man. She is also the wife who is trying to be the mother/lover/worker while keeping up her side of the marriage 'contract'. The male personas are many – men trying to find their way in a difficult economy where often their best efforts bear no fruit. The second part of the poem goes under the surface, back in time to some of the experiences that shaped the generations before us, and then comes forward to a fairly common family structure where the absent mother or father goes away to find work and the child is left vulnerable and feeling unloved.

JB: Perhaps here is a good place for you to talk about the work you did in setting up the Women's Bureau in Jamaica in the 1970s. What role did you play in setting it up and why did you think it important to do so? What is/was the Women's Bureau supposed to do?

CC: The Women's Bureau was set up during Michael Manley's tenure as prime minister to find out what Jamaican women wanted the government to do to support their progress. The launch of the bureau coincided with the first United Nations International Women's Year, 1975. There were just two of us – Peggy Antrobus was our brilliant director, and I was her assistant. We used local women's groups, NGOs, church groups, to set up committees in each parish. We then scheduled workshops in each parish. At the workshops, we asked the women simply – "What do you want for yourself, your family, your community?" I remember in one such workshop seeing a woman sitting quietly with tears rolling down her cheeks. She said, "It's the first time I've been asked what I want." There were so many women who were "doing for". Doing for the man, the children, the church, the political party. And as the years rolled on the "done for" were out doing nicely while they, the "doing for" were still living hand to mouth, letting out last year's dresses and polishing the year-before's shoes.

The whole experience of getting out of the office and into a wider understanding of my own island was tremendously enriching for me, and not all about struggle and hardship. I remember a workshop in Sav-la-Mar; I turned up early at the church hall which was empty save for a large cow wandering around the room looking at the posters on display. A few participants had already arrived and they stood around looking at me, wondering how I, Miss City Lady, exiting my little blue VW bug, was going to tackle the cow. They didn't know of my early St Elizabeth days. I strode in, ushered Bessie out and we began our workshop with a good laugh.

After a year, Audrey Roberts, who was interested in women in development issues, joined our staff, but the Women's Bureau was still so small that we had to rely heavily on the input and support of women who were already tackling the key issues in their own sphere. Gloria Cumper was working to set up the Family Court. Lucille Mair had done seminal research on Women in Slavery and was a strong force in politics. Women in the arts, communication, health, education, too many to name, were all making headway on various concerns. Although our office was so small, we did a lot of consciousness-raising activities which kept women's issues out at centre stage and stimulated a lot of debate and action on things like minimum wage, equal pay, access to non-traditional training and women in the military. It was a heady time of women networking and supporting each other in a very quiet, probably unnoticed, way. We had support from the top leadership in Michael Manley and his wife, Beverley Manley, who was a key player in the PNP Women's group. But we also had many detractors. We were most saddened by the "comrades" who wanted to dismiss feminism as the purview of white Americans, men-haters and bra-burners. And there were the church elders who wanted to quote scripture about a "woman's place" while relying on the women in the congregation to do the menial, unpaid jobs of keeping the church machinery clean and well-oiled.

JB: The collections return again and again to the many meanings of being "red" as opposed to "black" in Jamaican society. This can be seen at work in poems such as "Westmoreland" where the "red" female narrator carries "...the weight of the past/in that house and me, the product of both". In the poem "Mountain Lilies and Sand", the narrator speaks of a sick child who could be "... yours black sister/ and yours red sister", marking and denoting the difference between the two groups of women. What argument are you making about the privileges and possible pitfalls that can attend being "red" as opposed to "black" in Jamaican society? Is there a meeting place for both identities?

CC: There are so many castes, so many complexities in Jamaica about race, appearance, colouring, who has tall hair, who doesn't; the ridiculous list goes on and on. In all the mixes, red gal was not a term of admiration or approval. It's a real put-down; she is not pretty, not desirable. Yet, red gal can also be seen as a member of the privileged class. Back in the 60s she could get a job in a bank before her black cousin with the same or better qualifications. She is perceived as closer to the high-browns, the whites and nearly-whites, although those groups don't particularly want to include her. If she is seen in this latter group, then she doesn't have the authority to write of the 'black' experience. It's an uncomfortable place to inhabit and I early chose not to live there as I reject all those absurd categories. I acknowledge and call out the various castes to make a case for the inclusiveness of womanhood, of motherhood, of personhood.

JB: One of the tensions in the collection, for me, is between poetry and prose in works such as the poem "Kingston". A two-part question here: Firstly, in addition to being a poet you are also a fiction writer; do you have a preference for a particular form that you write in? Secondly, how do you make the distinction between a work that is a poem as opposed to a work of, say, prose/fiction?

CC: I play about with the prose/poem mix mainly in narrative pieces. In those cases, I like to think the prose still has a rhythm, a cadence that keeps it within the ambit of poetry. My first love is poetry but some material presents as fiction and others as poems and yet others as some sort of mix. I just try to be open to the ideas, those little whispers that play about on the edge of one's subconscious.

JB: In the poem "Diary of a Disturbance" you have a line: "Here in the anthology of our lives." One of the striking things in the collections is how much the narrator is moving across the island of Jamaica, and describing and recording what she sees, almost as if indeed a subconscious element of the collections is anthologising the island of Jamaica.

CC: Yes, you are right. That is exactly what is happening. I was trying to record and understand and sing about this place that is too complex to fit into one scene, one definition. I wanted to experience it in the here and now and also reflect a bit on the past in order to see how our present was shaped. Maybe that's all the writer can do: capture something of her time. Then our grandchildren will capture their own reality, and hopefully, as the years flow on, we will build up a sort of archeological trove for future generations. That sounds rather fanciful but it can be real. The first Jamaican novel I read was Roger Mais's *The Hills Were Joyful Together*, which was written years and years before I read it. I can't describe the big flash that went off in my head, the joy that came from recognising the beauty and pain as ours in a way that all the European literature I had grown up with, and loved, was not.

JB: As a writer, you engage floral images and floral imagery, particularly island flowers, as symbolic tropes of female lives. As a poet, I find that I do that myself, too. Can you discuss the beautiful poem "In the Frills of Jacaranda" and some of the ideas you were advancing about women's lives on the island, but also, presciently, about the delicacy of Jamaica's natural environment?

CC: My favourite subjects at school were botany and zoology. I had a wonderful teacher, Miss Rainford, who could make the structure and functions of these living things totally engrossing. Some of the references to flowers and trees are simply that – the "naming" of things in my world that I value and enjoy. But you are also right about the relationship between flowers and the feminine; the beauty, intricacy, their link to fruitfulness are all natural parallels.

"In the Frills of Jacaranda" is one of those poems that came out almost fully formed. Here the pretty flower images are hiding some nasty themes of men preying on young girls, particularly the "sweaty preacher", those men in positions of trust who, without conscience or remorse, savagely deflower their vulnerable young charges.

On the matter of the environment, it sounds trite to say that Jamaica is a paradise, but it really is and thankfully, though we come late to the job, many Jamaicans are taking the duty of keeping it an Eden seriously. I admire the enormously talented writer Diana McCaulay who has made it her life's work.

It's also not only how we keep our environment safe and beautiful but how we deal with ownership and stop seeing beaches and other prime land as "real estate" to be sold for commercial ventures. Anthony Bourdain put it succinctly in one of his programmes where he was visiting Jamaica. He was sitting on a beautiful beach which the local people were trying to prevent being sold for hotel construction when he asked, and I paraphrase,

"Who should enjoy paradise? Wealthy foreigners who can afford ritzy hotel rooms, or the local people who were born and live here, many of whom make their living from the sea?" It's a serious moral imperative that we not sell out our birthright.

JB: The poet you seem to look to and reference the most and try to dialogue with in your collection is Kamau Braithwaite, who turns up again and again in poems in both collections. Why is Kamau Brathwaite of such importance to your creative writing?

CC: Back in the 60s, when I was a young wife living in London, my husband, Jerry Craig, was older than I and already an art lecturer at a teacher training college and a prolific artist. Eddie Kamau Brathwaite had graduated Oxford and was living in London with his wife Doris. Kamau and a Trinidadian named John La Rose, and the Jamaican writer Andrew Salkey, started a group that came to be called CAM – Caribbean Artists Movement. We got involved and Jerry led the drive to get exhibitions set up for Caribbean artists and sculptors, including one at the House of Commons. As a teen, I was great friends with Dennis Scott and admired his work tremendously and so became interested in Jamaican literature. In CAM, I found a home that introduced me to the work of writers from the wider Caribbean. Kamau was a soft-spoken man with a knife-sharp intellect. I had never heard poetry like his: the rhythms, the thundering cadences, the whispered incantations, the complex themes. It was all heady, heady stuff. Years later, when I had started writing, I would find many writers whose work I also love, Derek Walcott being high up on the list, but Kamau's work, in some very elemental way, opened the door to what would be my lifelong love of poetry.

JB: Moving away from your collections for a moment, tell us a little about the series of Jamaican history vignettes you wrote and directed for children in the past? What was the idea behind the series? Why did you think it was important to do this?

CC: Before I met Jerry, he had produced the manuscript for a beautiful children's book called *Emanuel and His Parrot*. He had done the illustrations and an English friend had written the text from the story he gave her. He showed the book to Andrew Salkey, who gave him an introduction to an editor at Oxford University Press. She loved the drawings, but not the text. I rewrote the text for him so it was more Jamaican and the editor accepted it. It became the first full-colour children's book with a Jamaican theme on the English market. He produced a second book *Emanuel Goes to Market*. I also wrote the text from his original story. When we returned to Jamaica, I got a call one day from a producer on Miss Lou's TV show, *Ring Ding*. Would I bring an Emanuel book and read it to the children. Say what! Me, with Miss Lou? I was beyond thrilled. I went on the show, read the book and showed the pictures and as I was about to leave the stage, Miss Lou asked me to come back and tell more Jamaican stories. Who says no to Miss Lou? Of course, I promised I would and then went home and panicked. TV – a new story every week – what was I thinking?

I decided to find stories from Jamaican history. I hadn't been much interested in history at school so I was woefully ignorant about Jamaican history. I thought that if I could find stories that interested me, perhaps they would also interest my young audience. And maybe it would be a fun way for us both to learn about our past. So began my relationship with the amazing Miss Lou and my stint as a storyteller on live TV. The children seemed to love the stories and I was encouraged by the many adults who told me they would listen in every Saturday to the history stories.

JB: Your collections are suffused with the presence of Jamaica, but now another loved and complicated landscape – that of Florida, where you have lived for a number of years – has crept into your work. Does living in Florida at all complicate any notions of "home" that you might have? Where is "home" for you?

CC: Oh no, there are no complications! Home is Jamaica. I'm appreciative of the many good things I enjoy here in the US – I've been active in the "get out the vote" process as I do believe in active citizenship – but home will always be Jamaica.

JB: Finally, what is Christine Craig working on these days?

CC: It's been a difficult time here. The horror of contemporary American politics is deeply disturbing and it's difficult not to fall prey to cynicism and hopelessness. Why try to move forward and change anything if it can so easily be threatened and undermined?

But I'm trying to rouse myself from that malaise and am working on fiction, some short stories, a children's book, with – surprise, surprise – an environmental theme! I'm my own worst editor, destroying half of what I do and agonising over the few pieces that survive my purges. And I'm not good at getting my work out and published. Ah well, the rocky psychology of the creative! But let's leave that for another discussion.

OF HEARTS REVEALED:
AN INTERVIEW WITH OLIVE SENIOR

Olive Senior was born and brought up in Jamaica and educated in Jamaica and Canada. She is a graduate of Montego Bay High School and Carleton University, Ottawa. She started her career as a journalist with the *Daily Gleaner* and later entered the world of publishing. She was editor of two of the Caribbean's leading journals – *Social and Economic Studies* at the University of the West Indies and *Jamaica Journal*, published by Institute of Jamaica Publications of which she was also Managing Director. She left Jamaica in 1989, spent some years in Europe and since 1993 has been based in Toronto.

The Caribbean nevertheless remains the focus of her work, starting with her prizewinning collection of stories, *Summer Lightning* (1986) which won the Commonwealth Writers Prize followed by *Arrival of the Snake-Woman* (1989) and *Discerner of Hearts* (1995). Her novel, *Dancing Lessons* was published in Canada 2011 and *The Pain Tree*, a collection of stories in the spring of 2015 and by Peepal Tree (UK and Caribean edition) in 2017. Her illustrated children's books are *Birthday Suit*, *Anna Carries Water* and Boonoonoonous Hair (2019).

Her poetry books are *Talking of Trees* (1986), Gardening in the Tropics (1994), Over the Roofs of the World (2005) and *Shell* (2007). A bilingual edition (English/French) of her poetry was published in 2014 under the title *Un Pipiri m'a dit/A Little Bird Told Me*.

Olive Senior's non-fiction works on Caribbean culture include the *A-Z of Jamaican Heritage* (1984), *Working Miracles: Women's Lives in the English-Speaking Caribbean* (1991), *The Encyclopedia of Jamaican Heritage* (2004) and *Dying to Better Themselves: West Indians and the Building of the Panama Canal* (2015 OCM Bocas Literary Prize for Non-Fiction).

*

With Jacqueline Bishop and Dolace McLean

DM: Olive Senior, the first thing I want to ask deals with the issue of culture as related to your characters. Most of your characters are usually young children who are isolated and lonely, and the point of view from which they speak is one of what I call in my work, "Islandism" – the idea of being an island. It's almost if they're little islands in a sea of [adult] people who do not really care about them. Does that reflect something about Jamaican culture specifically or Caribbean culture in general?

OS: My first book of short stories reflected those kinds of characters but I would say, looking at the body of my work, I have a much more varied range of characters, though people tend to focus on the children. And I like the use of the term, "Islanded". In fact, I just wrote a whole set of poems called "Islanded" and I think that's what my young characters are. I don't think they reflect Jamaica, they just reflected me and how I felt as a child [who was] totally alienated from my environment. And although I'm not writing autobiographically, I think I've infused my characters with my own emotional states and feelings and so on. They reflected the fact that I felt like an isolated, lonely child. Totally alienated from adult culture. I don't know that it's more than that, really.

DM: So how would you then address someone who reads your work as somehow indicative of a larger Jamaican culture? Your work speaks for you as the writer who wants to break boundaries but at the same time it does seem to fit into certain categories...

OS: I wasn't writing about myself. I was writing about the people around me that I grew up with and so on. However, I'm just saying that as a writer I infused my feelings into the writing. I don't see it from the point of view of the critic who's reading it as a paradigm of something else. That's not how writers write. So, I'm [not sure if I can] answer that kind of question. It's for the readers and the critics to bring that to bear on the work. I am just telling stories.

DM: Oh so they're stories.

OS: Even my poems are stories. I'm a storyteller.

DM: Interesting that you should say that because it brings up a whole lot of questions, critical questions, which you say aren't [necessarily] "writerly" questions, but at some level, it seems that the writer has to almost consciously say, I'm not going to be a critical writer, I'm going to be a writer's writer. How do you make the distinction between just writing your work as stories and writing them for people? How do you negotiate that? How do you get your readers to know what it is that you're trying to convey? To get what it is that you are trying to say?

OS: Well, you see, I don't feel it's my job to negotiate anything. It's my job to tell a good story and to tell it in the best way that I can and to tell it honestly. I see my stories, or what I do, as part of a half of something and the reader then has to bring something to bear. It's a kind of contract between myself and the reader and it's up to me to be convincing and to touch the reader in some way. That's my job. A story isn't an essay. People can read politics into it, they can read all kinds of things into it but that's not what I set out to put in. I set out to communicate something about one human being to another human being. That's what I'm about.

DM: Interesting. So then who is your audience? The thing about writing is that writers write, they create. But it seems that writers actually have to create for someone and sometimes they have to think "How will I market this," To whom will I target [my work]," "Who is my audience?" and so I'm just wondering if you have an audience in mind?

OS: None of that enters into my mind. For me what matters is the writing. What I'm doing here and now. If it never gets published, it never gets published. I consider it my imperative to write and all these issues about getting published and so on have come long after I started to write. And I'm not even that concerned about them. I write what I want to write. I'm not writing for a particular audience. I'm not writing because I want to sell. That's not my motivation at all. I'm just fulfilling a need in me to accomplish the most important thing in life which is to put stuff down on paper.

DM: And if that never went anywhere beyond a, let's say, self-published copy to your family, that would be okay?

OS: Well, I've gone beyond that so it's not really an issue. However, the thing is [that] when I wrote my first collection of stories I didn't think of being published. You know in North America and in the metropole it's interesting to see how people approach writing. It's very different from how I approach writing. To me writing was something you did because you had to do it. It had nothing to do with a market. What's a market? I knew nothing about that. And I still have this attitude. I teach writing and have students who have not published anything handing me a card which says, "So-and-so. Writer". Or I know people who will say to me, "You're writing something and it's not commissioned? You mean nobody's paying you to do it?" So my attitude towards writing is, I guess, a very old fashioned one, which I will not advocate for anybody else, but it is also the attitude of the people that I grew up with, people of my generation coming from the Caribbean.

DM: And it's interesting that you should say that because, in very many ways, what you are saying ["I write because I write"] is pretty much a luxury these days.

OS: I agree that it is a luxury, but I don't think I write because I write. I think you become a writer because you can't help it. It's not a choice that you make, you are chosen. It's a burden that's placed on you, and you just fulfil it, you just get on with it. I don't see writing as a "career choice", which is the way some people see writing nowadays. I've never been to university to learn anything about writing. It's just part of who I am. I think I'm coming from a very different place, than where people nowadays are coming from, in relation to becoming writers.

JB: I agree with everything you are saying right now and indeed as someone who writes, I really do understand. So would you say then [that] you are writing to kind of understand something? For yourself?

OS: Yes. I guess [my writing] began as a way of understanding myself. I started writing merely as therapy, in a sense that I just needed to work out a lot of things about my identity really, and that's when I started to write. I didn't start to write for other people but in the process of doing that, I discovered not just things about myself but about my society, about the people around me. So in a way it's an interrogation, not just of myself but of my society and I think what has happened to me is that I've moved away from self. Very little of my writing now has anything of me in it and that's deliberate. Whereas, it's very much concerned with Caribbean society, both my poetry and everything I do. Because I feel my engagement now is with the society; trying to explain this society to myself really.

DM: That's actually really interesting because it brings me to the other large issue on our agenda, which has to do with living in North America but writing about the Caribbean. Why is it that you live in Canada and write about Jamaica from that place? Is it that you did not want to continue or could not continue to produce in the Caribbean?

OS: Well, the fact that I moved out of the Caribbean is really accidental. I sort of left for a year because I needed a break and the year became two and three. And you know now it's become ten. But everything I write is about the Caribbean, I've never written another word about anywhere else. I suppose I was a little bothered by the whole notion of living in one place and writing about another but then I read what someone said to the effect "the writer's country is writing" and that seems to apply to me.

DM: That is quite interesting. After all there are all kinds of reasons why it's difficult to produce in Jamaica or in the Caribbean. It is a frustrating thing not just because there's a lack of resources but because there's also a lack of critical appreciation for the kinds of work that people do. But it would seem to me that if writing is the only home that a writer ought to know, and if writing is a burden that a writer must express, then it would seem that it should be okay for all those writers to stay in the Caribbean because then it won't matter where one is placed as long as one is doing what it is that one is chosen to do.

OS: Well, to me personally it doesn't matter where I live because most of what happens to me, happens in my head. I live inside my head. And I spend a lot of time in Jamaica, so its not that I am so far away. Besides, I like travelling, I like going around the world, and I like seeing new things. I don't think I have to sit in Jamaica in order to write. And in fact I think I've had a much better perspective on Jamaica living outside of it because it has given me some space and distance. I wrote eight books living in Jamaica or seven books. So it's not problematic. And I didn't leave because I could not write there. It's accidental that I left. I didn't leave to leave. I'm still very much engaged with Jamaica and what's going on there.

JB: Speaking of what is going on there, Olive, there are some questions I want to ask about your view of life in Jamaica now. I am interested to know what you make of the crime situation in Jamaica?

OS: Well I don't know if that's something I really want to go into. Because what do I make of it? What does anybody make of it?

DM: What about the violence? Is it cultural and how so? In your work there's a sense of colonial disorder and imperial order and I'm just wondering is it that the violence is a natural outgrowth of independence, so to speak? That somehow the vernacular culture of Jamaica is taking over and that there is this [social] tension because the former structures of class positioning are being upset?

OS: It's extremely complex. But I think we tend to forget that violence is ingrained in our culture from the beginning. Columbus arrived and the first thing that he did was set dogs on the Tainos. Our history, our written history, is born out of violence. If you look at who the first settlers were, they were pirates, they were buccaneers, they were slave owners, and I think that Jamaica had more slave insurrections than any other country in the New World. So for us to look at violence today as if it's something new is, I think, ahistorical. I think we need to see it as a product of colonialism and of our history. Our failure at managing disputes in the home or larger society. I think what's different today is the form the violence is taking and the fact we are now equipped with deadly weapons of destruction. So now all disputes, no matter how small, are settled not with words or fists but with bullets. And, of course, there are all kinds of other elements involved, such as the drug trade.

When I was growing up I suppose there was a lot of domestic violence around me, but if there was ever a murder anywhere in the country, this was big news. I grew up in a place where doors were left open. I had no fear as a child, absolutely none. I never, ever, felt threatened or anything. So things have changed. But also, I think we have to look at the root causes of violence. I don't think it's a product of independence – unless it's a question of independence failing to meet people's expectations. But I do think it's a product of poverty, of injustice, of our failure as a people to provide for the majority of our citizens. To educate our children. To provide people with the basics of life. I mean food shelter and so on. Violence is bred out of those kinds of conditions. But what bothers me about the violence is that there doesn't seems to be any serious analysis on a national level as to the causes of violence and our collective responsibility and therefore we can't really address it. Collectively, we need to examine who we are and where we want to go, what kind of society, and what kind of culture do we want to create and we haven't done that.

DM: And why do you think that the violence is characterized the way it is? It seems that there is a rigid class structure that blames certain kinds of people for the violence, and in the face of the overwhelming amounts of violence that are there now, why do you think that those class structures still prevail? And what are they supposed to accomplish, especially in light of the fact that they are failing?

OS: Part of it is that the whole society has broken down in a way at the level of leadership and there are lots of other factors that we need to look at. For instance, the impact of migration on the socialization of children. Who is raising those children left behind? And of course there are serious economic factors which are getting worse and worse. What bothers me about all of this is the impact it's having on all the youth and the children and the kind of world that the majority of them will inherit. I think something like one third of the population lives in Kingston and a very significant portion of the population in Jamaica is under age fourteen. What are we giving them as adults? What kind of world are they growing up in? What values are they being given, considering that the old values are broken down and we haven't replaced them? I just see it as something very, very complex.

DM: Oh it's extremely, extremely complex. The thing that I feel is that in some way I have to try to make it better or do something differently to help to replace those [old] values. How does that happen? I'm not quite sure. But I do have classmates who have gone back and others who are in training who harbour some ambition to go back and contribute. So how are you trying to replace some of those [old] values with your writing, especially now that your writing has gotten more socially conscious?

OS: Well I'm not sure I myself am consciously trying to replace values. I think that my job as a writer is to hold the mirror up to society and to say this is how things are. But I don't thinks it's for me to prescribe. I also think, though, that part of the problem for countries like Jamaica are the people like us, the people who have left over a long period of time. We have to see ourselves as part of the problem.

DM: How so?

OS: Well, in the sense the people who leave are usually the people who are educated, the people with the skills, training or ambition – and when we leave [we are] draining the country of [our] talents. Let me hasten to say I am not blaming people for leaving – we all have to follow our dreams. But I personally feel the need to give something back. And that is why I've spent the last twenty years of my life working on the *Encyclopedia of Jamaican Heritage*. Because, in a way, I say, okay, I'm part of the problem, and this is my way of giving back something.

DM: Is that realistic? I have this strange feeling that the average fourteen and under youth will see attempts through literature and writing as some sort of romanticized part of our history that we can always look back to and say, "Oh that's how it used to be." I get this strange sense that writing and literature might not be as pertinent to modern Jamaica as it should be.

OS: One has to be optimistic. That's a very pessimistic view and I'm aware of it. However, my attitude is that if I can impact just one child, [that's good]. If one child is going to get interested and say, "Oh I didn't know this, I didn't know this, oh wow!" then it is enough. It is enough because he or she will read this book that is about everything – history, literature, plants, animals – [the Jamaican] world that I grew up loving and learning about. So although there are all these other cultural influences that have penetrated the society, I still believe we have to keep trying. We just have to believe that there are enough young people out there who are going to make a difference.

JB: It's so funny how I found out about you. I'd almost finished my bachelor's degree. I was living in France and I found a book in France that had one of your stories. You know it wasn't even here [in North America] it was all the way in France and when I found it, I couldn't believe it. I didn't know that there were writers from Jamaica and I especially didn't know there were women writers from Jamaica. I was a junior at that point in college and it did make a difference in my life to know that.

OS: It's good that you say that, because it brings me back to the question of who I write for. I don't write for anyone in particular. My work is read by people all over the world because I'm really writing about the human condition. I'm willing to touch anyone who is willing to be touched by it. But I must say that I'm really pleased when my work is taught in schools or universities and when young people say to me that they saw themselves reflected in it, because I grew up not seeing myself reflected in literature. So from that point of view I'm very pleased that this is happening.

JB: There's another way to look at it, also, that I have found in my life. Whenever I'm interested in a topic that topic seems to find me. And I feel that people who want to know more about Jamaica in the way that Olive Senior writes, will find Olive Senior and will find the Jamaica represented in your work.

OS: Yes. But part of our problem is that in the Caribbean we don't see literature as having that kind of impact, we no longer see culture as part of the development process.

DM: In Jamaica?

OS: Yes. You know, independence was really a wonderful time because we were engaged in a dialogue then, the whole society. People were talking about things we'd never talked about before and I found it very exciting and I was really caught up in it. For a while we were really trying to come to grips with who we were, with questions of identity. This was when all the cultural institutions, like the National Gallery, and training schools for the arts were set up, and I think that Jamaica has a terrific history in that regard. But the way I see it, it was like a window opening or a door opening for a moment and then it's slammed shut again. That is what is happening in Jamaica.

DM: And what happened... why did it slam shut?

OS: Well I think a lot of it is based on political decisions, because culture needs money to survive. And when the economy shrinks, as it has done in Jamaica, then it becomes a question of how you cut the pie. You need public support for what you're doing. If the public support is not there then cultural activities fade away, they die on the vine. But there also has to be a recognition in the society at large of the need to develop and promote what's local. The contempt that local booksellers seem to have for Caribbean books is a case in point. But... we haven't talked much about the writing... into trouble! (*Laughter*).

DM: Well, it's only because I think that work comes out of a context and work is put in a context as one reads and it's important to be able to pull out those things that are implicit in the text and make them explicit and say, well this is what this text actually does or can do and that is why I ask. (*Laughter*).

OS: Oh I understand. It is just that I think we should make it clear that the writer's perspective is different from the critic's perspective. I think part of the problem now is that critics assume that writers write politically. And that, you know, writing is this political act, as if I'm going "this is my post-colonial moment", which is nonsense. I mean this is something I try to make clear to people, that we writers are coming out of a different space and it is for the readers and the critics now to bring something else to it, which is not the same thing that the writers are bringing. I do think we need each other, and that writing develops best in a space where we have critics and reviewers and critical readers. One of the reasons that Caribbean writing has developed is precisely because we've had institutions like the University of the West Indies and critics who started to write about Caribbean literature. I think this is a very important part of the process.

I see that anything we as writers do is bound up with what other people are doing. People of my generation were very much influenced by music and by the voices that we were hearing. I can remember, as a seminal moment, the first time I heard certain Jamaican songs on the radio because these were raw country-boy voices. These were not BBC voices. And I think that was a liberating moment, a liberating experience for all of us who were being socialized to be English men and women [because] this is what high school did for you at that time. And suddenly to hear these voices and to hear that rhythm in the music, I think that had a lot to do with our thinking and the changes that took place in literature and in art.

JB: Olive, I have read all the books and my favourite story in the entire world is "Ballad" and I wonder if you can talk a little bit about how you wrote "Ballad" because I remember once you said that you'd been trying for a while and "Ballad" was your breakthrough story.

OS: Yes, it was. I decided at a very early age I was going to be a writer – when I was four I would tell everybody, because I learned to read at a very early age. Reading was a consolation for me and I used to bury myself in books. But I also listened. I grew up hearing stories, I grew up in an oral culture and I was very, very conscious of words and the power of words. As a child I wrote all through school and won prizes, the usual thing. But although I wanted to write, I just found I couldn't write using the third person, objective point of view... bit just didn't feel comfortable. And so that particular story... that was a breakthrough story for me. It's when I chose to allow my character to speak with her voice, which was the voice of a little country girl. I came to think of it as the "little tradition" bursting forth, for, like other people I had been raised on "the great tradition", which included the English literary canon. But the minute I allowed that girl to speak her story, to tell her story in her own words, that allowed me to enter the world of writing because it just opened it up. And then I felt more confident about allowing my characters to speak patois because those were the people I wanted to write about. These characters arrived with their voices.

JB: Another thing I've realized is that sometimes you write about characters who are not really given a say in Jamaican culture. For example, the main character in "The Arrival of the Snake Woman" – the snake woman herself. How did you come up with that title? Anyway, she's an Indian woman and she misses her country and she runs her hand over the map and expresses the kind of longing that I guess I feel here for Jamaica. But that's a character that we don't generally see much of.

OS: People have written a lot about that story because it was a sort of breakthrough for the Indian in Jamaican fiction. I remember meeting Indians in Portugal who read that story and they said that they were so touched because I had her crying and using the end of her sari to wipe her eye and they were asking "How could you have known this?" But the gesture just seemed natural to me. I say I write intuitively because a lot of what I do is not conscious. It's not because I think, okay I'm going to have her doing this. My attitude is that I'm recording everything as I go through life. And that is what happens. The fiction or poetry are products of all my life experiences, and you know that life experiences are not just existential, but it's what you've read, it's what you've heard, it's everything.

JB: My three favourites for the record are "Ballad", "Arrival of the Snake Woman" and of course "Discerner of Hearts", and they really do bring out a whole world when one reads them. But back to "The Arrival of the Snake Woman", I mean how did you come up with this Indian woman in the first place?

OS: When I was growing up in this little village, there was this Indian woman and everybody called her "Miss Coolie". I've been roundly criticized by various people for that but anyway... She was very old when I was small and I didn't know anything about her, but she was the village midwife who delivered babies so she might have delivered me, I'm not sure. But she stuck in my mind and I started to speculate about how this one little Indian lady came to be here in a village of mainly African-Jamaicans because [she didn't seem to] belong there. At the time I knew absolutely nothing about Indians, of course; it's much later that I realized they'd come as indentured workers. But it is just from speculating about that woman and deciding to give her a background that I wrote this story. Of course, this story is set much further back in time, it's set around the end of the 19th century and the beginning of the 20th century, but it was just from my imagining, knowing nothing about this woman, and thinking about how she got here – that's where that story started.

JB: Olive, I've read these stories and I've read these stories (*Laughter*) and sometimes I'm totally envious! I wish I'd written "Ballad" because it's my all-time favourite story in the world! And in another of your stories that I so love, "Zig Zag", in your collection "Discerner of Hearts", we have these girls growing up with all the contradictions of being a young girl in Jamaican society. On the one hand, the dark-skinned girl gets pregnant, and her mother is furious but proud at the same time. So how do you deal with all those contradictions in your characters? Are your characters always contradicted in some kind of way?

OS: I think so. I think I was always aware of these contradictions growing up in real life, and I think my stories mirror real life, although they are fictional creations. I think at a very early age I was very aware of social forces and so when I come to write I worry about my characters and the narrative and so on, but I don't worry about the background. I automatically know what the background of each character is – it's as if it's there, it's patterned, it's in my mind. I think I truly understand Jamaicans, in that sense. I suppose I've always been interested in asking "why", which is the most important question for a writer to ask. I've always asked myself "why" even as a small child and so I've grown up with a good understanding of how things operate. Of course I've also read a lot, and my reading and everything I do sort of fits in with everything else. When I was doing the research and writing for [the book] *Working Miracles: Women's Lives in the English-Speaking Caribbean*, that helped to inform my understanding of things that I knew from experience but I also think I was able to put a lot into that book from my creative self.

JB: And having been the editor of *Jamaica Journal* must have given you a whole wealth of information. I sometimes think well that's why Olive Senior knows so much! (*Laughter*)

OS: Well, yes it did, but I also know a lot because I've always been a voracious reader. And as I say, I've always been very curious. I'm tempted to put a picture on the cover of the Encyclopedia of Jamaican Heritage of me at age 4 and say this is when my research began. (*More laughter*)

DM & JB: You should... no you should.

OS: I'm the kind of person if I don't know something, even now, I'll go look it up because I cannot bear not to know. But there is a difference between growing up in a society where you just learn as part of the process of growing up, as opposed to moving to somewhere new where you have to start from scratch. And I think this is why I still write about Jamaica because it is already so much of my knowledge base.

DM: That's true and that's reflected in your work. You know the names of the birds, you know the names of the trees and it's even the way you describe the topography...

JB: You have a love affair with Jamaica.

OS: Yes, it's in my blood.

JB: What do you think of the idea that contradiction moves Jamaican society?

OS: Contradiction is at the heart of Jamaican society. It's part of what makes the country exciting, but it's also something that causes such pain. We are people who experience a great deal of pain precisely because of these contradictions. It's the pull that we feel between all these different cultures from which we've come and which have shaped us. And we have love/hate relationships with everything and everybody. So it gives us our "Islandism" and our excitement, but at the same time it also makes it difficult to move – to sort of transcend this, because we're so preoccupied with existence.

DM: And I think some of that is tied to the whole cultural values that we were talking about earlier, which are now missing.

OS: Yes. It is a different climate now; it's harder now and young people who are going to the universities have to be pragmatic and think, "I have to get a job." There are just so many things working against the development of national literature in those places.

JB: Can we expect a novel from Olive Senior?

OS: I have written one novel which is in the bottom drawer still and probably will stay there, but part of my problem is I don't have time. I mean I work for a living and novels require [a lot of time]. I know there are people who have ten children and write at the kitchen table every night, but that's just not how I function. I need a lot of headspace. And all the things I have in my head right now are long books, novels, but I don't know if they'll ever get written. I have a lot of things in my head I want to write. I'm interested in looking at events in the past or time periods in the past that were formative moments. But I might say that today, this is what I'm going to do and I might wake up tomorrow doing something else. Who knows?

THE MUSE OF MEMORY IS THE MUSE OF POETRY: AN INTERVIEW WITH POET LAUREATE LORNA GOODISON

Lorna Goodison CD is a Jamaican poet and a leading West Indian writer of the generation born after World War II. She was appointed Poet Laureate of Jamaica in 2017, succeeding Mervyn Morris. In 2019 she was awarded the Queen's Gold Medal for Poetry. She has also achieved many other notable awards including in 1999 the Musgrave Gold Medal, the 2013 Order of Distinction, the 2018 Windham-Campbell Literature Prize and the 2014 OCM Bocas Prize in Poetry. Poet and literary scholar Edward Baugh says: "one of Goodison's achievements is that her poetry inscribes the Jamaican sensibility and culture on the text of the world". Apart from issues of home and exile, her work also addresses the power of art to explore and reconcile opposites and contradictions in the Caribbean historical experience. Also a painter, Goodison has illustrated her own book covers, as well as exhibiting her artwork in the Caribbean, the US and Europe.

Her poetry collections include: *Tamarind Season* (1980), *I am Becoming My Mother* (1986), *Heartease* (1988), *Poems* (1989), *Selected Poems* (1992), *To Us, All Flowers Are Roses* (1995), *Turn Thanks* (1999), *Guinea Woman* (2000), *Travelling Mercies* (2001), *Controlling the Silver* (2005), *Goldengrove* (2006), *Oracabessa* (2013), *Supplying Salt and Light* (2013), *Collected Poems* (2017). Her short story collections are *Baby Mother and the King of Swords* (1990), *Fool-Fool Rose is Leaving Labour-in-Vain Savannah* (2005) and *By Love Possessed* (2012). Her memoir, *From Harvey River: A Memoir of My Mother and Her Island* was published in 2009, and a collection of essays, *Redemption Ground: Essays and Adventures* in 2018.

❦

JB: Lorna, I must say I was moved to tears when it was announced that you would be the new Poet Laureate of Jamaica. So I start this interview by asking you if there is any significance for you, personally, in being the first female Poet Laureate of y/our beloved homeland? What do you hope to initiate or achieve with this new platform?

LG: Thank you so much. I am honoured to be the subject of one of your interviews.

I too was very moved when Justine Henzell, Professor Edward Baugh and Winsome Hudson, former director of the National Library of Jamaica (NLJ), and Minister Olivia "Babsy" Grange asked me, on behalf of the Government of Jamaica, to become the Poet Laureate of Jamaica. Being made poet laureate at the same time that my *Collected Poems* – which is over 600 pages long – was published by Carcanet Press (UK) seems like a double blessing. As you yourself said to me, "If anybody asks you what you have done with your life, you can point to that book."

As the first woman to be given this honour, I am, of course, well pleased, and I have hopes, dreams and plans for what I'll do while I am Poet Laureate, and one of the first initiatives I've been involved with is the "All Flowers are Roses" Self-Defence and Poetry Summer Workshop. This was a workshop designed to teach young girls basic self-defence and poetry writing. It was taught by the well-known Jamaican poet and martial arts expert, Cherry Natural, and the poet Yashika Graham. The logo was designed by the British Jamaican artist Ruel Hudson, and it went so well that the current director of the NLJ, Beverly Lashley, is working with Abigail Henry, who does a wonderful job of running the Poet Laureate programme, and me to expand it this year.

As I see it, poets laureate are national praise singers and advocates of poetry, and I believe I have been doing something like that in my own work, in an unofficial capacity, for many years. I am particularly grateful that I've had the great good fortune to have been able to read my praise poems to Jamaica to wide audiences here at home and in many different parts of the world.

I have also been at this business for quite some time. My first collection of poetry was published in 1980, by the Institute of Jamaica Press, and individual poems of mine had been appearing in various magazines and in Jamaican Sunday newspapers for at least twelve years before that. From the very beginning, I was always writing poems inspired by aspects of Jamaican culture; even some of my most intimate and personal poems somehow manage to reference Jamaica. One of my poems, which appears on the London Underground, is called "Bam Chi Chi La La", and it is about a Jamaican teacher working as a char woman so that she can build her retirement home in Mandeville. Because I love how we talk, I try to write in a mixture of Standard English and Jamaican speech so that it resonates perfectly to Jamaican ears, but it is still accessible to non-Jamaicans. Somebody once wrote that I seem to be trying to inscribe Jamaican culture onto the consciousness of the world. I think that is a good thing!

JB: One of your initiatives as the new poet laureate of Jamaica is the Helen Zell prize for young poets. Can you expand on this and why you thought it important to initiate this prize?

LG: I was fortunate enough to have taught for many years at the University of Michigan in their Helen Zell MFA writing programme, which is consistently rated in the top two such programmes in the world. As part of the job I had to read and evaluate countless applications from highly gifted young writers who are very serious about developing their craft. As the current Poet Laureate of Jamaica, I thought that I would like to encourage our young writers to perform at the highest level, and I am grateful to Douglas Trevor and Linda Gregerson, at the University of Michigan, for agreeing to establish this prize. The details can be read online, but basically it is open to Jamaican poets between the ages of seventeen and twenty-five. Applicants are asked to submit a portfolio of between three to six pieces of original work to be appraised by University of Michigan MFA students and faculty, and the winner will receive a financial prize.

Since becoming Poet Laureate I have given a number of talks and readings in schools and libraries and I've met young people who are really serious about poetry. By establishing this prize, I am doing my best to encourage the development of a new generation of young Jamaican poets. The winner will be announced at a special function on World Poetry Day, March 21.

JB: I had the chance to read recently of your going to South Africa to deliver the Nadine Gordimer Memorial Lecture to the 5th African Women International Writers' Symposium. Huge congratulations on that. Can you take a moment here to talk about what that experience was like for you? As well, you seemed to be saying, in the lecture that I read, that women's stories add a necessary counterpoint to the male stories that you read about Africa. How necessary is it to hear female perspectives and voices in writing?

LG: Delivering the Nadine Gordimer Memorial Lecture at the 5th African Women International Writer's Conference in Johannesburg, or Jo'burg as South Africans call it, was an extraordinary experience. I had been blessed to travel to Southern Africa three times before, twice to give readings at the International Poetry Festival in Durban, and once when I accompanied my husband, who was a Rhodes Scholar, to a gathering of the newly established Rhodes Mandela Trust in Cape Town. Anyone who knows my work knows that I always felt a profound connection to the people of Southern Africa; and my poem "Bedspread", which was written for Winnie Mandela and that I had the honour of reading to her in person here in Jamaica in 1994, is a poem that I still get requests to read. I have over the years met and shared platforms with a number of African women writers whose work I greatly value because they write from their own very unique perspective. In 2000, at a Commonwealth

Conference organised by Michael Schmidt of Carcanet Press, I met and spent time in the company of Nadine Gordimer, and so I was able to speak first-hand about that experience in my talk.

Now, more than ever, it is important to examine things from the female perspective. The half that has never been told is now loudly demanding to be told. As someone who has been trying to tell my side of that half for over fifty years, I say this is a good thing. The world is experiencing something of a seismic shift when it comes to matters of gender, and if this movement is handled right, then the world just might receive a badly needed measure of nurturing and healing.

JB: I am sure you are familiar with "not being new to this, but being true to this". A little later on in the interview, I will take up the ways in which I see you continually experimenting in your work. But more and more there seems to be an explosion of Caribbean voices and Caribbean literature in the marketplace. I wonder how do you, as someone who has been around for some time, make sense of all the new Caribbean voices now vying for attention? What advice would you give to someone trying to make their way out into the world of publishing, as a writer from Jamaica?

LG: Speaking as someone who started writing when there was very little to gain from being a Caribbean writer, I am pleased that there are now so many more opportunities for publishing, prizes, fellowships, etc for our writers. Here is the thing: a real writer usually writes because that is what he or she has to do; and if this is so, they are in for the long haul. Personally, I resisted the idea of being a writer for a number of reasons, but no matter how hard I tried, I could not avoid writing poems and stories. I used to destroy them, but they kept coming. There were years when I was putting my energy into other things, years when I assumed writing had gone away and left me to my own ill-advised devices. As it turns out, what was happening was that my voice was just being cultured in a new and different way, and that culturing process takes time. When it was good and ready, poetry came out in that new way in the form of my 'Heartease' poems.

All I'm saying is that sometimes this writing business writes you more than you write it, and if that is so, what you produce is not going to be dictated by any marketplace. So, let everyone write and let everyone produce and some will be sprinters (but only one will be the Usain or the Shelly-Ann!) and some will be long-distance runners.

JB: But maybe I need to temper that question, because I can attest to the struggle that poets in particular face in getting published. Recently, someone I quite like asked me, why write poetry? What in the world can the writing of poetry do for you? What are the roles, function and uses of poetry to a place often in crisis like our beloved Jamaica?

LG: Why write poetry? Well, for one thing we need to accept that there is probably never going to be really huge audiences for poetry in our part of the world. But you never know. I was just in New York City taking part in a celebration in honour of the life and work of Derek Walcott that was held at the 92nd Street Y. It was a freezing cold night, but the huge auditorium was filled with people who had come to hear poets and writers sing praises to our great Caribbean poet. The best-selling poet in the world today is Mowlana Jalal ad-Din Balkhi known to us as Rumi, who was born in Afghanistan 800 years ago. All kinds of people today draw deep consolation and joy from Rumi's words. Who could have guessed that something like that would have happened?

Poetry is one of the gifts we human beings have been given to help make our lives easier, and people used to know this. When I was growing up everybody in Jamaica who had passed through primary school knew poems because they'd been made to memorise them. People knew memory gems – "Little deeds of Kindness, little words of Love, make the mighty ocean and the stars above". Think about that for a minute. What that little couplet is saying is the universe is created by acts of love and kindness; love and kindness are creative forces. Poetry is, as one poet said, "one person's inside talking to another person's inside". This describes that feeling you get when you read or hear something and your reaction is, *That is exactly what I was feeling*, or *That is exactly what I was thinking*. When that happens you do not feel so alone in the world. So, for as long as we are thinking, feeling human beings we will need poets to express people's innermost thoughts, to help speak for people who have no voice. Writing on behalf of people who have no voice is something that poets must do, especially in times and places in crisis. Real poets have to have a sympathetic imagination, they have to have the negative capability that John Keats spoke of, they have to be able to imagine themselves into other people's lives and into situations that they themselves have not actually experienced. To aspiring poets I'll just quote what Miss Lou used to say to me at various stages of my life when my career was not always moving forward: "Lorna, tek wey yu get, so till yu get wey yu want".

About publishing, there are more Caribbean writers being published today, both by mainstream and by smaller presses, than there were when I started out. And there is online publishing which is a great way to begin to get readership for your work. But I definitely agree that we have to try to make much more happen on that front for writers in the region.

JB: You have by now published fiction, non-fiction, and criticism. Your oeuvre as a writer is quite diverse. Yet "poet" is the title you seem to prefer, more so than "writer". Why is this so?

LG: It took me a long time to refer to myself as a poet. I felt that I had to earn that right. I also think that often you yourself cannot just decide that you are a poet; usually some acknowledged poet identifies you as such. The best example of this is to be found in the short story, "B. Wordsworth", by V.S. Naipaul. And yes, I have written non-fiction and fiction, but my default position is still poet. How do I explain this? Poetry is my darling? Love it like cook food? Seriously. Poetry has saved my life on more than one occasion; it has led me to the best parts of myself. There have been times when I found it hard to pray, but I am always able to pray through reading and writing poetry. Poetry gave me a structured inner life at times when I was experiencing chaos in my outer life. Poems I have written have helped to give shape to my inner turmoil. People have told me that some of my poems have helped them through times of loss and trials, and that they read my poems at weddings and funerals. Someone once wrote to me to say that he keeps a copy of "Heartease" next to his bible. Why should I not privilege the name poet above writer?

JB: One of the issues that invariably come up at conferences and such is that of writers who write within and those who write from outside the Caribbean. You have done both. A two-part question here: Firstly, do you believe writers who write outside of the Caribbean have any special responsibilities in how they choose to write about and represent the Caribbean? Then: Do you see developments in the Caribbean that are making it less and less necessary for writers to leave for the metropole?

LG: I am not sure that we can tell writers what and what not to do. Most writers are iconoclasts, and they value their own opinions highly. That is to say, some of them have big egos. But having said that, I have been known to get really upset at some dispiriting one-sided depictions of life in the Caribbean that are so sensational and weird that you have to wonder what would motivate someone to write some of those things. Money and fame? I once had a student in the United States say that, judging by the books he'd read from the region, the Caribbean must be the worst place in the world for a child to grow up. That hurt me to mi heart! I'd say that maybe writers have responsibility to at least be fair to their subject, and that writers who do not really know the area should do careful research before they write about us. I am strangely optimistic about the Caribbean, I cannot explain why. There is much evidence to the contrary, but I somehow believe that we are going to turn a corner, that good things are going to happen and this will create more opportunities for writers to remain at home and to thrive. Look at what happened when a visionary like Glen Mills decided that we should coach our athletes at home. Now the whole world is coming to him! This could happen with our writers. Why am I using so many sports analogies? Maybe because I have an old-girl crush on Usain Bolt?!

JB: As our writing tradition matures, one of the questions that I am faced with as a reader of Caribbean literature is how to draw the line between being influenced by a writer and not simply just making off with an author's imagery and style and techniques. When does influence become plagiarism in creative works? What words of wisdom do you have to offer on this issue?

LG: Many writers begin by imitating other writers they admire. But as you develop, you have to find your own voice or all you will end up being is a good imitator or somebody who uses tracing paper to copy over other people's words. I personally think that it is best to spend time cultivating your own voice, and the unique circumstances of your life are what will make your voice distinctive. Nobody else will have lived your life but you, so even when you are assuming a mask, you will be masking in your own one-of-a-kind way. Something else to consider is that many people come to poetry as a result of having been broken in some way, many poems are written from places of terrible pain, and that *cri de coeur*, or cry from the heart, is something that is hard won. It should be respected.

JB: Now, turning to your quite substantial collected poems recently published by Carcanet in the United Kingdom. In your very first collection of poems there is a poem entitled "A Brief History of a Jamaican Family", which seems to be the introduction in your work to the fact that history will become a trope that you will return to again and again. Why the fascination with history and what would you say is your muse?

LG: "A Brief History of a Jamaican Family" is one of my very early poems. I believe it was published in the Carifesta anthology in 1976. I'd thought about reading history at UWI but I decided to study art instead, and to do what some scholars call "history from below". I have done jobs which required me to do field work, so I've ended up interviewing people from all walks of Jamaican life who have versions of history that are not found in books. All my work is engaged at some level with history. The muse of memory is the muse of poetry. History and memory are fellow travellers. I suspect that for as long as I keep writing, I will be drawing inspiration from our heartbreakingly tragic yet strangely redemptive history. I feel deep love and undying gratitude to all my ancestors who suffered and struggled and refused to give up so that I can be here. If I can honour them by writing about them, I am going to, as we say, "do my endeavour best". Also, writing poems that are inspired by historical events is another way to teach others about our history.

JB: You know, Lorna, one question that I have always wanted to ask you is, where for you is Heartease? Is Heartease an actual place in Jamaica? Similarly, what can you tell me about search-mi-heart flowers? Are those for you real flowers? How did you come up with that name? To me, those two things, along your guinea woman great grandmother, are indelibly linked to your work.

LG: I was a trainee bookmobile librarian at the Jamaica Library Service – my first real job after I left school – when I was sent to work in Manchester, St Elizabeth and Westmoreland and I saw the signpost for "Heartease" through the window of the big bookmobile as we were driving through Manchester. I was so moved by the sight of this place with such a blessed name, that years later I began to write about it as this mythical place of goodness and light. I believe there is actually more than one Heartease district in Jamaica. For me though, Heartease is internal, it is a site of Peace, Hope and Possibility, and some days I feel close to it, some days it seems very far away. Still, I know now that it is the journey to reach that Heartease state that is important. The glimpses of it we get along the way are what keep us going.

As for the search-mi-heart, it is a real plant, a type of bush used to make tea. It is supposed to be good for heart palpitations or fluttering. I have come to believe that it is very important to search one's heart on a regular basis, and by heart I mean our internal life.

JB: The actual Jamaican landscape stands out in your poetry, particularly Jamaican fruits and flowers and of course the Blue Mountains. But one huge revelation in reading your collected poems is your fascination with the constellation, with stars, the moon and with light. What is behind this fascination?

LG: You know, when I started to teach at the University of Michigan, I got into the habit of reading, for at least two hours every day, some poetry or fiction I'd never read before or some book about a subject I find interesting. I went to a lot of great lectures and readings during my time in Ann Arbor, and if I found those talks or lectures engaging, I'd go off and read more about the subject. In 2000, I got married to Ted Chamberlin, who is a brilliant literary critic and social activist. He is also my great encourager, so when for example, I was asked by the South Bank Centre to take part in a special celebration to commemorate the anniversary of the publication of Dante's *Inferno*, Ted got me every English translation of the *Inferno* ever written and I spent time in "hell" reading multiple translations of Dante's *Inferno* for weeks! I ended up rewriting Canto 12-Brunetto Latini, and setting it in Jamaica. Since then I have rewritten three other cantos, and I might be ready to tackle another now. I have come to believe that in order to write and to teach creative writing you have to be interested in, and to have a fair amount of knowledge about almost every subject, including the constellations and what the King James Bible – I am a big fan of the King James Bible – refers to as "the great lights", that is the sun and the moon and the stars.

JB: Your mother was a seamstress, and she returns in one form or another in all of your collections, to date. Sewing arises forcefully as a trope in your works, particularly so in your later writings. So, tell us, Lorna, a little about your mother Dorice. How did she learn to sew? What were some of her notable creations that you remember? Do you still have some of the things that she created?

LG: My mother was a great and generous soul. She was powerful and beautiful. Very strong, you did not mess with her, but she was amazingly kind-hearted and she was highly intelligent. She had been a teacher before she got married to my father Marcus – I want to put in a word for my father here, he was one classy guy, caring and loving of all his children – Barbara, Howard, Carmen, Vaughan, Kingsley and Karl, Keith, Lorna and Nigel. He had a great work ethic, he was a trusted friend in whom many important people in Jamaican society confided, and he had a killer sense of humour which we all inherited along with his love of music; everybody in my family is passionate about music. Anyway, I learned many sweet little poems and all sorts of stories from my mother Dorice. Her family, the Harveys, were big-time Anglicans, so she was very familiar with the language of the Book of Common Prayer and her speech was rich with all sorts of high and low references. She is the person who encouraged my eldest sister to become a journalist, and I believe if she had lived at another time, she would have become a writer.

I learned much from watching my mother sew. One of my favourite definitions of a poet is that of "maker". I like the idea that you are actually making something when you write a poem. When my mother and her sisters Cleodine, Albertha – also called Jo and Ann – sewed dresses (only Aunt Rose never sewed) they paid close attention to everything from how the fabric looked in different lights, to how it would fall if you cut it on the bias as opposed to just cutting it straight, and they made sure that the inside was finished as neatly as the outside, all kinds of things like that. I think I try to do something like that when I write poems. I'm not sure where they learned to sew, but my aunt Cleodine had gone to a special school run by an English woman and maybe she learned sewing there, because she was actually a world-class seamstress, who had a highly-developed aesthetic sense. She was the eldest so she may have taught her younger sisters. My mother used to sew the most gorgeous dresses. I remember one off-white damask linen dress with a circular skirt that must have had at least five yards of cloth in it that she made for my sister Barbara. It could have been in the pages of Vogue! I lost all the beautiful dresses she made for me to Hurricane Gilbert.

JB: In the later poems, there is a lot of transience, restlessness and movement. On the one hand, I read these as the natural outcome of partaking, perhaps unconsciously, in the triangular trade route travelling among Africa, Europe and the Americas. Yet, there is a resistance to the notion of exile by the narrator of these poems, who insists she is not in exile from Jamaica, simply "making life" away from Jamaica. How is exile different from making life and how do you as the poet of these poems understand the restlessness and the constant movement and travel, particularly in the later poems of the collected works?

LG: Other people have drawn attention to the themes of transience, restlessness, and constant movement in my work, especially the later work. The fact that I have been doing a great deal of moving up and down, working and living in several different places during the second half of my life, has come as a great surprise to me, because I never thought that I'd ever live outside of Jamaica. But as my beloved cousin Joan Moran once said to me when she came to visit me when I spent a year at the Bunting Institute in Cambridge Massachusetts, "If God can't move you, God can't use you". That is the only explanation I have for all the restlessness, etc. My dear son Miles, who moved back to Jamaica a few years ago, says he is in no hurry to go travelling anywhere. I think this may be because he has lived with me in so many different places.

JB: Continuing on the theme of travel, there is a deepening understanding of what New York City means to the consciousness, writing these poems. But it suddenly occurred to me that most artists going abroad to study when you did perhaps most likely went to Europe, specifically England, for their training. But for you that was different. Why did you choose to study in New York City as opposed to England? What was your time in New York City and at the Art Students League like? Who did you study with and what kind of work did you produce? Were you writing poems at this time, as well as painting? If yes, how did you juggle doing both art forms at once? Do you still paint today?

LG: I went to New York because I wanted to go to the School of the Art Students League. I believe it was Karl and Seya Parboosingh, who were good friends with my sister Barbara and her husband Ancile Gloudon, who recommended that I go there. Jamaican painters like Cecil Cooper, Vernal Rueben and others had also studied at what I believe might be the oldest art school in the USA. So I guess I was just doing what some others before me had done. I'd done art and art history for "A" levels and taken private lessons with artists like Moira Small and Valerie Bloomfield before going to the Jamaica School of Art where I was taught by people like Colin Garland, Kofi Kiyiga, Fitz Harrack – who was courting the brilliant Norma Harrack in those days – Vernal Rueben, Winston Patrick, and Gene Pearson. At the School of the Art Students League in New York, I studied portrait painting with Robert Brachman and I took a class with the great African-American painter Jacob Lawrence, who taught me many important lessons. For example, I learned from Mr Lawrence not to spend too much time over-thinking things. He'd always tell me, "Just go and do the work." I live by those words. I have never been inclined to get into too many discussions with anybody about my creative endeavours. I have always kept that to myself. I just try to do the work.

Strangely enough, I wrote a lot of my early poetry when I was studying to be a painter. Many of the poems in my first book, *Tamarind Season*, came from that time. In a way, I became a poet in New York. Today I no longer consider myself to be a painter, but I go to museums a lot, and I think and write a great deal about painting, about all the arts. I have, for example, been thinking a lot about public monuments, and the effect they can have on a society. But that is a whole other interview!

JB: Another thing I noticed is that you write many poems about visual artists and their work, but overwhelmingly, the visual artists you write about are male, with the exception of a quite moving poem about the work of Petrona Morrison and the poem, "So Who Was The Mother Of Jamaican Art?" I am wondering what your thoughts are on this observation, and if you can unpack for us the reason you wrote that quite powerful poem questioning the matrilineal provenance of Jamaican art?

LG: My poem "Who Was The Mother of Jamaican Art" was inspired by some of the thinking I've been doing about where art comes from. I read about enslaved women making carvings of human figures representing the children they had sold away from them, in an article by Tekla Mekfet, and the poem came out of that. I knew Edna Manley quite well during the 1970s, and I'm sure she'd agree that the first mother of Jamaican art would have been an enslaved African woman whose art was born out of unspeakable circumstances and whose work would have been unsigned. I wonder about things like that a lot. Can you imagine how many gifted people were lost to the world because of the abomination that was the Atlantic Slave Trade? I am grateful to historians like the great Philip Sherlock, Lucille Mair, Swithin Wilmot, Patrick Bryan, Rupert Lewis, Maureen Warner-Lewis, Verene Shepherd and Hilary Beckles for the influence their work has had me; and yes, although I have written a poem for my dear friend Petrona Morrison, and I've credited Kara Walker, you are right, I do need to engage more with art made by women.

JB: Finally, there are praise songs in many of the poems in your collected works, but two that really stand out are dedicated to your contemporary poets Velma Pollard and Derek Walcott. It is indeed breathtaking that one poet should "turn thanks" to other poets in her work. Why did you feel the need to do this?

LG: I learned a very important lesson after the publication of *Tamarind Season*. In that book, I dedicated poems to people who were just friends and, in some instances, almost casual acquaintances, people I was not particularly close to, but whom I maybe just liked. I discovered after that, that there is a kind of reader and/or critic who reads a lot into a dedication, and they usually read way more than I actually intended. So, since then, I have become very careful about who warrants a poem from me. It goes without saying that Derek Walcott more than deserves praise poems by the bushel for all he has done for poetry. My poem dedicated or 'livicated' (as Rastafari would say, and Velma Pollard being a boss of dread talk would agree) to her, came about because I once heard her give a very funny and smart reading of the loincloth worn by Bombo, the little boy who lived in the Congo, a story taken from The Royal Primer, which we used to read in primary school. It is meet and right to praise; writing praise poems is something all good poets are bound to do.

EXPLAINING OURSELVES TO OURSELVES

EXPLAINING OURSELVES TO OURSELVES: AN INTERVIEW WITH WRITER MARCIA DOUGLAS

Marcia Douglas is the author of the novels *Madam Fate* (Women's Press, 2000; Soho Press, 1999), *Notes from a Writer's Book of Cures and Spells* (Peepal Tree, 2005) and most recently, *The Marvellous Equations of the Dread* (Peepal Tree Press, 2016), which was shortlisted for the 2017 OCM Bocas fiction prize. In 2018, New Directions brought out a US edition of *The Marvellous Equations of the Dread*. Her poetry collection, *Electricity Comes to Cocoa Bottom* (Peepal Tree, 1999), won a Poetry Book Society recommendation. The collection explores the recuperation of Jamaican place and voice from the perspective of a young woman in urban America in resistance to culturally annihilating forces in that society.

Marcia Douglas's more recent awards include an NEA Fellowship. She performs a one-woman show, *Natural Herstory*, based on her fiction and poetry, and currently lives in Boulder, Colorado, with her husband and daughter. She is an Associate Professor at the University of Colorado, Boulder.

JB: Marcia, I am very much taken with the non-linear narrative and multiple perspectives in your novel *Notes from a Writer's Book of Cures and Spells*. In that regard your work seems to me a cross between Erna Brodber's and Toni Morrison's. Am I correct in reading these influences in and onto your work? Also, I am curious how you characterise this work – is it a novel, for example?

MD: I have never consciously thought of Brodber or Morrison as major influences as such; however, I do admire their work. They are both important in that they have cleared a path for others to follow. I particularly love how Brodber engages fiction in ways which challenge certain assumptions about how narrative works. In that sense, we are kindred spirits. My particular approach to form comes from an interest in pushing the boundaries of what it means to tell a story, fusing multiple genres – poetry, fiction and visual art – as well as multiple points of view – first person, second person, epistemology and so on. Interwoven within that are the places where history, memory and the imagination meet. In the process, I break a lot of so-called, "rules", and invite my artistic rebel to come out and dance. The result is what might be described as a hybrid novel. This aesthetic is also conscious of offbeat patterns such as those found in certain African textiles and other visual art. The beautiful "offbeat" is all around us, if we begin to look. It is in the delicious meal served with knives and forks which do not match, or in the grandmother by the side of the road in a floral blouse and striped skirt. This, I feel, is part of my aesthetic lineage. So, in answer to your question – yes, this is a novel! – albeit my unique contribution to existing understandings of what a novel can look like. In today's publishing climate, which values lyrical realism, this is a risky path for a writer to take, but it is the sort of work I am interested in pursuing. I am very much engaged in questioning what else can be done with form, and how form can be in conversation with my experience of the world. In addition to all of this, I am also committed to writing stories which are accessible and meaningful.

JB: Can you please explain to the readers who the character "Old Story Ma" is?

MD: The character, "Old Story Ma", can best be understood as a muse. She inspires creativity in others by appearing at unexpected moments and in differing forms. Most times, she appears as an old woman, but she may also be male, or even a baby. In whatever form she appears, her role is to motivate, and she tends to do this by provocation. There is a poem, "La Muerte, Patron Saint of Writers" by Clarissa Pinkola Estés, in which the muse is an old woman who agitates and rouses the writer with, among other repulsive things, her garlic breath. Old Story Ma is exactly that kind of muse!

JB: Your work incorporates many whimsical drawings of particularly Jamaican animal and plant life. I loved these drawings very much, but found myself wondering how integral they were to the text. In other words, I was wondering what would be lost, in your mind, by not having these drawings in the work?

MD: This novel is a meta-fiction – a story about storytelling – but in a broader sense it can also be understood as meta-creative – creativity conscious of what it means to create. As such, the novel is structured around the concept of a writer's notebook. Hence, there are snippets of prose or extended "notes" as well as drawings and photos. The drawings are integral to how the work functions as a concept. In fact, I wish I had included more of them. Furthermore, their appearance also connects to the offbeat patterning I mentioned earlier; the quiet inscrutability of the unexpected, random or mismatched.

JB: There seems to be a conscious attempt in this work to invoke the trope of the "folk" here – whether it is folk knowledge, folk remedy, and most of the characters seem to be, for lack of a better term, "folksy". Why such a strong insistence on the "folk" in the work?

MD: I understand what you mean here. Though I grew up in Kingston, I was raised by "folksy" parents very much connected to the land and to certain ways of being, and this novel reflects that sort of merging of urban edge (eg much of the story takes place among squatters in a Kingston cemetery) with rural/folk knowledge. There are ways in which these two strands tend to coexist in Jamaica in interesting ways. And too, folkways are doorways, tracing us to our African roots; and sometimes, transforming into other permutations (such as in the journey folk/mento took, fusing with other popular music forms to become reggae). So, you are right – I do tend to spotlight the "folk" (yes, for lack of a better term) in my work. The function of our "folk" connectedness deserves more acknowledgment. For this reason, I am inclined to reach for another word besides "folk," which so easily gets categorised as the provincial or quaint or yesteryear. The "folk" touches in *Notes from a Writer's Book of Cures and Spells* reach for something deeper – connected with agency and empowerment. Though "rootsy" has a somewhat different usage, for all the reasons stated above, I prefer it to "folksy," and see how one could extend its meaning to include something of what I am interested in exploring in my work. One of the terms I use in the book is "natural herstory" (which is also the title of my one-woman show); a turn of phrase which reclaims and (re)roots.

JB: As someone who has lived away from Jamaica for some time now, what is your relationship to the island? By that I mean, I found myself wondering if all the folk elements in your work was an attempt to ground not only the reader – but more so yourself – in and on the island?

MD: Jamaica can be seen and understood through many lenses, and that folk/natural herstory lens is the one I chose to use for this particular book. While my first novel, *Madam Fate*, shared certain elements in common with *Notes*, in subsequent works, the lens I utilise varies and is unique from project to project.

But reflecting on your question further, I should add that there is a way in which writing and other creative forms are always a way of explaining ourselves to ourselves, so there is certainly that aspect of the work too.

JB: Dolls hold pride of place in this work. Dolls cry, they have longings – in other words, the dolls are quite animated here. You are, in this work, shown as well to be quite a gifted maker of dolls. When did you start making dolls? Why did you start making them? What particular relevance do you think that doll-making has to Jamaican society?

MD: For readers unfamiliar with the book, I should preface this response by explaining that the main character, Flamingo, is a storyteller who makes dolls to represent her characters. Photos of Flamingo's dolls are included in the book. Originally, I had no intention of including the photos. The doll-making was simply an interesting side project, which I thought could perhaps draw me closer towards an understanding of my character, Flamingo, and thereby further immerse me in the world of the story. A former writing teacher of mine once advised that if your fictional character is sitting in a bath tub, you might need to stop writing and go and take a long bath just to be in the present moment of what that feels like. So, I began making the art dolls out of that sort of intent. And subsequently, I discovered that I really loved making these dolls and the project developed with more seriousness from there. As far as possible, I incorporated Jamaican-derived (natural and found) materials into the artwork, eg, ackee pods/seeds, sea grape leaves, coconut husk, various shells, bottle tops etc. I believe that all creativity – whether writing, visual art or performance – comes from a similar place, so the same passion which fuelled my writing also fuelled the making of the dolls. It all felt very synergistic. In making the dolls, I was not necessarily drawing from a Jamaican doll-making tradition as such, though I was certainly tapping into what it means to create out of consciousness of Jamaican space. Also, the creative impulse has long memory, and these dolls have been understood by some as having connection to certain West African artistic traditions. This was my first venture into making art dolls. In addition to being included in the novel, some of them have also been featured in *Art Doll Quarterly*.

JB: The dolls in your book are represented in colour photographs. They are quite stunning. What do you hope the images of the dolls do for the reader? Do you worry at all that having the characters portrayed as dolls will lessen the strength of such strong characters?

MD: Ultimately, the decision to include images of the dolls came out of the same intent as the decision to include Flamingo's drawings. The dolls are part of the aesthetic fabric of the book, as well as part of the meta-creative concept. So I don't worry about the dolls lessening character strength. It's a risk I'm willing to take. For me, art involves risk. Lyrical realism is based on keeping the reader in a certain dream. Don't jolt your reader out of the dream, we are told. This advice can be useful, and has resulted in some beautiful novels, many of them favourites of mine. Still, I, on the other hand, am interested in saying, Look, reader, this is a dream and it's okay to be conscious of it. I call it "lucid reading".

JB: In fact, many of the characters here are unforgettable – Alva, Born in China, Carmen Sister Innocencia Shane – what is your relationship to and with these characters? Specifically, I remember Paule Marshall once telling me (and I think she wrote this somewhere) that one of her characters was walking about in the world. Do you too feel that these characters are real? That they live on outside of the pages of the text? I confess that I expect to buck up Alva one of these days!

MD: As writers we use heavy doses of imagination, but our characters may also include aspects of ourselves and of people we have observed or met. To be a fiction writer is really a multidisciplinary venture, calling upon so many fields of knowledge to breathe life into characters on a page. The result is that sometimes we think we might in fact "buck up" one of them. This has happened to me at least a couple of times. I have come across someone who feels like the manifestation of a character I thought I had simply imagined. I suspect many writers have this experience.

JB: Am I correct in thinking that the act of writing and storytelling in general are their own characters in this tale? Do you believe, as does one of your characters, that "writing is a cover for necromancy"?

MD: Yes, it is certainly correct to say that creativity is its own character in this novel. Creativity is power. However, beyond the bounds of the story, I would not go as far as saying that "writing is a cover for necromancy". In the novel, that statement is Sister Innocencia's judgment of Flamingo, and it is said out of both fear and respect for her gift. Speaking personally, though, what I would say is that writing comes from a deep place, and can be a sort of spiritual practice. When my writing is going well, I feel more centred and grounded. Writing can also heighten one's understanding of and compassion for others in that it invites the sort of interrogation that taps into the true roots of human angst.

JB: You seem to be making the point with the powerful soliloquy by Mrs Ying that the Chinese are more fully integrated into the Black community on the island than other groups that also call the island home. What accounts for this, do you believe?

MD: I am not necessarily suggesting that the Chinese community is more integrated into the Black community than other groups (though that is an interesting conversation to take up). I am more interested in exploring the fact that many of us arrived here on this island, via various paths of sacrifice and pain. In the novel, though on the surface Mrs Ying is a successful shopkeeper, she has come to Jamaica carrying the burden of a very angst-filled personal history. As humans, our pain connects us. Here, too, I am also exploring the complexities inherent in migration. Mrs Ying journeys from China, and likewise, the character Alva, in a parallel journey, goes to New York. Mrs Ying, by the way, is based on my memory of an elderly Chinese couple who used to live in a small house behind my aunt's shop in Waterhouse. I was about six or seven years old at the time, but recall that the woman always seemed somewhat forlorn, and I wondered about her history and how she arrived there. Little did I know that she would surface in my imagination many years later.

JB: As well, the soliloquy by Carmen Sister Innocencia Shane is quite powerful. I found myself wondering at times if, in fact, she was a nun. If she is indeed, how do you explain her willingness to so openly embrace her sexuality without any seeming worry about violating the rules of the church?

MD: Perhaps my portrayal of Carmen Sister Innocencia Shane is a result of what happened to my imagination after Catholic education! Seriously though, CSIS (as she refers to herself) is a woman with a past full of secrets. Most of the exploits you refer to took place before she became a nun; in fact, they are what drove her to the church. The theme of double identity or camouflage runs throughout the book. Part of what allows CSIS to speak so openly about her past is that she knows Flamingo will hold her story in confidence. She also knows that telling her tale will free her. In a letter to Flamingo she says, "Here is a bargain: change my identity in your little book, and I will tell all." In a similar manner, Marion Tate Rice (aka "Bad Rice"), the mysterious woman in the cemetery, keeps her true identity secret. In fact, up until a certain point it is not even clear whether she is really dead or alive. I enjoyed developing and getting to know both of these characters very much. It was as if they confided in me, as they did with Flamingo.

JB: One really lovely surprise in the book is the incorporation of the endangered endemic Jamaican butterfly, *Papilio homerus*. In fact, you link this butterfly quite movingly to Madda Shilling who eventually dies. Are you using Madda Shilling's death to call attention to what is happening to this butterfly?

MD: Yes, and I am also using the endangered butterflies to call attention to the possible fate of our stories and histories and herstories – if we do not honour them and tell them. This is a book about the act of storytelling, and storytelling is medicine – art is a medicine – and necessary for personal and cultural survival. The swallowtail/*Papilio homerus* is magnificent and we, as a people, should honour that which is powerful and magnificent within us and among us.

WRITING HELPS ME MAINTAIN MY SANITY:
AN INTERVIEW WITH POET ANN-MARGARET LIM

Ann-Margaret Lim is the author of two poetry collections: *The Festival of Wild Orchid* (2012) and *Kingston Buttercup* (2016). She has been published in journals, anthologies and her country's two major newspapers. She has a BA in English Literature and has benefitted from workshops conducted by Wayne Brown, Mervyn Morris and Kwame Dawes and the poetry of such greats as Derek Walcott. In 2018, she was featured in *Ebony Magazine*: 6 Caribbean Writers to discover this summer.

She lives in Red Hills, Jamaica with her daughter.

❧

JB: Ann-Margaret, in your most recent collection, *Kingston Buttercup*, and your collection before, *The Festival of Wild Orchid*, a lot of effort is expended in tracing the Chinese story in Jamaica. Why is telling that story so important to you? Like the narrator in *Kingston Buttercup*, have you ever travelled to China, and if so, what were you, the poet, in search of in going to China? What did you learn or find in doing so?

AML: Whilst I may not do much prose (none published, at least), I'm a lover of the narrative poetry book – the book that tells a story. My story – that of a woman who happens to be a mother, daughter, lover and a witness and testifier of the Caribbean, more precisely Jamaican life – includes the somewhat expected mixed ancestry of the typical Caribbean resident. In this case the mixture includes the Chinese gene pool. My father is half-Chinese, with his father coming directly from China in the 1930s, and my step-grandmother (*popo*) is Chinese, coming directly from China during the 1940s. I grew up with my father and his wife's family. My grandmother was the family matriarch, until her sudden death in 2014. She is very important in my life. My story has a lot to do with her and how she treated me, not as her step-granddaughter, but as her granddaughter. Although my times with my paternal grandfather were limited (he died when I was ten), they were also memorable and remembered fondly.

Consequently, in the books, I really try to trace my story, who I am and what echoes in me. I can't pretend that I'm trying to trace and tell the Chinese or African story, because that would be a huge undertaking, requiring grants, fellowship, funding and serious research time, meaning no full-time work, but full-time research and writing, which actually would be ideal.

Yes, I travelled to China – jumped at the opportunity offered by the Chinese government to press officers from developing countries. I was happy to be in China, but many times felt that the experience would have been so much richer if my father and grandmother were there too. Their absence was very much present then. In the poem "At The Karoake Bar 21st Century", I tried to capture what being in China was like for me. I learnt a lot about my father and grandmother's background – and the reasons why migration was necessary for the Chinese born in the rural areas, in a feudal system that ensured that your province of birth dictated your job prospects in the future. So I found out for the first time, whilst in China, the reason why so many Chinese migrated to the Caribbean, for example, and are still doing so, which was to better their prospects.

While in China I also saw why my father loved music so much, played instruments and sang Chinese opera, since almost every station I switched to had some music talent show throughout the day. I even saw it in the communities and community centres – the heavy dependence on recreational music. Being in China, I got closer in spirit to my father, deceased grandfather and grandmother.

JB: One of the things that stands out quite clearly in your now two collections of poems is the centrality of gardening to your writing. Flowers as metaphors also abound in your work. What's their importance?

AML: Maybe it all started with that same grandmother/popo of mine. She loved gardening, and I spent much of my time, both in adulthood and childhood, gardening with her. I remember my first essay in prep school about the person you love the most, and it was about spending time gardening with my grandmother.

I love nature and flowers immensely. They affect me greatly. I also find that the names of flowers can be quite intriguing; like Bizzy Dizzy, Prayer Plant, Joseph Coat, even the weed Shame Ole Lady, for example. The Kingston Buttercup, with its beautiful yellow flower but thorny undergrowth, for example, represents Jamaica and Jamaicans – a beautiful place, with a not-so beautiful underbelly.

JB: *Kingston Buttercup*, the collection, is divided into four sections: Spirit Trees, Violet Blue, Neem, and Night Blooming Cereus. Can you explain the meaning behind the title of each section? What do you hope readers take away from each section?

AML: All section titles are named after trees or have the name of a flower in them. The tree and flower image is constant throughout the book. I think we need to use our trees and flowers more to beautify

Jamaica. We in Jamaica should give more thought to landscaping – because nature relaxes and it pacifies.

In Spirit Trees, I look at events and people that have shaped my life. These include the Tainos; the violent introduction of my ancestors to the island; my mentors, my heroes, my lost loved and still living loved ones, and so on. In *Kingston Buttercup*, as in my first book, I try to place the individual, the voice in its environment, and that placing includes tracing from the original inhabitants of the island to the individual's genealogical lineages in Jamaica today.

Spirit Trees documents the people and events that formed the person and is named so to reflect the spiritual connection of an individual to its geographical location. The name Spirit Trees is actually taken from the poem "And They Inhabit The Landscape Still" which is of course about the Tainos who knew that their ancestors inhabited the guava tree.

Violet Blue seeks to place the voice in contemporary Jamaica. The title is taken from a poem in the section, in which a magnificent violet blue-flowered tree leaves me speechless and spellbound. I can never forget seeing those blue flowers on Red Hills Road that long-ago evening. I fell in love and was thankful to God for being alive and experiencing this pure pleasure of this violet-blue blossom that stilled Red Hills Road.

Neem is the section in which I deal with that bitter sweet thing called eros and romantic love. The neem plant is bitter, but it's sweet, because it is good for you. The name neem, for me, is also very sexual. (Say it under your breath, or with your morning voice.) "Neem" is also a poem in that section. I was hoping to get potent and relevant section names for my book and hope I have done so.

JB: The native inhabitants of the island of Jamaica, the Taino, are also a central preoccupation in both collections of poems. Why are the Tainos so important to you?

AML: I live in Red Hills and feeling and being convinced of their presence in my yard, I researched and found that the Tainos also lived in the area we now call Red Hills. Most people know about the Tainos' Spanish Town settlement, because of the museum that was once in operation in that area, but many Jamaicans may not remember that Red Hills is connected to Spanish Town through Plantain Heights. So it's really one trail from their houses in Red Hills to fishing in the river at Caymanas. All of that knowledge informed the writing of these poems.

As fate would have it, I was given a gem of a story whilst attending the launch of Lesley Gail Atkinson's edited compilation of essays on the Tainos, *The Earliest Inhabitants: The Dynamics of the Jamaican Taino*. Then president of the archeological society, Ainsley Henriques, was talking about the Taino family that he found as a developer dynamiting the Red

Hills, back in the day. That confirmed it for me, that what I was sensing was real and that evolved into "Tainos of Red Hills" in my first book.

JB: One of the strongest themes in your published works is an absent mother. I am wondering why this theme might be of such centrality and importance to your work. Also, in your new collection, the abandoned daughter is raised by her father. Are you trying to change or challenge the way that Caribbean men in general, but Jamaican men/fathers in particular, are often portrayed in literature?

AML: I'm not using the theme to consciously make any point. The biographical poems are written from a position of truth, and an absent mother is painfully part of my truth.

I realised a while back that, in writing about my family life, my father somehow will be seen as a figure quite different from the stereotypical post-slavery, but still slavery-culture-inspired Caribbean absent-father type. My father sat me down when I was probably twelve or thirteen and explained that he asked my mother to leave me, whilst she went to Venezuela, because she wanted to bring me with her. He convinced her that I would be better off with him, since he had his own small business. That conversation put many things in perspective for me. It confirmed what I had suspected, that my mother never abandoned me; that she wanted me with her, but my father also wanted me in Jamaica with him. Unfortunately, however, in my mother leaving Jamaica for Venezuela, we lost contact with her.

God alone knows why I went to Venezuela, but whilst in Venezuela, I was told by different persons that many Jamaicans and Caribbean people went there in the '70s and '80s, when things were booming. It seemed to have been a good move for those thinking of buying and selling or improving their lives, back then, but apparently the economic boom took a nose-dive in the 1990s and thus many of the migrants moved on to the US, etc. I don't know if my mother is dead or alive. I don't know if she is still living in Venezuela or if she has moved on. There are so many things I do not know about my mother, but I prefer to think of her as alive and that she will be found soon.

JB: Several poems in the collection are for well-known writers – "Night Blooming Cereus" for Kwame Dawes and "The Warner Woman on Port Royal and Premonitions" for Eddie Baugh, for example. In reading these poems, though, I am a bit puzzled by the dedications, as if I am an outsider not privy to a private joke. Can you explain what you would like an outsider to the situation to get from the dedication of these poems?

AML: I consider Kwame Dawes a mentor and sometimes I'll send him poems that I feel are incomplete, or just not there as yet and "Night Blooming Cereus" was one such poem. Without Kwame's contribution that poem would not have been what it is today. I was so taken by how he got the poem and the direction the poem was really aiming for, that I dedicated it to him. Eddie Baugh has a poem called "The Warner Woman", so it was obvious that my warner woman poem had to be dedicated to him, because maybe if it wasn't for him, I would never have known the term warner woman.

To further answer this question, Jacqueline, I am thinking that maybe it doesn't matter to me if the outsider gets anything from the dedication, as long as those who it's dedicated to get it. I'm okay with that. Nothing is wrong with a poem sometimes beginning and staying as communication with a fellow poet.

JB: Finally, the narrator in "Kingston Buttercup" takes immense pleasure in domesticity – in raking the leaves of her yard, washing the clothes and hanging them on the line, in cooking dinner for her daughter. There was something very wholesome about this. The domestic pleasures invoked in the poem made me wonder about whether you, Ann-Margaret, take as much pleasure in domesticity? When does your writing get done?

AML: My pleasure in domesticity is directly linked to its purpose. If it's washing my daughter's clothes, sure there's pleasure in that, because it's for the apple of my eye; while ironing my own clothes most of the time is really a chore. Those times I would rather be reading or writing. I write everywhere and anywhere. If I can't write at a particular moment I try to keep the thought in my head until I can jot it down. I read and write mostly when my family is sleeping, so yes, I sport bags under my eyes. It's a cycle, really; you stay up for weeks, then give it up, get some rest for weeks, then stay up again. The ideal for me would be to write and write and write around the clock and read and read and read, but that's not my reality now. And the truth is, if I'm not reading and writing, I'd be dead, at least mentally and emotionally. So, for life and sanity, I read and write.

THE BLESSING AND BURDEN OF BEING A POET
FOR MILLICENT A.A. GRAHAM

Millicent A. A. Graham lives in Kingston, Jamaica. Her first collection, *The Damp in Things* was published June 2009 by Peepal Tree Press. It was followed by *The Way Home* (Peepal Tree, 2014).

She is a fellow of the University of Iowa's International Writing Program, 2009 and was awarded the Michael and Marylee Fairbanks International Fellowship to Bread Loaf Writer's Conference, 2010. Her work has been published in: *So Much Things To Say 100 Calabash Poets*; the *Jamaica Journal*; *Caribbean Writer*; *BIM*; *City Lighthouse*; *Callaloo* and *Bearing Witness II*. She is the organising, founder member of a writers' workshop, The Drawing Room Project.

❧

JB: Millicent, congratulations on your most recent collection of poems, *The Way Home*, published last year by Peepal Tree Press in the UK. This is your second collection of poems, and I always find a second collection of poems particularly interesting because there is often a solidifying of the voice and the themes of the poet's work. This certainly is so in your case. Certain preoccupations begin to stand out in your work, one of which is an ambivalence towards the natural world. On the one hand, there is a thick rich sensuality in a poem like "Inheriting the Stewing Pot", but on the other hand, the natural environment can be quite ominous as in the long beautiful title poem, "The Way Home". Can you please explain this seeming contradiction in your work?

MG: Thanks, Jacqueline. The book came at a busy time for me. A group of us had just finished coordinating the Drawing Room project's inaugural writers' retreat with poet Christine Craig at Country Thyme in Highgate, St Mary, which was a tremendous experience. Immediately afterwards I had read along with Jamaican poets Velma Pollard, Ann-Margaret Lim and Professor Mervyn Morris at the Calabash International Literary Festival in Treasure Beach, and then took part in his Poet Laureate Series which arranged for distinguished poets to read across the island. It has been an active year and I feel that I am just now having the time to reflect on what it means to have a second book published, and to reflect on the reactions from readers.

I have never thought of myself as "ambivalent" towards nature. Rather, I see the diversity of the natural environment as reflecting our individual emotions. So yes, sensuality is there, as well as a foreboding element, which I hope reflects the multiplicity of our response to the world around us – the environment in which we live and breathe and feel. There is really no contradiction at all, in my mind.

So a girl replanted in a new place with unfamiliar relatives in "Inheriting the Stewing Pot", is undeniably stirred at an immediate sensory level by everything. This is a different experience from that of the adult in the title poem, who is triggering the memory of childhood and recognising the trajectory of events that places them in the present, which can feel uncomfortable while being curiously personal.

JB: Staying with the title poem, I note again and again that Eve's expulsion from the Garden of Eden is a theme you return to from time to time in this poem and in this collection. This preoccupation made me begin to wonder if you saw Jamaica as a modern-day Garden of Eden, and, if yes, who might Eve be in this modern-day Jamaican garden? Do you, for example, take on the persona of Eve in these poems?

MG: Oh, goodness! I would hope that Eve is equally as interesting as Adam! For me 'Eve' is a symbol of time or a verging on possibility and in another way, she is an archetype – Jung's mental image that comes from way back in the world of myths and dreams. It is her doubt, her defiance, her choices and the ease with which she becomes compassionate that betrays her, very often. So, if Jamaica were the Garden of Eden, then consider Eve the blessing and the burden of living here as a woman, with these complexities. Here is a world of women condemned by whispers. I would expect that we all take on the persona of Eve, and so, there is a universal truth in there somewhere.

JB: Oftentimes, Millicent, when I am reading your works I feel as if there are secrets in your poems. This is particularly so for me in the poem "News". Is this a conscious decision on your part? Do you agree that there are secrets in your poems?

MG: Of course! A thing should have a secret to be alive... and more often than not, you don't have to be told to know... Some secrets we are all in on, though we might not care to admit. Secrets – mysteries, things that are hidden and left unsaid – are certainly there in my poems and in that way they are as much about what is missing as they are about what is present.

JB: Along with secrets, there is often wonderful word play and wonderful word juxtapositions in your poems. Can you explain to us, for example, what "Nanny colonies" are in your title poem? Somehow I feel it has to do with more than the ants that you reference in that poem.

MG: Do you remember that chant: Nanny, Nanny, come fi yuh rice an' peas? It is a literal reference to that ritual of stirring and waiting as a child, the expectation of this little creature rising up out of the earth. There is also the sense of a spiritual summoning and a nod to that heroic figure in us all that must be summoned in moments when we feel small and defeated. A Nanny colony is that spirit accrued! But, without giving too much away in terms of an explanation, there is, in that fifth part an arch in the poem, the persona's perspective and the transformation towards womanhood, towards home.

JB: Another tension in your work is that of staying or leaving the island, referenced quite movingly in the poem, "Bird". Is this a personal tension that you struggle with?

MG: I do struggle with that tension, as a professional trying to make her way in the corporate world; as a woman trying to be both man and woman to provide security and create stability and family; as an emotional soul aware of the important act of burying my emotions so that I may survive; and certainly as a writer, writing in the Caribbean, in Jamaica, where opportunities and support for the writer and the artist are slim. You are faced with the choice to give up here and build away from home in the hope of returning in the end; or of continuing that relentless pursuit to make an impact here in Jamaica. That choice is a luxury that ought not to be a luxury, but it is.

JB: On the face of it these poems are almost apolitical. Yet, on closer examination, politics is deeply implicated in them. For example, in the poem "Catadupa" you write about a sense of decay that has obtained on the island after "the '90s" when the country "bartered" things away. Firstly, can you explain and locate the title of the poem, then explain the politics of it?

MG: Hmm... politics is in everything. I would say in my work politics sits on the sideline, a bystander; it is not the main focus. But if it does get shot down by a stray bullet or a car runs over it while dodging a pothole and riding to the bank, then that is an accident, as in life. Catadupa is a small town in the mountains of St James, about twenty miles from Montego Bay; it was once a well-known and colourful stop on the railway line. I was told of women who would make clothes from cloth that the tourists en route to Montego Bay chose; tourists could collect their clothes, handmade in Catadupa, on the return journey. The town was also famous for its medicinal herbs, which were sold along with fruit and crafts to those travelling on the train; the wooden birds! In 1992 the railway line was closed and now Catadupa is illustrative of the long-term effects of the choices we make, and the lives and worlds that change as a result of these choices. Some people's worlds thrive while others' decay. I would hope that the tone is more a reflection on balance rather than a critique of the lack of it.

JB: I found the poem "Mind the Guinep Fly..." quite interesting since it is the only time in the collection there is a lapse into patois. Yet, for me, it is not a very convincing lapse, because the poem quickly recovers into standard English. What were you trying to say with the way this poem was written? Why isn't the entire poem, for example, written in patois? Have you or would you write an entire poem or even collection of poems in patois?

MG: Particularly in this collection, the voice is relaxed and focuses on the turn of a phrase, the "how" of the language in use, but subtly so. This I think is because my work is not a dialogue or narrative from a set of characters with distinct voices. It is more of an introspective, thinking voice heavily grounded in images (and more and more, in the actual landscape) and a kind of inspired idiom for a voice or 'I' that is the observer.

The first line of that poem, "De next-door-neighbour" is more an attempt to domesticate the tone to suggest "a forbidden temptation". I tried to do the same thing that "Once upon a time" does to a story. But to answer your question on writing in patois, I perhaps came closest in my first book *The Damp in Things*, with the long poem "Boy Pickney", but even then, it was more the lyricism and idioms that defined the voice. Recently in a workshop I am part of, we looked at dub poetry, the work of Jean 'Binta' Breeze, Linton Kwesi Johnson, Michael Smith, Kamau Braithwaite and others, experimenting with music and language; maybe there will be something in the next manuscript!

JB: Trying to negotiate what or where "home" is, is a constant preoccupation in this collection. So I will just ask you: is "home" an actual place for you? Where is your "home"?

MG: Where is home is an important question for me and for Jamaicans, particularly with possession being such an evasive target. Some of us lose home as a means of survival or regain it through the reimagining of an ancestral home. For me, home is not merely a physical place, but more a moment or a state of being – that sense of personhood, or rather, the prosopón, which is the creative self, and how it manifests and extends through the people, objects, actions and passions we deem valuable.

JB: For me, perhaps the strongest poem in this collection is "Prayer for Morning". This is a poem that goes by really quickly, and is dazzling in its word play. Can you speak a little bit about how this poem got written? My sense of it is that this is one of those poems that poets talk about in terms of the poem writing them. Also, can you explain to the readers what that lovely mellifluous word "kibber" in the poem means?

MG: It is one of those, indeed! The poem woke me up and demanded to be written and try as I might to ignore it, it wouldn't let me be until the first draft was done. That doesn't happen often, and that they are keepers even less often! Well, between Walcott's Maman and McNeill's diminutive Dresden, I think the images of the spider and fearful children lit my imagination. From this came the poem's refrain "Let the morning find us here." This refrain is a prayer we all know, likely planted in a time of power-cuts and gunshots, though that could be today as well as long ago depending on where you live.

"Kibber" means to shut or close, but the word commands an abruptness and immediacy with its striking staccato sound that shut and close do not accomplish. This is a way that patois works for me in a poem, not just as voice but as sound. Incidentally, in July 2014, I was invited to participate in the Empire Café project in Glasgow, Scotland, just around the time of the Commonwealth Games. This was an initiative that explored Scotland's relationship with the Trans-Atlantic Slave Trade. While there I visited the Gallery of Modern Art and saw a *Maman*, a piece by the artist Moyna Flannigan. The image was striking! It brought to mind Edna Manley's *Ghetto Mother*. This time, the children squirmed under the protection of a womanly spider and although there were clear contrasts, the image flooded me with the poem. I love when I feel that connection with art!

JB: I find the artwork on the cover of your book simply gorgeous. How was the cover chosen? What can you tell us about the artist? And, finally, is your poem "Negro Aroused" a nod to Edna Manley's famous sculpture and, hence, Jamaican nationalism?

MG: I'm so happy you love the cover, Jacqueline! Coming from an artist, it is much appreciated! We are so fortunate to live in a country rich with the creative endeavours of artists. I find a constant source of inspiration in the work of our fine artists, musicians and artisans. When I shared my poetry with Michael Brooks, an eminent visual artist, and asked him to do the cover art I thought he would laugh at the concept of the Cassia Park Bridge (this bridge in Kingston being close to where I grew up and now live), but he was delighted and embraced the collaboration both as a document of our history and as a metaphor for this journey. The mystique of the bridge left to span two eras into perpetuity is wonderfully represented by this intuitive artist. The damp in the gully, the mountain across the skyline, the light all hold meaning for me. Michael's work brings that to the book with a different power and palette.

"Negro Aroused" is one of my favourite monuments in the city, set against the seascape in downtown Kingston. There is so much happening along this pier; the throes of lives torn from home, a labouring existence so close to a romanticised sea. Why did Edna choose him, or Van Gogh the potato eaters? Was this nationalism or truth? I imagine there is a kind of independence to be able to honour and celebrate ourselves through art. Perhaps that is why we always lean away from the cold and in the direction of home; whether we can possess a comfortable house, or live day to day from a bucket and a chamois. Here, in Jamaica, we have the dignity of broadening our backs, lifting our heads, owning our lives and being our creative selves.

KEISHA-GAYE ANDERSON BELIEVES IN MAKING THE MAXIMUM IMPACT WHILE WE ARE HERE

Keisha-Gaye Anderson is a Jamaican-born poet, writer, visual artist, and media professional based in Brooklyn, NY. She is the author of *Gathering the Waters* (Jamii Publishing 2014), *Everything Is Necessary* (Willow Books), and *A Spell for Living*, which received the Editors' Choice recognition for the Numinous Orisons, Luminous Origin Literary Award, and is forthcoming from Agape Editions as a multimedia e-book, including music and Keisha's original artwork. Keisha's poetry, fiction, and essays have been widely published in national literary journals, magazines, and anthologies. Keisha is a past participant of the VONA Voices and Callaloo writing workshops, a former fellow of the North Country Institute for Writers of Color, and was short-listed for the Small Axe Literary Competition.

❦

JB: Keisha-Gaye, I am so delighted with the arrival of your collection of poems, *Gathering the Waters*. I have known you for some time now, and know that this book has been long in the making, so congratulations! There is something very ancient and wise about these poems. So maybe we should start there, in the fact that reverence "For the Ancestors" is not only the dedication to your book but percolates throughout the entire work. Can you speak both specifically for yourself, and more generally, as to why you believe it is important to remember the ancestors?

KGA: Indeed, this work represents many years of close listening. I have learned that writing is much more about my receptivity to certain truths versus the mere assertion of my own limited opinions. What is forty years of life? A speck of dust in time. So, it was only right to start at the source and honour what I know to be the reservoir of the inspiration that has been distilled through me into these poems. As a Jamaican woman of African descent, acknowledging my ancestors is particularly important to me because of the violent disruption to our family structures that came with slavery.

   The unnamed bodies carpeting the Atlantic floor, the mothers whose babies were torn from their breasts and sold away, the husbands hanging from cotton trees, the musical and ancient languages silenced by colonial laws, the sleeping African gods buried alive under Christianity – these all require witnessing. They demand to be acknowledged. And because I stepped through the doorway of these ancestors' experiences into this life I am living, my voice is for them.

On a very mundane level, I also believe that the more a human being learns to regard himself as part of a continuum of human experience that stretches back endlessly while, at the same time, pushing the world forward, the more that person will be invested in living as the highest expression of himself. We all have a role to play.

JB: Equally important in your work is the act of memory and remembering, even when some memories are quite painful ones. One could argue that it is time to move on from some of the really painful places that your work takes us to. Why do you feel, then, that it is important to linger in those places?

KGA: There are marks that trauma – both personal and familial – make on the psyche, and this is just a part of life. Though these scars do not vanish, we can learn to view them differently with the passage of time. It is important for me to understand life experiences from every possible angle, even when they are hideous. My poems offer me a process for turning these happenings upside down and inside out. And for those who have walked the same difficult path and are playing a certain record over and over in their minds, this work may assist them in changing that tune from a funerary hymn into a ballad.

JB: The role of women, both as nurturers and the source of conflict, is a running theme throughout these poems, and links it to a lot of works by other Caribbean women authors. How do you explain this duality and outright contradiction in your work?

KGA: Isn't it wonderful that life is so messy? That love and hate are identical things, if you really look at them closely? Caribbean women are master tightrope-walkers in an experience that has been defined by paradoxes. In many ways, we have done the impossible – remained the gatekeepers of half-remembered culture and the fierce nurturers of new generations, while surviving through hundreds of years of physical and psychological terrorism, incorrectly named "slave societies". We are still sifting through that untreated and unacknowledged trauma, which causes, for instance, the total rejection of the black body by its inhabitant.

But I also feel that Caribbean women are freer than many other women to transform themselves into anything they can imagine because they are not constrained by any particular traditional template of womanhood. We are so many things! And through that tension and duality emerges a beautifully complex and unpredictable individual, which is sometimes loving and sometimes terrifying, like any other force of nature.

JB: Given that women are the central characters in this book, what do you think men and boys can learn from reading this work?

KGA: This question also makes me think of duality. I believe men and boys can learn that we are not that different from each other, in terms of our need for love, our search for identity, our experience of pain or alienation, and our desire to expand and improve ourselves as human beings. I want those readers who are not female to see their own reflections in the faces of the women and girls in their lives, and love the totality of "us" as two sides of the same coin. It takes two legs to walk; we are not going anywhere if we aren't going together, and we need to begin the journey with empathy and tenderness.

JB: Nostalgia for the past and for a childhood in Jamaica is a very strong theme in this work. How do you explain this sadness and nostalgia, and do I see in the works hints of a hope of some kind of eventual return to Jamaica and a kind of disillusionment with migration?

KGA: Well, I think it's important to first understand that Caribbean immigrants in the United States, when we were growing up at least, lived largely in communities with other Caribbean immigrants. New York tends to have very distinct ethnic enclaves. So, while the Caribbean culture was ever-present amongst the people we interacted with daily, I only understood those people through the framework of the circumstances that brought them to America – from the tireless worker planning to one day "return home", to those putting down roots while supporting family back home, to others seeking to fully assimilate and blend into this new home, which tended to collapse all prior identities built on class, culture, or colour into one tiny box: black.

"Home" became like a skyscraper casting a long shadow – one could feel the effects of the structure blocking out the sun, though the structure itself was difficult to see in detail. And I, like many immigrant children I grew up with, lived in a shadowy limbo of sorts, not fully American, not fully Jamaican/Caribbean, unsure of how to identify in this Western culture that demands labels above everything else.

Much of the remembering in my writing is an attempt to get a clear picture of my essential self and distinguish my hybrid identity as a "Jamerican" from my parents' memories and experiences. Actually, it has been a wonderful vantage point from which to critically view both of the cultures that have helped to shape me into who I am. I regularly spent a lot of time in Jamaica with family as I was growing up, but visiting isn't the same thing as living in a place.

As for any disillusionment with migration, I would say that, while this journey is different for each immigrant, I have observed that a large portion of Caribbean immigrants in America are what I call "urban nomads", who get entangled in the web of urban primacy but don't ever achieve the prosperity they envisioned when setting out on the journey. There are many well-documented reasons for this, but my disillusionment is with a much wider global problem, of which Jamaica is just one microcosm. It doesn't have to take shape in this way, if we begin to think differently about our talents, resources, and our place in the world.

In the end, I'm pleased with the journey of my life and wouldn't change a thing. But I will always have one foot in Jamaica, no matter what.

JB: I was struck throughout the book by a spirituality that was not Christian-centred. Can you explain to me what you understand spirituality to mean and how your understanding finds its way into your work?

KGA: To know that the costume of your countenance is the very same as the earth you walk upon is a humbling and fantastic thing. That became apparent to me at a very young age, five or six, when I came down with a very serious illness. I only remember my mother on her knees at the foot of my bed, praying fervently for my life. As I grew, I increasingly wanted to know: Who or what sees through these eyes of mine, and why? To me, there was always a distinct separation between the person "I" whose reflection I studied in the mirror and the person inside of me asking questions like, "If God made me, then who made God?" I was about eleven when I posed this question to my very pious Christian grandmother, who promptly shut me up and said I was never to ask such things. My parents were Christian and I attended Catholic schools my whole life. As a lover of words, biblical stories appealed to me intellectually and morally, but they didn't move me – not even the way a beautiful song moves you.

It was only after experiencing a Kumina ceremony as a child that something stirred in me. Maybe it was the drums, the dancing, the people gathered together. I'm not sure. But it set me on a path that I'm still walking and I learn something amazing each day by allowing myself to drop some of the blinders of the Western, Christian world view when examining the wider world, other cultures, and most importantly, my inner world.

JB: One of the recurring themes in your work, perhaps unconsciously, is a woman covered in gold, often gold dust. Want to hazard a guess for our readers why this woman is covered in gold and the significance and symbolism of that colour in your collection? It does not seem simplistic in so far as the gold means materialism for you.

KGA: It is quite unconscious, so thank you for making me take a look at it consciously! As I think about your question, I now remember vividly an iconic image I saw as an adolescent in a *National Geographic* magazine. It was a picture of a gorgeous Ghanaian woman, adorned with gold objects in her hair and gold jewellery around her neck, and also, gold dust brushed all over her skin. The image was regal, yes, but it is also ironic because this gold dust was one of the things that attracted European slave traders to Africa's gold coast. And as we know, Africans were also complicit in the trade, as much as we don't want to acknowledge that reality. Women were often the casualties of this greed exhibited by both Europeans and Africans involved with the trade. The gold dust is a rare and beautiful adornment but also something that attracted negativity.

JB: As someone who had an amazing relationship with her grandmother, I found your poems to your grandmother, which you call your "children's poems", quite rich and moving. Throughout the collection, the main ancestors seem to be women, mothers, rivers, the River Mumma. All of this leads, inexorably for me, to the Garden of Eden. So is Jamaica a present-day Garden of Eden for you? How do you view your homeland?

KGA: The Garden of Eden has always struck me as a very dull place. I think we can agree that Jamaica is thankfully anything but dull! For its size, Jamaica has made, and continues to make, an incredible impact on the world in just about every discipline that exists. I'm exceedingly proud to hail from such a dynamic, creative, and resilient culture, which I consider to be essentially matriarchal, though it presents as largely patriarchal. The mothers have kept the culture alive, whether unconsciously or consciously. The mothers are the first teachers. And the feminine part of humanity has the singular ability to take anything and transform it into something new and useful in order to nourish the wider society. That is what women do. It has always been this way.

I love Jamaica dearly, in spite of its challenges. Growth is never painless. But considering our humble roots, I think every Jamaican should be exceedingly proud of our collective contribution to the world and stand firmly in that truth as we continue to better ourselves, no matter where we live on this planet.

JB: While reading your collection, I paid keen attention to the fact that you had a poem called "Mama Adisa". Maybe this particularly stood out for me, because I read your book shortly after reading Opal Palmer Adisa's most recent collection of poems. By chance, were you directly referencing Opal Palmer Adisa in this work? Who are the literary Mama Adisas that you are paying tribute to in this poem?

KGA: I love Mama Adisa! I'll tell you how I met her, or how I remembered her. There's a woman I would see in my dreams from time to time.

We're a culture of dreamers, aren't we? She appeared as a six-foot-plus, striking black woman. She always seemingly had important information for me and usually I didn't want to hear it or made no effort to remember it after waking up.

"How many mothers should one adult woman have?" I thought to myself. "One telling me what to do when I'm awake and another scolding me in my sleep." (Because you know, Jamaican mothers don't care how old you get – they are still going to tell you what to do.)

Well, one morning, after seeing this woman again in my dream, standing in my very own bathroom, I decided to get her out of my head by writing her into a poem. I ditched work and sat in a café. I looked around and saw that the café was pretty empty, so I said out loud, "If you want me to write about you, you should at least tell me your name." At that moment, the name Adisa popped into my head. I'd never heard the name before. Anyway, I wrote a poem that I was proud of, and it later got published in a literary journal. Out of curiosity, I looked up the name's meaning. It turns out that it's a Yoruba name meaning, "One who is clear" or "clear spoken". That information coincided with me receiving the results of a matrilineal ancestry DNA test I'd taken two months prior, which revealed my maternal lineage to be Yoruba/Fulani. Imagine my surprise. When Mama Adisa shows up, I'm a much better listener now.

JB: Finally, being a witness is a predominant theme in this work. In fact, there is a school of thought, led mainly by Carolyn Forche and Adrienne Rich, that one of the most important roles of poetry is, to paraphrase Rich, to help people see what they are living through, and help give voice to experiences we would rather overlook. Do you consider yourself a witness poet? Why or why not?

KGA: I am absolutely a witness! If I hadn't had the work of others in this literary tradition to turn to in my formative years, I don't know what I'd do. Writers helped me to feel connected to a larger experience and to make sense of where I happen to find myself in this story, and also know that my individual story was vital to the whole.

Though much has been written about the immigrant experience, it's always changing and evolving. My particular experiences represent just another phase of an ongoing process, as Caribbean people have been moving throughout the Americas, for one reason or another, for hundreds of years. Each movement has its own story to tell and its own larger truth to impart, and I'm just grateful to be a part of this journey. Through my writing, one of my hopes is to help unravel and demystify our more challenging experiences and place them in a wider social, political and historical context so that we can properly calibrate ourselves to make the maximum impact while we are here.

KERRY YOUNG'S HISTORICAL NOVELS SHED LIGHT
ON A VIBRANT CHINESE COMMUNITY IN JAMAICA

Kerry Young was born in Kingston, Jamaica, to a Chinese father and mother of mixed Chinese-African heritage. She came to England at the age of ten. Kerry's background is in youth work where she worked both locally and nationally, and has also written extensively. She has Master's degrees in organisation development and creative writing, and a PhD in youth work. Kerry Young is a Buddhist in the tradition of Vietnamese Zen Buddhist master Thich Nhat Hanh. Her interests include Tai Chi, weight lifting and golf. She also loves jazz and plays alto and tenor saxophone.

Kerry is a reader for The Literary Consultancy, a tutor for the Arvon Foundation and a Fellow on the Royal Literary Fund Fellowship Programme where she is writer-in-residence at The University of Sheffield (2014-2016). She is also Honorary Assistant Professor in the School of English at The University of Nottingham and Honorary Creative Writing Fellow at the University of Leicester.

Her novels are *Pao* (2011), *Gloria* (2013) and *Show Me a Mountain* (2016).

❧

JB: Kerry Young, thank you so much for this interview, which will focus on your three novels *Pao*, *Gloria* and *Show Me A Mountain*, all of which, to varying degrees, examine the Chinese experience in Jamaica. I want to start by asking why did you feel the need to tell essentially the same story from three different points of view? What did you think would be gained by doing this? Which book would you suggest a reader start reading first, and why?

KY: I didn't start with the idea of telling the same story from three points of view. That emerged organically over time. I think after I finished the first draft of *Pao* I had some vague notion that there might be three books, but I hadn't configured in my head that it would be the same story. I don't know what I thought, really. Maybe I was seeing it more like a sort of family saga. Who knows?

Anyway, I wrote *Pao* first. That was the book I had in mind when I decided to try to write a work of fiction. Then a couple of things happened. Firstly, the publishers loved the character of Gloria Campbell and together we decided that would be the second book. Secondly, I realised that Gloria would give me a great opportunity to further explore the issues of race, class, wealth and gender – of Gloria's life and experiences as a woman of African heritage from a poor background in Jamaica at the time in which the books are set. And since I'd always seen *Pao* not only as a social and political commentary on contemporary Jamaica, but also as exploring those kinds of cross-cutting societal issues, it seemed to make sense to look at them from Gloria's point of view. In writing *Gloria* it became very obvious that Gloria Campbell and Fay Wong (because of race, shade, wealth and class) lived in two different Jamaicas. So I wanted to take the opportunity with *Show Me A Mountain* to examine the personal, social and political similarities and differences between the lives of these two women – and Pao as well.

So it is one story, but it's also three stories, as Pao, Gloria and Fay all have their own tale to tell. Yang Pao is a fourteen-year-old Chinese boy who arrives in Jamaica in 1938 and grows up to become the godfather of Chinatown. Gloria is sixteen when a violent act forces her and her sister to run away from Westmoreland to make a new life in Kingston, where, in 1945, she meets the racketeer Yang Pao. They begin a relationship, which Pao's stepfather is unhappy about; he wants Pao to marry a nice Chinese girl. Fay Wong is the extremely poor choice that Pao makes: a wealthy woman of mixed Chinese and African heritage who is trying to escape the constraints of her privileged upbringing. In the process, Fay's eyes are opened to a Jamaica she never knew existed. When Fay's mother tells her to marry Yang Pao, Fay finds herself on a journey of self-discovery, sacrifice and betrayal.

I don't think it matters which book the reader reads first as all three are completely independent, stand-alone stories. That said, reading them in order would be fine. *Pao, Gloria, Show Me A Mountain*. Certainly, *Pao* before *Show Me A Mountain*. Although I know people have read them in a different sequence – and indeed, some readers tell me they read *Pao* first, and then re-read that book after reading the other two – there is so much more you learn about Pao when reading the stories of the two women.

JB: I would describe your work as compulsively readable; that is, it is hard to put the novels down once you have started reading. This is a hard feat to achieve with historical works, yet you have managed to do this, while making the works also feel very contemporary. Why did you think it was important to spend the looking at the period leading up to Jamaican Independence that you do in your works?

KY: To me, 1938 to the early 1980s was a hugely significant period in contemporary Jamaican history. That time span takes us through the disturbances over employment, wages and poor conditions across the English-speaking Caribbean, the forming of the first national political parties, the right to vote under British rule, the West Indies Federation, Independence, two states of emergency, two Michael Manley administrations. That was our road to Emancipation as a nation. That was the story I was trying to tell. I wanted to help the reader to understand what happened to us as a country – from British colonialism to US fiscal policy in the Caribbean. I wanted to explain why our history has been so chequered, and latterly so violent. I wanted to show that our domestic problems are not strictly of our own making. That is why the Karl Marx quote appears as an epigraph at the beginning of *Pao*.

> People "make their own history, but they do not make it as they please; they do not make it under self-selected circumstances, but under circumstances existing already, given and transmitted from the past."

That said, I was also very aware that I wanted the books to be entertaining – not just, or primarily, educational. I wanted the books to be fun and as you say "compulsively readable". So I really focused on the characters and their stories. Working hard to make them come alive as real people with real lives, real challenges and real triumphs. People the reader could relate to and want to care about. And I tried to do that with respect, humility and humour. For everything else that Pao is, he is also very funny.

JB: Sticking with the history in your works, one of the things that your books do very well is bring to life a Chinatown and a vibrant Chinese community that existed in downtown Kingston that maybe many of us were not quite aware of. Can you give us some insights into the formation of this community, what led to its demise, but also what remains in downtown Kingston of this community? In the process, can you talk about the two main riots that have taken place against the Chinese in this community in the past?

KY: That is funny isn't it, that people outside of Jamaica are often unaware of the Chinese presence, even though the Chinese have been there for so very long. In fact, Ray Chen's book published in 2005 was titled *The Shopkeepers – Commemorating 150 years of the Chinese in Jamaica 1854-2004*. And that is all across Jamaica, urban and rural, not just in Chinatown in Kingston.

What I know of the history of the Chinese in Jamaica comes mostly from Ray's book. After the abolition of slavery, the British needed cheap labour to work the plantations of the Caribbean and many were recruited from southern China. Some of these workers were forcibly taken off the streets without their consent while others were indentured labourers contracted with the ship's captain to work on a specific plantation for a period of five years (and, later, three years on other plantations). Some, like my grandfather, got free passage on British ships on the basis that they had the resources to start a small shop.

It seems to be a pattern of the Chinese to create Chinatowns wherever we go across the globe. Whether it be Kingston, London or New York... or anywhere else for that matter. Those Chinatowns provide services not just for the Chinese but for all people who want to eat or shop for Chinese food. Or maybe use the laundry or bakery or wholesalers. So I guess Barry Street was just another one of those places. Of course, times change and a lot of Chinese Jamaicans left in the 1970s, mostly for Canada and the USA. This is pure conjecture on my part, as I had already left in 1965, but perhaps people didn't feel as "at home" as they had done previously. That was certainly Pao's take on the situation:

> "The other thing that strike me 'bout the way Jamaica changing is how everybody start talking 'bout Africa. Is like we 'Out of Many', but the 'One People' seem to be just the Africans. Is Africa this and Africa that. Marcus Garvey and Haile Selassie. And ever since the world discover Bob Marley, everything turn to Rasta and reggae. It like they think the only true Jamaican is a African. Like they forget that the original Jamaican was the Arawak Indian and after the Spanish and British get through murdering all of them we was all imports. Every last one of us. But it no matter, all I see and hear every day now is how we got to get back to Africa."
>
> (*Pao*, Bloomsbury, 2011, p. 243)

A part of that sense of feeling ill-at-ease was most probably amplified by the anti-Chinese disturbances. In my view, that is in the nature of communities under pressure. When we are having a hard time, we look to our neighbour to see if they are having a better time. And if, in our opinion, they are, we turn on them. We blame them and we punish them for the hard time we are having. We don't always see the shared oppressions we experience and the ways in which the class structure operates to set different communities against each other while those at the top continue to reap the benefits.

This was how Pao saw the troubles in the 1960s.

> "Killing your neighbour not going solve unemployment and all the misery that go with that. Their enemy not their neighbour. Their enemy is the masa that is making himself rich while all them boys bleeding to death in the street. If you want talk 'bout brothers in arms then maybe we need to get together and go get back the land that still owned by British landlords. And maybe we need to go see 'bout how we going stop these foreign investors from just taking out all the profit as fast as we can make it for them, so Jamaica can get to keep something for herself. And then maybe we wouldn't need so much foreign aid. But the ordinary man can't do nothing 'bout these people. He don't even know where to find them. All he can do is take up a gun and fire it at the people he see every day. And the worst thing about it is he doing it with a gun he get from the CIA. The masa don't even have to beat the slave himself no more. We doing it for him." (*Pao*, p. 157).

JB: It seems as if most of the early Chinese in Jamaica were Hakka

Chinese. What can you tell us about the Hakka Chinese and their reasons for migrating to Jamaica? In what ways would you say that earlier community is similar to or different from the more recent Chinese arrivals to the island?

KY: I have to go back to Ray Chen's book to answer this. The Hakka people are long-time migrants who travelled south from their homeland in the north of China because of famine most likely caused by drought, flooding or pillage by invading armies. According to Ray, there were five migration periods dating from around 317 to the end of the Taiping Rebellion in1864. "This was by far the most important event to affect the Hakka, and had a bearing on why our fathers and grandfathers emigrated to the Americas, the Caribbean, India and other parts of the globe". (*The Shopkeepers*, Periwinkle Publishers (Jamaica) Ltd, 2005, p. 5). Why and how they ended up in Jamaica, I already mentioned above.

Honestly, I don't really know anything about the more recent Chinese arrivals to Jamaica. My understanding is that they are mainly Chinese workers employed by Chinese construction companies contracted to undertake development initiatives on the island. To my mind, these are, therefore, migrant workers who (most likely) will return to China, which is a completely different situation from people transported by a third party (willingly or not) to meet the third party's labour needs.

JB: *Pao* is written from a male perspective, and I really have to commend you, because oftentimes when the writer is of a different gender than the central character it can be jarring and unconvincing, but I did not have these problems with the book. Yet I found it very hard to get a sense of Pao's mother in the book, who always seems to be in the background, so what can you tell us about the character of Ma to bring her forward a bit?

KY: I can't really tell you any more about Ma other than what already appears in the book. She was "a hard-working girl from an honourable family; a believer in the Republic; a supporter of Dr Sun Yat-sen" (*Pao*, p. 50). She married Yang Tzu (Pao's father) after Sun Yat-sen gave way to the warlord Yuan Shikai. She lived through tough times working in the fields while the warlords increased the land rent and other taxes, and the Japanese took control of Shandong and Manchuria. She had two sons, Yang Xiuquan and Yang Pao. Her husband was killed by British and French soldiers while supporting the Guangzhou-Hongkong strikers at Shaji. She stayed in China until her husband's childhood friend, Zhang Xiuquan, sent passage for her and the two boys to come to Jamaica in 1938. When Fay asks her if she misses China, she says:

"Every day. The rice fields and the open sky. The village, the family and their father. He was a good man. Honourable man. Good farmer. Like Xiuquan. He make good farmer like his papa." (*Pao*, p. 85)

When asked if she misses her son, Xiuquan, she says:

"Ah miss, miss, miss. Too much talk 'bout miss. What good it do you? This happen, that happen. War, death, a new country, a son leave, a baby born. Who tell the world to make these things happen? That is why the Buddha say to be happy is to suffer less, and to suffer less is to be free from wanting. You accept what you have. Now I am here with Pao and Zhang." (*Pao*, p. 85)

Ma is a good Buddhist. She accepts that this is it. Everything is as it is.

JB: Creolisation often takes such intriguing forms in your work. Not just in language or even in the multiplicity of races and their mixing, but in smaller more seemingly insignificant moments as well. For example, I read Pao's gift of a jade necklace to his black lover, Gloria, as such a moment of Asian-African creolisation.

KY: Is that what it was? Interesting. To me, it was just a beautiful gift. Something Pao could and would purchase in Chinatown. Something he would feel really pleased about buying and something that would look amazing against Gloria's dark skin. That's how I saw it. Gleaming around Gloria's neck. Maybe you are right. Maybe there was something subconscious for me about the significance of the jade, but it wasn't how I was thinking about it.

JB: One of the things that stand out in all three books is the needlework, particularly embroidery and crochet, being done by Ms Cecily throughout. Can you address in depth the kinds of needlework you saw being done by women on the island, which groups of women engaged in what forms of needlework, what they made and why? There is that amazing scene in *Show me a Mountain* where Fay asks her mother if embroidery was what slave women did? In addition, the reader never actually gets to see what it is that Ms. Cecily is embroidering in all three books, so can you take a moment and give us some understanding of what that might be?

KY: As a child, I saw a lot of basket-weaving for the tourist industry and a lot of crochet by church-going ladies like my grandmother. There always seemed to be a lot of white doilies around – on the tops of side tables, under ornaments and covering food. As far as Miss Cicely's needlework is concerned, Fay comments on her mother crocheting:

"A tiny section of what I knew would grow into a magnificent centrepiece to be washed and starched in epic fashion to grace someone else's dining table." (*Show Me A Mountain*, Bloomsbury, 2016, p. 54)

And much earlier in the book Fay, as a child, is described as having wrapped her mother's half-embroidered table-runner around her waist (*Show Me A Mountain*, p. 11).

The comment about slaves comes in the middle of one of Fay and Cicely's famous arguments – after Fay, having been relentlessly beaten by her mother as a child, tells Miss Cicely that "brutality has been bred into the Jamaican psyche since slavery". "What do you know about slavery?" Miss Cicely asks and then continues:

> "All you ever worried about your whole life was how to parade yourself as white. Making your father board you at Immaculate even though the school only little way 'cross town. Running all over the place with your rich friends dancing and partying and playing tennis and God knows what. Like tennis is any kind of pastime for a girl like you." (*Show Me A Mountain*, p. 212)

Miss Cicely says that Fay thinks she's better than everyone else in the house because she has light skin, not dark skin like her mother. And this is Fay's rebuke. Fay is chastising and mocking her mother.

> "My light skin? Is that what worrying you? More like you doing battle with how you so black. Sitting on that veranda with your embroidery and crochet. Is that what the slave used to do on the plantation? In her spare time after she finish working in the field, or cleaning the great house, or cooking the massa's food or serving at table. Seeing to the laundry. Tending to the mistress and the children. And lying on her back for whoever wanted to defile her. Is that what she did? Embroidery and crocheting? And drink Earl Grey tea in the afternoon? Is that what the slave did that you are following in her footsteps?" (p. 212)

JB: I have to be honest and say of the three books, I find "Gloria" the least convincing. I guess this comes from a number of reasons. When I was collecting oral histories of Jamaican women for a book, I interviewed Chinese-Jamaican women who spoke openly of the hostility and racism that many in the Chinese community had towards particularly dark-skinned Jamaicans. So I find it hard that this was absent in Gloria's interactions with the Chinese men in her life and how easily and readily they accepted her and provided for her, absent of any discussion of race.

KY: "Out of Many, One People", that is the Jamaican national motto. So, what does that tell us? Jamaica is a very multi-cultural society. A society about which Pao comments, on Independence Day: "That day was our future, and it was full of hope that out of the many, that the British bring from all corners of the world to serve them, we could be one people" (*Pao*, p. 114). Of course, after 300 years of British colonisation, Jamaican society had been well stratified, so much later in the book Pao comments, "And even though we still struggling to sort ourselves out after the English come here 300 years ago and set everything up so careful and tidy – Africans on the bottom, the Indians, the Chinese, English on top…" (*Pao*, p. 266).

Social stratification does not only occur in colonised societies. You only have to take a casual look at the British class system to appreciate that. The problem is that as long as people are differentiated into different social groups based on socioeconomic factors such as occupation and income (or indeed race, shade or class heritage), and as long as these different groups are linked to different social status that give rise to different access to opportunities, privilege and power (social, political and economic), then misinformation and prejudices will be bred and sustained. As long as group A is considered to be better than group B, but not as good as group C, then societies can expect intergroup antipathy. And that's always a two-way street. It runs both ways.

So, you mention the hostility and racism you perceived towards "particularly dark-skinned Jamaicans" from the Chinese-Jamaican women you interviewed, and also the "riots" against Chinese people. This is what I mean about the antipathy running both ways. But my main point is that such divisions and resulting animosities are not designed by those who experience them. They are designed by those who benefit from them. Those for whom such hostilities serve a purpose. Like that well-known phrase – and tactic – divide and rule. Like Pao said: "The masa don't even have to beat the slave himself no more. We doing it for him." (*Pao*, p. 157).

I wonder if you would have had the same reaction from Chinese-Jamaican men. I ask this because as well as race and class, gender also plays a part in societal divisions – impacting not only on men's view of women and women's view of men, but also women's view of other women and men's view of other men. This also applies to other issues – for example, sexuality, religion, disability, and so on. These are all major cross-cutting issues that impact on the way individuals and groups perceive and relate to each other. And these are the themes that all three books seek to explore.

JB: Also, I struggled somewhat with the transformation of Gloria and all the women around her. It started to seem like all the prostitutes, every last one of them, were just good freedom-fighting people. Even the mean old woman from Back-O-Wall is tamed into a sweet grandmotherly figure.

KY: I don't know what I can say about that, really. I was trying to explore the way Jamaica was changing politically, and the relationship between Jamaica and Cuba during those years. I wanted to represent the "love affair". Hence, Gloria and Ernesto Sanchez. I suppose for me, people are rarely what they might seem at first. There is always something else to them. And you don't really get to know them until you understand their back story – as is the case with Aunty (from Back-O-Wall), and Sybil and Beryl. When you understand their back stories, then you understand why Aunty is so cantankerous and why Beryl and Sybil find themselves in the place they do.

I think that's a constant theme for me. This idea that we are many things – some good, some bad – all stemming from the sufferings of our past. There are many examples of this in my work. Not just concerning the main characters but also people like Isaac Dunkley and Louis DeFreitas. I suppose I'm just interested in trying to understand how people deal with the things that happen to them. How those experiences impact on the decisions and choices they make. How one thing leads to another. What sense they make of their experiences. And importantly, how they can use their understanding of their experiences to create a positive force in their lives. That is what I saw Gloria and Sybil trying to do. And Aunty too. But in any case, who says that a prostitute cannot also be a revolutionary? I think anybody can be. Anybody who becomes aware of the inequalities and injustices that surround us, and wants to do something about it. In Gloria's case, she is taking a stand against the social and economic conditions that created the circumstances of her becoming a prostitute. Of course, Sybil always was a revolutionary – from the moment we meet her. After all, it is Sybil who tells Gloria:

> "It like yu back in slavery. A hundred years ago they free the slave but they nuh free the woman. The woman is still living her life under the control a the man, under his law and regulation and goodwill. And her body is occupied. It is his. It belong to him just like the body a the slave belong to the slave master.
>
> And when yu suffer that realisation day in day out, year after year, life after life, what it do is shape how every woman see herself. Weak and subservient like she cyan do nothing without him say so, she cyan even think nothing for herself. She completely relying on him to know who she is, and all she can do is carry on just the way him want her to and hope for the best. Just like the slave. (*Gloria*, p. 52)

KB: For me, the real bookend to *Pao* is *Show Me a Mountain* which I was sure would be anticlimactic, having read the other two novels first, but it truly was not. I also was sure that there was no way that I would come to care for Fay as a character based on the first two books, and again I was proven wrong. At what point in writing these three books did you realise that Fay warranted the telling of her own story? What did you learn about Fay in telling her story? Are there other characters that you could foresee telling their stories? Mui? Henry Wong?

KY: I'm so glad that *Show Me A Mountain* changed the way you felt about Fay. Actually, that is exactly what I was talking about when I said (above) about knowing a person's back story in order to understand why they are the way they are and why they make the choices they make.

As I said earlier, I think I always had this third book in the back of my mind somewhere, but it wasn't until I'd written *Pao* and *Gloria* that I started to understand what Fay's story was. To be honest, it all came as rather a surprise to me. The thing I learnt about Fay was how strong she was. She was really determined to learn and understand more about Jamaica and her position of privilege; she was tough in coming to terms with her situation and dealing with it.

The other thing I learned was about "free will". What is "free will" and how much "free will" do we (any of us) really have? How much of what we think and do is determined by "free will" as opposed to ideas we have based on the past, flawed memories, mistaken perceptions, ill-informed opinions, bad habits, irrational thinking, fear, anxiety, worry, shame, guilt, loyalty, pride, revenge, anger, jealousy and all sorts of other (not necessarily appropriate to the situation) feelings – like how someone else/other people will regard us if we do X instead of Y. Do we ever make truly rational decisions based on free will? And if we don't then how alive are we? Hence, the St Thomas Aquinas quote at the beginning of *Show Me A Mountain*.

> The highest manifestation of life consists in this: that a being governs its own actions. A thing which is always subject to the direction of another is somewhat of a dead thing.

Plus, I understood more clearly the core values being explored in the books. For Pao: Can we be forgiven (or forgive ourselves) for the hurts we visit upon others? For Gloria: Can we forgive ourselves for the hurts visited upon us? For Fay: Can we forgive ourselves for the hurts we visit upon ourselves?

I'm not sure about telling the stories of other characters. But actually, that has been suggested to me, both Mui and Henry Wong. It has also been suggested that I produce a book of short stories with each chapter being a catch up on the lives of some of the minor characters like Hampton, Judge Finley, Clifton Brown, Miss Sissy, Sybil & Beryl. I have no such plans at present... but who knows?

JB: One of the really interesting things with having essentially the same story told from three different perspectives is that this lends itself to rich moments of reinterpretation and inter-textuality. Take for example the character of Isaac Dunkley. In one text he can be written off as a callous child pimp, in another he is a rising revolutionary. What is fascinating to me about the revolutionary Dunkley, though, is that his revolution does not seem to justify the same revolutionary rights to women. How does he square that circle?

KY: That is funny isn't it, how these things go? There are so many instances of campaigns that are pursued with a narrow or myopic vision. It puts me in mind of the 1982 book edited by Gloria Hull, Patricia Bell Scott and Barbara Smith: *All the Women Are White, All the Blacks Are Men, But Some of Us Are Brave: Black Women's Studies* (The Feminist Press). That is what I was trying to show. Isaac isn't any different from any number of men (or women) who pursue "one issue" while ignoring or forgetting that the people they purport to represent are all sorts of people. So, whether we want freedom for the "masses" or workers' rights, we have to remember that our interest group includes all sorts of people – black, white, mixed, women, men, gay or lesbian, differently abled, different ages, different nationalities from differing class, cultural or ethnic backgrounds and religious commitments, etc. This was why Sybil said, "A hundred years ago they free the slave but they nuh free the woman." (*Gloria*, p. 52) She was trying to acknowledge that challenge. And truth is, we don't need to look very far to see how "single issue" perspectives are enacted each and every day. I guess that's part of the contradictions of life. It seems people find it very hard to see beyond their own particular circumstances. Find it very hard to envision and represent a world beyond their own. No matter how right or noble their cause might be.

Anyway, Isaac was a changed man. And that transformation we appreciate when we understand his back story as it appears in *Show Me A Mountain*.

JB: Violence is an ongoing theme in all three books and you do a really great job of tracing the many routes and many modes of violence in Jamaican society. I am wondering, though, if you can foresee a time when Jamaicans can overcome our violent founding and stop enacting terrible acts of violence on each other? What would that Jamaica look like to you, if you can imagine it?

KY: I think it's really important to keep emphasising what I said earlier – that Jamaica's problems are not strictly of our own making – given our colonial past and historical relationship with the USA. As a researcher, I feel (relatively) confident in looking backwards, but I'm not convinced that I am qualified to gaze forward. After all, what do I know? Especially since I haven't lived in Jamaica for over fifty years.

JB: Although you have lived most of your life in England, I think it is fair to say that you are positively fascinated with Jamaica, a country you left at the tender age of ten years old. Tell us, why does Jamaica remain so central to you and your writing life?

KY: When I decided to write a work of fiction I had to figure out what to write about. I had written a lot of non-fiction previously and knew I wanted to continue addressing the kind of cross-cutting societal issues we discussed earlier, as these themes were often in my non-fiction work. I was told that your first novel should be something that you really care about. Mostly because it takes so long to write and you have to be able to sustain yourself. So, I thought about it and after a couple of false starts, came up with the idea for *Pao*, which actually took seven years to write.

Why? Because I came to England when I was ten years old and have always felt that people here misunderstand Jamaica. To them, it was either some kind of backward jungle or latterly (and increasingly) an island of terror where tourists can't be let out of their hotel compound for fear of personal and sexual assault. I also knew that Chinese Jamaicans are not a very familiar group to people in the UK. In fact, almost no English person believed that I was Jamaican. So, that was it. I wanted to put some kind of record straight about the reasons for our chequered journey.

When my mom read the first draft of *Pao* she said, "I can see where you got the idea, but your father was nowhere near as successful, or as clever, or as funny." So *Pao* is not my father. But that is where the book comes from. A father distantly remembered and mostly invented. *Pao* is the story an adult creates and weaves from a child's misunderstood, misremembered and half-forgotten memories. *Pao* was a gift to my father – a gift of a life longer and better than the one he had.

JB: Finally, my dear Dr Kerry Young, what are you working on these days?

KY: Something completely different. A book set in Malaya during the Japanese occupation. A story about a white English rubber planter who hesitates long enough to miss the British civilian evacuation in December 1941 and who lives out his time up to 1945 in the limestone caves of Penang and in the kampung village where the plantation workers hid and protected him.

What do you do in such circumstances? You sleep and you dream and you remember. How you got to be where you are. And why.

IN PAMELA MORDECAI'S WORK ISSUES
OF BELONGING AND IDENTITY EMERGE

Pamela Mordecai writes poetry and fiction. Born in Jamaica, she went to the US for undergraduate studies, returning to Jamaica to obtain a diploma in education and, eventually, a PhD in English from the University of the West Indies, Mona. She has published six collections of poetry, *Journey Poem* (1987), *de Man* (1995), *Certifiable* (2001), *The True Blue of Islands* (2005), *Subversive Sonnets* (2012) and *de book of Mary: a performance poem* (2012). This is the second in a planned patwa trilogy, following *de Man*. She has also published a short story collection, *Pink Icing and Other Stories* (2006), a novel, *Red Jacket* (2015), which was short-listed for the Rogers Writers' Trust Fiction Award, and five children's books. She has edited and coedited collections of Caribbean writing; published academic articles; and authored/coauthored numerous textbooks. She and her husband, Martin, wrote *Culture and Customs of Jamaica* (2001), published in Greenwood Press's Culture and Customs series.

She and Martin live in Toronto.

JB: Pamela, I must confess that while I have read some of your works in the past, this is the first time I've had the chance to read three of your books at once – the novel *Red Jacket* and the two poetry collections *Subversive Sonnets* and *de Book of Mary*. Reading all three books was an absolute revelation for me. I want to start off where I always seem to start in these interviews, by asking you to tell me a little about where in Jamaica you were born and grew up and what your childhood was like.

PM: Is me must thank you, Jacqueline, for reading and looking closely at the three books!

I was born in my grandparents' home, at the bottom of Elletson Road, close to Rae Town, not far from Kingston Harbour. The first manatee I ever saw was beached on a little black sand bay in Rae Town. The house was round the corner from Tower Street Prison, where at some point in time both my father and my uncle worked. The tramcar line, which I remember now with nostalgia, came down Elletson Road and turned the corner on to Tower Street. The woman who delivered me was Nurse Belisario, the only other person I've ever heard of with the same name as Isaac Mendes

Belisario, the first Jamaican-born artist who drew those amazing Jonkanoo figures. In many ways, this was the house of my childhood, though I didn't live there. It was old, with a parlour with wooden shutters that ran all across the front, as well as a living room. It had very high ceilings and a deep cellar, a well (never mind it wasn't very far from the salt water of the harbour), outbuildings that contained a big brick oven, and a gigantic concrete bath in which I can remember my grandfather bathing. It had a big back yard with lots of mango trees, a fig tree, calabash trees and breadfruit trees whose "man" blossoms my grandmother collected and used to make a sweet dessert. There was a barge tree as well, its pods of sour green fruit bearing straight off the stem. In our family, anything very sour was described as "sour like barge". No one outside the family seems to have heard of a barge tree, however. The small untidy garden had a rain tree – a bush with white flowers that bloomed whenever it rained. Also, there was at least one pomegranate tree, and holly bushes at the bottom of the front stairs – which, along with the front door, no one ever used.

The first actual family house of ours that I remember living in was on Mountain View Avenue in Vineyard Pen – in time, Vineyard Town – where we went to mass and novenas at the church of St Theresa, the Little Flower, and deposited our small savings at the branch of the government savings bank in the Post Office near the corner of Deanery and Antrim roads. We grew up in that house, climbing the huge poinciana tree in the front yard and playing house in its branches. It had a big yard in which my father kept chickens in a sizeable fowl coop, as well as a goat for which he grew lush guinea grass near a pipe. There were many lignum vitae trees, a grape arbour that hardly bore, an ebony tree that bloomed before the rain, sweet and sour sop trees, a coolie plum tree in the backyard, and a "good" orange tree under which Papa kept his carpenter's bench, as well as a Seville (civil) orange tree. Papa was an accountant, but he was also a fine carpenter who made lots of our furniture, for we couldn't afford many things. My father had the most able pair of hands. He could build a house from the foundations up, take a car apart and put it back together – until they put computers into cars. He could repair small appliances, mend our school shoes, look after fowls if they had yaws, tend to our toothaches and our minor illnesses. He extended our little house as the family grew to five children, adding a living room in front and a back verandah and converting the wooden, sand-dashed walls to concrete nog. We weathered the 1951 hurricane in that house, with Papa battening it down and hurrying outside in the lull when the eye was passing over to shore up whatever had come apart. He loved aphorisms and raised us on sayings: "Anything worth doing is worth doing well." "The graveyard is full of indispensable people." "When you have done your best, the angels can do no better." "What is fi-yu cannot be un-fi-yu."

I started school at Alpha Prep pretty early. My mother taught Spanish at Alpha Academy, and I began school when I was about four, by which time I could read a newspaper. I think I can remember walking to the bus stop at the corner of Deanery Road and Deanery Avenue with Mama, my older sister Betty and my younger brother Richard, murdered in Botany Bay, in the parish of St Thomas in 2004. My fourth book of poetry, *The True Blue of Islands* was written for him. I never liked school. Our starched white shirts under our navy tunics were scratchy and I was always losing my beret, much to the chagrin of my parents, for berets were expensive. I was almost always the youngest in the class, bright and rather goody-goody – a recipe for disaster! I had a temper and terrible nightmares, in the middle of which I would scream. My sister and I shared a bed at first, and it couldn't have been much fun for her. Papa would come and pat me back to sleep. Two happy memories have to do with poetry. Papa read us a poem most nights before we went to bed from *The Best Loved Poems of the American People*. I can still recite long portions of "'Twas the Night Before Christmas" and "The Gingham Dog and the Calico Cat" and all of Longfellow's "The Day is Done". And once having met the poems of Louise Bennett, I learned them by heart and recited them up and down the house. I often say that if I write poetry it was because of my father reading us poems and discovering Louise Bennett.

JB: It seems to me that in recent times one book follows another for you. A two-part question: What accounts for the enormous burst in creativity? Secondly, for someone known mainly as a poet, why have you chosen now to venture into short-story writing and novel-writing?

PM: Martin and I never planned to leave Jamaica. Ever. How we came to emigrate is still a bit of a mystery. However, as it turned out, immigration was crucial to both of us being able to write. Had we remained in Jamaica, we would not have written as much, and certainly not have published as much. Canada's generous funding for the arts is what has made a creative writing career possible for us both. I'd have continued to write textbooks, still my major source of income, and so the poems and stories for children that appear in these books would have been written. But I'd not have written six books of poetry and two works of fiction as well as a children's play that was lavishly mounted in Toronto in 2010 – and produced in Jamaica last year by students of the School of Drama at the Edna Manley College for the Performing Arts. That said, the books that, appearing quite quickly one after the other, create the idea of "a burst in creativity" are in fact the result of long-ago investments of time and effort. Though it was published in 2015, I was writing *Red Jacket* (working title, Cipher) as long ago as 2000. I had hoped to publish *Subversive Sonnets* in 2007 to coincide with the celebration of

200th anniversary of the abolition of the slave trade. It appeared in 2012. The only really recent work, therefore, is de book of Mary (2015), and even that I had been thinking about since right after finishing de Man, so from the late 1990s. I was encouraged to venture into prose when I heard a very famous Caribbean-Canadian poet friend say she began writing prose because "nobody ever made a living from writing poetry!" Recently, thinking back, I've concluded that writing de Man perhaps nudged me in a narrative direction but I won't go any further with that since I may be anticipating the response to one of your later questions...

JB: Issues of belonging are at the centre of Red Jacket – whether the main character Grace Carpenter belongs on the island of St Chris, in Africa, or in Canada. Whether she is truly black and what blackness means for someone who is "red" as she is. What are you trying to examine about issues of belonging and skin colour in the novel?

PM: I was and am most interested in what makes identity, what contributes to the construction of a self. Inside that larger question are the more focused questions: what part does belonging have to do with me being me? What part does blackness have to do with belonging and with me being me? I didn't want the story to be a tale about a dark person not fitting in with white or lighter-skinned people. That was (and in some parts of the world, like India, continues to be) a function of attitudes cemented by history and mores. Power and powerlessness don't participate in quite the same way in the circumstances in which Grace finds herself. Power resides in her community, being first, her family, and then those in the town of Wentley Park. Not everyone in her adopted family likes her and some in the community don't, because they are black people and she is red. It's true their attitudes might also be a function of inherited prejudice, but she is in so many other respects exactly like them, and she is only a child. I've just read Chimimanda Ngozi Adichie's *Americanah*, a novel that provides a nuanced perspective on blackness, written as it is by an African contemplating the behaviour of Americans, including African-Americans. If I understand the book, her female protagonist, Ifemelu, sees blackness (as Americans conceive of it) as phenotype, dark colouring, because that is what the non-black world responds to – mostly recoiling from it. Gramps, Grace's adopted grandfather in *Red Jacket*, describes blackness differently. For him, blackness is not just skin colour but language, culture, ethnicity. (I guess those qualities that led Toni Morrison to say Bill Clinton was America's first black president?) If that's not so, Gramps says, any tar-brushed white person could be from St Chris. Though she is otherwise "black", Grace experiences a phenotypically black community's negative response to her red phenotype: in this case, black people do the rejecting. The disavowing is not of an "other" – white, Asian, Jew – but of one of their own in all respects except in how she looks. How important is it that the young person physically resembles those who nurture her? Might it be that in an animal kind of way, looking like the pack is important for belonging? These days, we see stories on the Internet of foxes raising chickens, so maybe that's not so, or not so anymore, as animal-kind evolves... Maybe we humans are behind in that as well... So without giving away the story, though Grace is very much part of St Chris, its language, its customs, its people, and very attached to her adopted family, Gramps especially, she still lacks a basic emotional anchor and she spends her life searching for it.

JB: Why did you choose to set *Red Jacket* in two made-up countries, Mabuli and St Christopher?

PM: I've always said it was because I wanted to avoid having to be answerable, accurate. I was born and raised in Jamaica and have spent most of my life there, so I know it well enough. Still, people can be picky, especially about places, a language, culture and customs that are dear to them. Kamau Brathwaite, an old friend, once called me on a geographical inaccuracy in one of my poems. In "Jus' a Likl Lovin'" in *Certifiable* (2000), I had the Mona moon rise out of the sea, because I needed the rhyme. It doesn't, of course – which he and I and all the folks who know Mona know. I didn't want the need for that kind of truth to bog down the writing of *Red Jacket*. Similarly, in inventing Mabuli, I could feel some freedom, never mind it is in a very specific location in West Africa. There's another way of looking at that question. In an imagined place, it is possible to make physical context answer narrative needs, and to design setting for that purpose. That was a big part of what I enjoyed, especially in inventing Mabuli. I'd never been to West Africa, so to create the tiny country that I conjured between Mali and Burkina Faso, sharing a short border with Côte d'Ivoire in the south, I had to work from books, videos, photographs, maps, articles and so on. Overall, I had to be on top of old and contemporary history (including history of weather), climate, topography, vegetation, agriculture, architecture, cultures and ethnicities, in the real spaces (the Caribbean, West Africa) in which I'd placed St Chris and Mabuli, during the time period in which the novel is set. (When the novel says there were floods in West Africa, and a hurricane in the Caribbean, both things are true of both places at the time.) I did a lot of research in an attempt to avoid misrepresentation, but within the confines of what had to be, I could also do some inventing. Atunkle, Jimmy's father's forebear on his mother's side, claimed to have met Napoleon on his campaign to

Egypt. It was fun and entirely plausible to imagine that. There's also a story that explains how Mabuli came to be bilingual. It involves the Tellem, small red people who could reputedly fly and who lived on the Bandiagara Escarpment in Mali between the 11th and 16th centuries. I love it!

JB: Now turning to *de book of Mary*, you are carrying on your examination of notable Biblical characters which began with *de man*: a performance poem about the life of Jesus. Interestingly enough, your examinations take the form of "a performance poem" which brings up several interesting questions. Why the interest in Biblical characters (you are writing a trilogy)? In addition, I notice that this collection is dedicated to Kamau Brathwaite. Can you tell us a little about what went into this dedication?

PM: I am writing the Jesus story as a trilogy, a generational story beginning with Joseph, whom I picture as an old man when he married Mary, with Mary in fact being the next generation, and Jesus, the third. I'm very much a disciple captivated by Jesus, for one thing because of the status he accorded women, beginning with his mother. In a huge break with tradition, Jesus made them persons with agency, striking individual selves, from the anonymous woman caught in adultery, to Magdalen, who washed his feet with her tears and dried them with her hair, to Martha, the enabler, and Mary, the one who was mindfully present. The other New Testament characters, including the villains, are also riveting. It's probably because of how it came about that my accounts of the Jesus story are for performance. In the early 1990s, after a Good Friday service at the Church of St Thomas Aquinas, the university church near Papine, Fr Ollie Nickerson, SJ, pastor at the time, asked me to write "something for Good Friday". Since the something he was asking for was meant for the congregation, it had to be performable. When the first line of de Man dropped into my ear, I knew it would be that way. As for the dedication to Kamau, he is an old friend as I've said, but more than that, he has influenced not just Caribbean poetry but my own work in seminal ways. He gave poets permission to get on bad, as bad as we wanted, needed to. Miss Lou may have showed us the way with the use of poetry in patwa, but Louise, never mind her earthiness, was a lady. Kamau taught us to be noisy, raucous, leggo negroes, to cuss, to sing, to chant down Babylon. From he let loose in *Rights of Passage* with his "fucking negro man", Caribbean poetry has not been the same.

JB: What, for you, defines the contours of a performance poem and why do you believe Bible stories and characters are particularly rich for this genre?

PM: Performance poetry is different things to different people. It's not one genre. It seems that, for many people, the performed poem is less than the poem on the page, because – they say – it's theatrical and needs to be acted to get across to the audience. This applies even to poems that, like mine, begin life on the page. (A similar criticism was made when Bob Dylan got the Nobel Prize for Literature: because his lyrics needed melody, they couldn't be as good as poems for which the words had to stand on their own, unaided.) Theatre uses more than words as a medium; it uses lights, sets, sound effects, costumes, which combine to make the theatrical statement. Performance poetry isn't theatre, because however much the performance poet uses voice and gestures, he uses them to get across the meaning of what the words say. Judgment about a poem's worth should depend on the poem itself – not whether its audience read it or heard it. After all, poetry began everywhere as "spoken word" and in every tradition in the world poetry has never stopped being performed. For me, performance poetry lives on the page, but it lives more fully in the mouth of a performer or performers. They make the poem come alive by making it soulful – to use a word that's perhaps lost currency. Performance poetry makes an audience into a community by passing through a soul or souls, to other souls, and magically knitting them together. I don't know if I'd say Bible stories and characters are particularly rich for this genre but they are very satisfying to work with. Once I started rewriting Bible stories in patwa – I first translated the Christmas story from Luke in the mid-seventies – they broke open in more meaningful ways. So perhaps it's that patwa suits the stories, making them real and vivid, more than that the stories suit patwa and so, performance. (For me, patwa and performance can't be separated.) Because Bible stories are well known and beloved by many, people feel an ownership, and so an eagerness to see what there could be in them that's new and different. The newness of them is not achieved just in getting them up off the page, for Bible stories have been the subject of every kind of theatre over the centuries, up till now. The newness is in the patwa in which they resurrect.

JB: How do you explain the seeming contradiction in de Book of Mary, in which the book (and the exact same events) seems to be unfolding simultaneously and contemporaneously in the Middle East and on the island of Jamaica?

PM: It's not a contradiction, is it? Jesus commands the re-enactment of the Last Supper, after all, so you could say he foresaw multiple unfoldings of that event at least. He tells the apostles, "Do this in remembrance of me." He intended that part of the story to be replayed and replayed, everywhere, in every time and every cultural context. In a way, every reading of the crucifixion story – indeed, of the entire Jesus story – in every language, at every time in history, is such an unfolding. (I'm convinced that with every translation of the Bible into a new language, some meaning we couldn't see before becomes evident.) We all make old stories ours, including the Jesus story, if we choose. For some folks, this happens especially in Lent and on Good Friday. For others, it is the Christmas story that offers itself for repeated re-enactment. Looked at in another, perhaps more important way, Jesus is teaching, healing and preaching in and through us now, in languages and cultures everywhere, just as he was doing in his time. He is Gandhi, Sojourner Truth, Harriet Tubman, Martin Luther King Jr, Oscar Romero, Rigoberta Menchú Tum, Malala Yousafzai. He is good people everywhere, working for a better world.

JB: Now I'd like to turn my attention to your astonishing collection, *Subversive Sonnets*. I find this collection deliberately inventive in how it plays with and skirts the conventions of prose and poetry – quite deliberately so. On the one hand, these poems are a readily identifiable poetic form, the sonnet, but on the other hand they are grouped together to form prose pieces. Can you take us through the process of how these poems were made (why you decided, for example, to group so many of the sonnets into prose pieces instead of letting them stand as individual poems) and in so doing explain the title of the collection?

PM: I started to say earlier that after writing *de Man: a performance poem*, I drifted towards storytelling poems. I can't explain this satisfactorily to myself: it simply is so. Many of the poems in my next collection, *Certifiable*, were story-poems, as were poems in *The True Blue of Islands*, and, as you point out, *Subversive Sonnets*. There is the question, though, of why I'd choose to write the stories in sonnets. Black American poet Marilyn Nelson wrote a sequence of sonnets ("a heroic crown of sonnets") called "A Wreath for Emmett Till" about the 1955 lynching of young Emmett. He was an African-American teenager, just 14, and they lynched him for supposedly whistling at a white woman. Marilyn Nelson says, "The strict form became a kind of insulation, a way of protecting myself from the intense pain of the subject matter." Something similar is true for me. Traditional forms help me work my way through the harsh subjects of the poems, at the same time that they help me keep a distance, because I'm having to pay attention to them, as well as to what I'm writing about. I wanted a contrast between the stately traditional form and rougher subject matter. I've done this before, notably in a poem about abuse called "The Story of Nellie". It reads like a nursery rhyme. Sonnet sequences that tell stories are not new, though in the beginning the stories were often about romantic love, doomed romantic love in many cases. An example of a romantic sonnet sequence many people know is Elizabeth Barrett Browning's "Sonnets from the Portuguese". And there are some (happy) romantic poems in *Subversive Sonnets*. I like to think that there is a Creole voice behind all the poems, even those that seem to be in English, and that the patwa undertone, working the traditional English form is also subversive.

JB: In the poem "Old Diaries" the reader is asked to consider both sides of a very complicated issue – that of Paul Bogle, and why he instigated the Morant Bay Rebellion. But interestingly enough, while the narrator of the poem claims allegiance with Bogle, she is left to contemplate too that she has a relative who fired onto Bogle. What was the importance of bringing forward this relative (the militiaman) that maybe many people would probably have pushed to the background?

PM: The poem doesn't really cover Bogle's motives. There have been some very odd matings in the history of the West Indies – of white masters and black slaves, of black slaves and higher status white women. "We all have our white grandparents!" as a friend of mine likes to say. Some of those forbears forced themselves upon their sexual partners and raped them, but others, more than we think, were part of mutually agreed relationships. Of course, except perhaps buried deep in the mind of the narrator, this isn't a poem about that kind of pairing. It's a poem about, on one side, a white grandparent who shot at black rebels who might have been relatives of a black grandparent on the other side. The white man was an army officer who did what he was told, one of millions of soldiers throughout time who did bad things on the orders of their superiors. The Caribbean is full of ancestors of many colours who did bad things to one another and other people. Are we going to somehow erase them?

JB: You know, Pamela, more and more I find that I am personally interested in needlework culture in Jamaica and the larger Caribbean. How it is shunted aside and not taken seriously oftentimes. Indeed, I am finding out that one of the places I have to look to find out about that culture is in Jamaican women writers' works. Imagine, then, my absolute delight and surprise in coming up on a poem like "Lace Makers" in your collection. Can you tell us where you went to high school, what that experience was like, and if indeed lace making was something that you engaged in at high school, as did the narrator in the poem? Lace making is not something often associated with Jamaica. Why is this poem dedicated to Tony McNeill?

PM: I'll take the last question first: the late, brilliant Jamaican poet, Tony McNeill, another close friend, came up with something he called an "Embroidered Line" with which he ended some of his poems, though, by and large, his poems don't have a pronounced concrete quality. He described the embroidered line, which is always the last one, as "achieved by superimposition", that is, printing the line on top of itself. His explanation for the line is part of a complicated account of the development of his poetry, but he does say he "considered 'The Embroidered Line' as a kind of resounding 'yes' at the end of each poem". So you could say these lines finished the poems the way lace finishes a piece of clothing or fine linen. I went to high school at Alpha – correctly, "Convent of Mercy, Alpha Academy". We had nuns from Malta and they taught the girls at the approved school how to make Maltese lace. I remember something a bit like a lectern, with a curled-over top, and spindles anchored at the front that fell over the surface of the "lectern". Threads were attached to the spindles and the girls tossed the spindles to – miraculously, it seemed to me – create the lace. Nowadays I often doubt this memory, vivid though it is. My memories of school are not especially happy ones, though I did well enough. My salvation at school came about because of a unique Alpha characteristic. The Alpha Cottage, which began the whole Alpha project in the late 19th century, was one of the places where indigenous theatre first developed. Alpha maintained this focus on theatre into the 20th century. The school staged homemade and ready-made plays and so I had the opportunity to act all through school, taking part in productions entered in the All-Island Drama Festival and the French Drama Festival, and participating in the All-Island Speech Festival. I can remember the shape and taste of the army's Garrison Theatre at Up Park Camp, where school plays were performed before they moved to Ward Theatre. I was good at acting and it gave me a chance to be somebody. I had a voice, presence, identity on stage that I didn't have elsewhere – I grew up as a bit of an outsider. I've recently become aware that theatre decidedly influences the voices of Caribbean poets who are also actors (eg, Baugh, Bennett, Ford-Smith, Walcott, Young). As for lacemaking, though I come from a family of women who worked with their hands – they did sewing, embroidery, knitting, crotchet, tatting (which is a kind of lacemaking) – and though my daughter does all but one of those things, as well as needlepoint, carding wool, spinning wool, and weaving, I do only some, and lacemaking isn't one of them. It's the image of young women under a big guango tree making immaculate white lace that has stuck with me, and the idea that women, by making something with their hands, could achieve economic freedom.

JB: One of the things that is often said and maybe offered as a critique of writers of your generation is that the writing is often so genteel. In your case though, this is decidedly not so! Curse words are used without pause in such poems as "Reading at 4:00 AM" and there is a raucous abandon to sexual pleasures. Indeed, the very landscape in the poem "Cockpit Country – A Tasting Tour" is both eroticised and sexualised and sacred mothers are themselves sexual individuals! This made me wonder, do you feel in step or out of step with most writers of your generation? Where does the bravery come from in tackling such taboo subjects?

PM: I take it you mean women writers. It's not for me to say who is genteel and who isn't, though it is true that I'm perhaps more like, say, Tanya Shirley in that respect than some others of my age. It may also be true that women writers of this generation are not constrained in ways their earlier sisters were. They were breaking ground, after all, and audience was a consideration. Perhaps because I was abused as a child and an adolescent and I've also had a fairly challenging adult life, I've always felt called to explore the nitty-gritty in my work and to do it in an uncompromising way. The Jamaicans I know are all capable of being foul-mouthed, so why eschew curse words? Sex, gender and sexual matters, and the consequent orderly or disorderly childbearing and child-rearing, have been at the centre of our post-slavery being. Why tiptoe round those facts? Nor are these things true only of us. They probably apply to most of the world. Our writing must address our being as it is. Writers need to go boldly – and if it's where no one has gone before, well, so be it.

JB: Speaking of taboo subjects, the poem "Thomas Thistlewood and Tom" really stands out in the collection in this regard. Can you explain what this poem is all about and why you felt the need to write it? In so doing, maybe you might want to engage with the complexities of the system of slavery that come into full view in the poem "Great-Granny Mac" where a young enslaved girl is sold into a family that looks just like she does?

PM: "Thomas Thistlewood and Tom" is my favourite of the four love poems in the book. The slave, Tom, loves his woman enough to literally eat her shit. Thomas Thistlewood, author of the infamous 14,000 page diary, The Diary of Thomas Thistlewood, was a particularly brutal plantation owner. One part of a preferred punishment for slaves, called Derby's Dose, was forcing another slave to defecate in the miscreant's mouth. The offender would then be gagged for hours, to chew on shit. While we push on with the tribulations of our lives, there are people who have faced and survived unimaginable horrors. Derby's Dose is one of them. I wanted to overturn the punishment by making a triumphant thing of it. In this poem, Tom overcomes his master by inviting him to "watch me do it!" as he eats his woman's shit. Ironically, Thomas

Thistlewood, who began as a plantation overseer and went on to become a plantation owner himself, purchased a slave, Phibbah, from his original employer, Cope, had a son, Mulatto John, with her, eventually made a life with her on his estate, Brednut Island, and in the will in which he freed her, referred to her as his "wife". Phibbah is not the only slave who made a consort for a powerful white man. There was, if I remember rightly, a highly-placed official in one of the Danish Virgin Islands who also had a black woman as a partner. Slavery was a complicated business and enslaved women must have faced many challenges negotiating it. Great Granny Mac is about another triumph, this time of a young enslaved woman fleeing from a black plantation owner who debases his own people by owning slaves. I was never taught very much of any country's history, with the exception of a little West Indian history early in high school. As a consequence, I never knew that there were black people on this side of the Atlantic who owned slaves till I was an adult. I was of course revolted. How could one think of enslaving one's own kind, especially having suffered the experience of enslavement oneself? What kind of soul poisoning could achieve that? Still, I remember Prof Emeritus Patrick Bryan of the history department at the University of the West Indies, Mona telling me once not to forget that within the system of slavery, where whites oppressed blacks, was a second system of oppression: everybody oppressed women. Routes to enfranchisement were not simple, but once a male slave had been freed or had bought his freedom, one of the things he might have done to improve his status was buy property, including slaves. So, to become somebody, he would have had to dehumanise his own people. Bellmartin, Great Granny Mac's owner, is one such. Like I said, slavery was complex and it is perhaps too easy for us to make retrospective judgments.

JB: One of the things that I noticed in *Subversive Sonnets* is a sense of voyaging and moving from one place and one country to another, and recording what is going on. What do you think is at the root of the wanderlust of the female narrators in these poems?

PM: Some of the female narrators are pretty much stuck in one place, or else passing through – Barcelona, Calgary, Cozumel, Gloucester-on-Sea, the Zambesi, Darfur, and various places in Jamaica. However, some do indeed travel about within a poem, except that their wanderings are not so much the result of wanderlust but on account of some kind of necessity. In "Temitope", for example, the young woman is stolen from her hometown in West Africa, is hauled across the Middle Passage in a slave ship and "comes home" when her female descendant is born generations after in America. In "Great Granny Mac", the narrator is the great-grandchild of Madeleine, whose story she tells. As a child,

Madeleine is torn from her family who are scattered to various parts of Jamaica. She is forced to work on the estate of her new owner, a black man named Bellmartin. Quick-witted and determined, she teaches herself to read and cipher, though it is against the law. She grows up there, is in due course raped, and though pregnant as a result uses her knowledge of poisons and their antidotes to engineer her escape. She lives as a free woman to make a family and to see the next three generations.

JB: Your books are published and available in Canada where you now reside. Have you made attempts to have them published and available elsewhere, as in the United Kingdom, the United States or even in the Caribbean? Why or why not?

PM: The books are supposedly available anywhere as almost all Canadian publishers, including small presses, have distributors in the UK, the US and the rest of the world. Most publishers require authors to give them world rights, after which it is for the publishers or the authors' agents to sell rights elsewhere, though some authors do manage this. The Caribbean is perhaps the trickiest place to distribute one's books. I've tried to arrange launches for my books in Jamaica (both *Subversive Sonnets* and *de book of Mary* were launched there) but most of the expenses for this and any other kind of promotion must come out of the writer's pocket, with publishers able to help in a very limited way as they are often small publishers surviving on government support. When regional distributors add their mark-ups to the RSP of the book, the prices end up being very high. I know a little about this, as we had a small company that, inter alia, were distributors of Canadian books in Canada before we immigrated. The selling price of any book includes cuts for author, bookseller, distributor, as well as the publisher. For books that are exported, shipping and handling costs also become part of the equation. The result is that only very big presses that can afford deep discounts (because they have large markets elsewhere to pick up the slack) are able to put their books into the Caribbean market at an affordable price.

JB: Finally, what is Pamela Mordecai working on these days?

PM: Too many things at once! I am completing a novel, The Tear Well and a second short story collection, Goat Mouth, but also working on de book of Joseph, the first book and the one that will complete the trilogy on the life of Jesus. And further down the road, there's a YA novel and a YA play.

WRITING A NEW JAMAICAN STORY

FOR SHARON LEACH, WRITING IS HOLDING
A MIRROR UP TO SOCIETY

Sharon Leach is a Jamaican writer and essayist, born in Kingston. In addition to being a featured columnist for the *Jamaica Observer*, she is the coordinator and editor of that publication's weekly literary arts supplement, "Bookends". Her fiction has appeared in several journals, including: *Jamaica Journal, Caribbean Writing Today* and, most recently, *AfroBeat Journal*.

Sharon Leach was one of the first recipients of a scholarship to the Calabash Writers Workshop and, in 2011, she was awarded the Musgrave bronze medal from the council of the Institute of Jamaica. Her first collection of short stories, *What You Can't Tell Him: Stories*, was published in 2006. This was followed by *Love It When You Come, Hate It When You Go*, published by Peepal Tree in 2014.

JB: Sharon, thanks so much for your second collection of short stories *Love It When You Come, Hate It When You Go*. The stories are very contemporary. Indeed, they are set in what I would call the "now" Jamaica, and they are very urban, upwardly so. I guess my first question to you is, how representative do you feel these stories are of the average Jamaican in Jamaica?

SL: Thanks, Jacqueline, for reading it and including me in your series of interviews. I really don't know how representative my stories are of the average Jamaican in Jamaica. But I don't know that my stories are necessarily required to be representative of any particular grouping of people. My first duty as a writer, I think, is to tell stories. And to tell them well. It's really that simple. If you tell good stories, people who don't necessarily share your background, race, social status, creed, whatever, will appreciate them. I tell stories about the world I live in now: I tell stories about people, especially women, who are trying to navigate their way through a world that's vastly different from the one their parents came up in.

JB: Your work has been credited with occupying "a new territory in Caribbean writing", in so far as your characters "are neither the folk of the old rural world, the sufferers of the urban ghetto, or the prosperous brown and white middle class of the hills rising above the city, but the black urban salariat of the lands in between". How did you come to carve out such a unique position for yourself in Caribbean literature? Why is it important to tell these stories?

SL: This country has produced so many sterling writers, so I wonder why it is that I find there's such a lack of writing that reflects the experience of these people, the urban salariat that I find myself a part of. Our stories were by and large not being told. So, imagine my absolute delight when I first laid eyes on Colin Channer's *Waiting In Vain*. I remember that book, written by a Jamaican, giving me permission, even as I was honing my craft, to write about an urbane world, one like the one I knew about, one in which there was a black intelligentsia, and where men and women discussed, openly, sexual mores, single women lived on their own in apartment buildings and entertained married lovers. This is the world I understand, the world that keeps me endlessly engaged. I have lots of stories to tell that are different from the stories that are described as typically "Caribbean", the ones I grew up reading. My world wasn't rural at all, and I would be disingenuous to write about life on a farm, for example. Or spending summer holidays in the country. Nor did I grow up in the ghetto. I can't write about that stuff. The stuff of my life is seeing my parents work tirelessly to build a business and make a middle-class life for my sister and me, sending us to good schools, bundling us off for holidays abroad. But I also remember my family not quite fitting in with the denizens, the old-money families, of those same hills in upper St Andrew where we eventually moved to when I was eight years old. This is where I'm coming from, and this, to a great extent, is where my characters are coming from, middle-class Jamaicans in multiple roles, who deserve to have their stories told too.

JB: Secrets are at the core of many of these stories. Especially secrets involving sexuality and sexual encounters. Why this emphasis on secrecy and sexuality in your work?

SL: I've always thought that if Jamaica were to be blown up in some horrific nuclear event, the only thing that would be left in the wreckage would be skeletons falling out of closets. Well, skeletons and the bloody cockroaches we can't seem to get rid of! I don't know one family that doesn't have secrets. And oftentimes, these secrets are tied to sexuality: a husband who impregnated the helper; a wife secretly pining after her son's college-age best friend; an underage daughter who's sexually involved with her classmate; a son who's keeping the secret of his parents' business partners' sexual proclivities; and other such permutations. I find it important to write about these things, however un-pretty they are, because if, as the American writer Alice Walker says, we are here not just to survive, but survive "whole", then we have to look at things that oftentimes we'd rather look away from, and confront them.

JB: Similarly, you explore what I guess can be characterised as a "transgressive sexuality" in many of these stories – particularly so between parents and their children. What is the commentary that you hope these stories make about sexuality? What would you say to the charge that this focus on transgressive sexuality is specifically sensationalist?

SL: Real talk: I don't think transgressive sexuality is as sensationalist as we'd like to believe. It is in fact very commonplace. But it's ugly; we would rather not have to deal with it. I know three completely different sets of people who have admitted to me that they had, in their childhood, sexual relations with grandfathers. Admitted this in the most matter-of-fact way possible. So much so that I wondered, after the fact, whether I'd heard them correctly. In one of my stories, "Sugar", from my first book, *What You Can't Tell Him*, the mother knows what her daughter has done to make that extra money she hands her after she's slept with the tourists, but she turns a blind eye and belts out a hymn that somehow absolves her of any guilt or responsibility. And I think this is reflective of recent headline-grabbing news stories about all those underage girls being found dead and pregnant, especially in small communities. Everybody knows what's going on, or at least, they have a notion of what's going on with these young girls and the older men who are abusing them. Why the secrecy and silence? Who benefits from it? Certainly not these young dead, pregnant girls in these communities. The secrecy and silence, perhaps borne out of shame, can only be deleterious to society. But, remember, it crosses borders, this secrecy and silence, appearing in middle-class communities, as well, which, in a sense, let's just put it on the table, makes a mockery of the notion of class superiority and inferiority, doesn't it? I think my work is very clear-eyed, and rather than aiming for sensationalism, if anything, simply addresses this silence wherever it occurs.

JB: Is the character of Sugar in the story "Comfort" (in your second collection) a carry-over from the character of Sugar in your first collection? If yes, what do you find so engaging about that particular character?

SL: Yes! I just made mention of Sugar from the first book. She does appear in "Comfort", as well. She's a character I happen to really love. Of all the characters I've conceived, she's the one I can't let go, and in fact, I've done an elaborate workup on her, how she transitions to being the person she knows she has the capacity to become. She will appear in successive collections and we'll see how she grows over the years.

I don't know why I love Sugar so much. Actually, I've come to love her. I didn't really before because that story was always the story I was asked to contribute to anthologies. And I was always annoyed because I felt like my other stories, of which there are many, were being overlooked. But in time I came to see the character's allure. This character is unlike most of the people of my stories who are already upwardly mobile in their lives. Sugar is poor. Her family is poor, like, seriously poor. There is a lot of shame and, yes, secrets, surrounding them. But she is determined, although she makes many missteps, to become someone she can be proud of. I guess I'm fascinated by the potential journey. I plan to stay with that character until I can't write anymore about her.

JB: Your work also seems, for lack of a better word, "episodic" and located in an immediate encounter. These stories rarely progress beyond the moment. Is this a factor of the form (short stories) that you are working in? Do you believe that a form such as the short story can incorporate a more expanded narrative of years, decades even, this despite the brevity of words?

SL: I do realise that my work is episodic; it's something my mentor, the late great Wayne Brown, and I spoke about. He always wanted to see the way I'd deal with a story that unfolded over a stretch of time. And in fact a story I wrote, not in either story collection, "Thursday Evenings with Donald", was in answer to a challenge from him. It catalogues the tender love affair a spinster lady has with a married man, over many years. Wayne was particularly fond of this story because it not only covered a long time span, but it also employed the omniscient for point of view, which was a POV Wayne dearly loved, and which isn't often used by us "modern" writers. So, yes, the short form does and can lend itself to an expanded narrative, and for the next collection I am consciously working on making the time span of the stories longer.

JB: Your characters move easily between the island of Jamaica and other spaces outside of the island. Is this a commentary on your part on the spread and proliferation of Jamaican culture – and a recognisable global Jamaican identity – outside of the island? Also, am I correct in my reading that many of the characters in your stories are filled with anxiety and their anxiety, it seems, is laden with trying to prove how cosmopolitan they are, not only to themselves but to a larger world?

SL: You know, Jacqueline, these people have no such lofty concerns. I travelled every summer since I was ten, and sometimes also at Easter or Christmas. It was just the way it was. I had classmates who packed up and went to visit relatives in the country. That wasn't part of my reality in the '70s, '80s and '90s. My country relatives and our family, on both my parents' sides, were, well, estranged. But the friends and "courtesy" relatives who lived abroad were who we were close to. It wasn't about expressing a global Jamaican identity outside the island. I don't think that was even a thing back then! It was simply what you did if you were in a certain social milieu. That fluidity of being here one day and waking up somewhere overseas the next is, I suppose, just me projecting onto the characters. But I think that's happening more these days, however: Jamaicans are unquestionably cosmopolitan. Jamaica and Jamaicans have definitely become a global brand.

JB: Many of your characters seem contained in a middle-class bubble – as seen most clearly in the story "A Mouthful of Dust" – where issues of everyday survival do not trouble them. Furthermore, when members of what can be called the lower class show up in your work they are often compromised, angry or violent. Is this a commentary on class and racial politics in Jamaica?

SL: Again, I don't like the idea of making deliberate class, racial, or even political, statements. I'm not an anthropologist; I don't give reports about the ills of society; I don't make judgments. What I am is a writer, and consequently, my duty is to tell the truth, to simply hold a mirror up to the society – hey, this is what I see going on here, are you seeing this? – and the society can make what it will of what it sees in that mirror.

JB: I know that you have worked as the editor of Bookends for several years now, showcasing the talents and voices of not only Jamaican writers, but writers in general. Can you speak to the importance of the publication in fostering an appreciation for writers and literature in Jamaica, and beyond? What kinds of work do you aim to showcase in Bookends?

SL: This year Bookends turned nine; I am amazed about this! When it started I was convinced it wouldn't have lasted six months. A magazine with the name Bookends was always, as far as I was concerned, going to be a hard sell in a landscape not readily identifiable with a big reading culture. As you can see, I was wrong! Books and literary pursuits are slowly and steadily coming to the forefront in Jamaica, and I'd like to think that Bookends has had some small part to play in this! Over the years the magazine has been scaled down somewhat, in line with the paper trying to keep production costs down. Still, we soldier on. I love what I do. I think, as does the *Jamaica Observer*, that it is an extremely important forum not only for readers, but also for writers, as we provide a platform for them – those from the region in general and Jamaica in particular. I remember when I was first published in the Literary Arts, the publication that predated Bookends. It was the first time I'd been published anywhere; how thrilled I was! That was where I found my voice and where I started to hone my craft, under the expert guidance of Wayne Brown, who was the then editor. Where would I be today if I hadn't been afforded an opportunity such as the one Wayne gave me? So I think a publication such as this one is vital for identifying new voices, new talent. It's also good for more established writers, so they can connect with their readers. It's also a great way to keep abreast of books, locally and internationally, and it provides a platform for book reviews, as well, as a way of disseminating information on launches, news and keeping them up to speed on literary festivals and competitions, which are becoming increasingly important for our writers to get involved with as we establish our presence on the literary world stage.

As it concerns the writing published in the magazine, if the writing is clichéd, forget about it. I'm open to work that showcases fresh perspectives, unique voices that will make me get excited and sit up and take note.

JB: Finally, what is Sharon Leach working on these days? Can we expect, for example, to see a novel from you?

SL: Ah, sweet mystery of life! But seriously, Jacqueline, I really do want to write a novel. And I'm pretty sure I will someday. I have so many ideas rolling around in my noggin. But for now, I'm slowly collecting again for another short-story collection. More immediately, however, I'm expanding my portfolio and building my résumé as a screenwriter. I'm presently working on a screen adaptation for my story "Sugar", which is a wonderfully enriching and fulfilling experience. I told you how much I love that character; I can't wait to see her on the big screen!

MOUNTAINS, LAND, SEA AND SAND:
AN INTERVIEW WITH POET TANYA SHIRLEY

Tanya Shirley was born and lives in Jamaica. She is a graduate student and lecturer in the Department of Literatures in English at UWI, Mona. She was awarded an MFA in Creative Writing from the University of Maryland, USA. Her work has appeared in *Small Axe* and *The Caribbean Writer* and in *New Caribbean Poetry: An Anthology* (ed. Kei Miller, Carcanet, 2007) and more recently in *Unwritten: Caribbean Poems After the First World War* (Nine Arches Press, 2018).

She is a Cave Canem Fellow and a past participant in Callaloo Creative Writing Workshops. She has published two collections of poetry with Peepal Tree Press, *She Who Sleeps with Bones* (2009) and *The Merchant of Feathers* (2014). The former was named as a 2009 Jamaican bestseller in the *Jamaica Gleaner*: "Local books did it big in 09".

JB: Tanya Shirley, thank you very much for a strong, indeed very strong, second collection of poems, *The Merchant of Feathers*, published recently by Peepal Tree Press in the UK. Your book is divided into three parts, and in the first section what struck me the most was how politicised these poems were. Whether it was the politics of weight, but, even more intriguingly, the politics of race, colour and class in the Jamaican society. My first questions to you then are: Can poetry ever be too political? And do you have that fear about your work?

TS: Thank you. I love your work, so praise from you is greatly appreciated. If we think of the political in terms of the distribution of power, governmental responsibilities, the "total complex of relations between people living in a society", etc, then the poet cannot escape from the political. What I am cautious about is sacrificing craft in the name of politics. I don't want to become so didactic that my poetry is more of a sermon and less of a poem. So I am always balancing the demands of poetic technique and the thematic concerns of my political messages.

JB: One of the themes that stood out quite forcefully in this collection is the violence that Jamaicans transact against each other. I am thinking of the ironically titled poem, "Sweet Sweet Jamaica", which is all about the brutal, at times deadly, violence that children, particularly, can face in Jamaica. How do you account for or make sense of (by way of an explanation) this violence, particularly towards children?

TS: I am not a sociologist so I can only speak from the point of view of a humble observer. Jamaica is a wonderful country, but it is hard to live here with this paradox of beauty and tragedy. There are only a few rotten apples but they make it hard for the majority of good citizens to live with a sense of peace. I think those inflicting violence on others are numb, frustrated and see no hope for their future, and as a country we make it too easy for them to get away with their cowardly, criminal acts. My role as a poet is to place a mirror before the society so that we don't ignore what is happening and we may be more inclined to demand protection for all our citizens, especially the most vulnerable among us.

JB: This collection of poems has a really rich variation of female characters in it, from near-white uptown ladies, to tired bedraggled prostitutes going home early in the morning with dark scandal bags. One of the most empathetic and moving female characters in the entire collection is found in the poem "The People Are Deading". You recoup the woman made famous by that statement and what she is saying as a profound problem for Jamaicans, regarding the Dudus incursion. Given that what she has to say is, in your telling of the story, so important, why then do you believe that she became the object of so much laughter and derision?

TS: I can't imagine life without laughter. It's certainly a coping mechanism, but the danger is in not going beyond the laughter. One hopes with comedy that people will laugh but at some later stage assess the pain behind the laughter; sadly, that does not always happen. Too often we use laughter as a dismissive trope. I think some of us are still caught up with colonial ideas about language and if a serious message is not delivered in the Queen's English then it is fodder for derision. I was also struck by the idea of performing for the cameras and the microphones and the assumption that we have to "speaky spoky" to deliver a message (think of "Nobody Canna Cross It"). So in laughing at "deading" I think subconsciously we were also laughing at ourselves and our skewed perceptions of representation. I could go on more about class and race as well, but basically I wrote the poem to encourage readers to re-examine the YouTube clip and see that here is a woman who was expressing the anxiety that we were all feeling and even if we laughed we should still be aware of our common humanity.

JB: I confess that my favourite poem in the entire collection is "Matie Shall Not Conquer". This is so, even though I find highly problematic the female-on-female attack in the poem. Yet, there is so much energy and authenticity in that poem! So my question for you is, do you know where this poem came from? Is there an inciting moment or incident for this it? Did you do research to write this poem?

TS: I did a bit of research because I am fascinated by rituals and the many ways that women attempt to assert power in their relationships. For some women, "tying rituals" such as "oil a hold him" and "oil a never lef' me" give them a sense of control in their relationships. I am also quite interested in deconstructing notions of respectability in women's poetry: the idea that female writers should only portray women in monolithic and essentialist ways when women are complex and multifaceted. As writers, being feminist does not mean that we only write about women as saints and saviours. The truth is that many women are forced by patriarchal ideologies to believe that they must compete with each other in order to get attention from men. The reason the poem seems authentic (and thank you, by the way, for your kind words) is that we all have lived through or heard about similar situations and in this poem, the wife figure is seen as triumphant, which reflects society's disdain of the mistress/matie figure; however, both are implicated in the act of vying for a man's affection.

JB: I also like very much the mysticism in several of these poems. Women come walking out of the ocean to offer advice. Indeed, women are swaying and sashaying and are oftentimes deeply self-assured in these poems, particularly so in their sexuality. What accounts for this self-assuredness in so many of the female characters in your book?

TS: I have benefited from observing my mother and her female friends, who, over the years, have given each other support, and I've seen the confidence that comes from knowing you are rooted in a strong female community. These women have an almost surreal power and awareness of themselves that I find truly fascinating. I was also blessed to have a mother who spoke quite freely to my sister and me about female sexuality and we were encouraged to embrace all aspects of our identity. There is something magical about a woman who exudes self-acceptance and that kind of woman will always appear in my poems.

JB: Another aspect of your work that I really enjoyed was the effortless mixing of patois and standard English. Was this deliberate on your part? Did you find that mixing easy to do while you were writing these poems?

TS: I found it very easy because I am always code-switching. I think and speak in a combination of both registers and, thanks to poets like Louise Bennett, Mervyn Morris, and Lorna Goodison, I have no hang-ups about the legitimacy of patois in written poetry.

JB: The things that deejays say in some of these poems crack me up, even though at times the poems that come from what the deejays have to say are quite charged and painful. Still, in reading your Jamaican deejay references, I wondered what you believe the role of deejays, as distinct from musicians, is in the Jamaican dancehall scene?

TS: Well, far more people have access to deejays (I'm including sound selectors) than they do to musicians in live performances, and there is something electric about that space where the deejay has a mic, is on an elevated platform and the people are like acolytes. The deejay then has the power to circumvent the singer's voice and he and the rhythm are the authority in that space. I wanted my poems to explore many of the irrational things that those deejays say in the heat of the moment and how sometimes we respond to them because of the rhythm and the euphoria of the communal space. What happens when we remove those sayings, "Bruk off yuh head, mi buy it back a mawnin'" from that space and examine them on the page? It's also my way of bridging the gap between "high-brow" and "low-brow" art because the deejay is a creative artist.

JB: A lack of comprehension regarding the intense homophobia in Jamaican society stalks several of these poems. I am thinking, specifically, of the "The Merchant of Feathers II" poem. I am trying to get you to answer a question I have long struggled with myself: How do you account for and make sense of the intense homophobia in Jamaican society?

TS: I don't really understand it, so perhaps I can't answer your question. Religious hypocrisy, maybe? A threat to perceived notions of masculinity and femininity? I know that in "The Merchant of Feathers II" I wanted to explore what happens behind the scenes to people who have to endure homophobia. Basically, as a writer, I want to remind my readers of our common humanity. I am also interested in this fascination that we have as a society with policing people's bodies and sexualities when there are often far more pressing concerns that we neglect.

JB: In the third section of your collection of poems, there are several love poems, which I read as not only love for a physical person, but by extension, love for one's self, one's country. If nothing else, Jamaica comes out of these poems as a place of immense, almost unbearable, contradictions. I say to you then "Jamaica" and you say what?

TS: Let me make a random list: verdant mountains, fertile land, sea & sand, untapped potential, political corruption, fastest man & woman, talented, resourceful people, likkle but tallawah, don't know what to do with the marijuana, reggae, Rastafari, rum, doctor, lawyer, scientist, t'ief, mongrel dog, mango, Obeah, household helper, heat, heart, art, dancehall, church, crime, jerk chicken... this list could go on till mawnin!

JB: Finally, tell us about the gorgeous cover of your book. Who chose the cover image of your book? What can you tell us about the artist? Why was this cover image the right one for your book?

TS: I chose the cover image and Hannah Bannister from Peepal Tree Press did the layout for the cover. I bought this painting a few years ago and immediately I knew I wanted it to be the cover of my next poetry collection. I love how it portrays a woman gracefully carrying her load. It's an unsigned painting and because I purchased it from the estate of someone who died I was unable to find out anything about its origins.

YEMOJA SITS ON MY HEAD: AN INTERVIEW
WITH POET OPAL PALMER ADISA

Opal Palmer Adisa is a Jamaica-born, award-winning poet, educator and storyteller. A performance poet and writer, she is the author of five novel and short story collections: *Bake-Face and Other Guava Stories* (1986), *It Begins with Tears* (1997), *Until Judgement Comes* (2007), *Painting Away Regrets* (2011) and *Love's Promise* (2017). Her individual poetry collections include: *Tamarind and Mango Women* (1992), *Leaf-of-Life* (2000), *Caribbean Passion* (2004), *Eros Muse* (2006), *I Name Me Name* (2008) and *4-Headed Woman* (2013). As well as a number of books for children, her poetry, essays and stories have been anthologized in over two hundred journals; she travels and shares her work internationally.

*

JB: Opal, your most recent collection of poems, *4-Headed Woman*, published by Tia Chucha Press, is some of your strongest work to date. The poems are like pure fire and ice, and are sharp and clean. I guess my first question for you is: Can you explain the title of the collection for our readers?

OPA: As a woman, I feel as if I need at least four heads to function, and that is true for many women, as we juggle the various roles of being artist, first and foremost, then wife or partner in any domestic relationship, then professional – in my case teacher/professor – and then as mother – for me, it is mother to three and even though they are young adults and scattered, I am still on call constantly. So the title emanates from this reality, that in order for a woman in these contemporary times to be grounded, she must be in possession of at least four heads – possession is key, not just to have four heads, but be able to switch from one to the other with ease.

JB: In these poems there are many instructions to women and girls, and you bring us, quite intimately, into their lives. What would you hope men and boys take away from this collection?

OPA: There are many men who say they admire strong women, but in reality the admiration appears, when probed deeply, to be from a distant, nostalgic place... I don't want to be admired as a strong woman because often what that means is that I am expected to handle everything, and I do, when I am really looking for partnership. I think this is true for many women who are capable, but we would like men and boys to respect our capabilities without thinking that makes us less desirable as mates or that means we can and should handle everything. I hope boys and men will love us skin-deep, and admire and respect how multifaceted we often are, and how much we handle daily.

JB: Many of the poems in the collection are very sensuous. There are many poems conflating food and flowers and the female body, for example. How deliberate was all of this on your part? What is the importance of sensuality (and the centrality of sexuality) to your work?

OPA: From the very beginning, sensuality and sexuality have been central to my work, to my life, to how I show up in the world. We are sensual beings and while these days vulgarity – men humping girls like dogs in carnivals and on the dance floor is normalised as entertainment or acceptable behaviour of liberation – is sometimes appropriated for sensuality, for me there is no comparison. Growing, preparing and eating food is one of the most sensuous acts, and I certainly believe my body, women's bodies are delicious fruits that must be enjoyed, and therefore I was very deliberate about exploring and exposing this aspect of womanhood. Women were and many still are agrarians.

JB: Apart from perhaps Lucille Clifton and Sharon Olds, I have never read poems so breathtakingly celebratory of menstruation, even with all the complications that menstruation can mean for some women. Why do you think that menstruation remains such a taboo subject in poetry? And was it difficult for you writing so many poems on this topic?

OPA: Menstruation is taboo because despite what many of us would like to believe, the notion of woman from the Bible still dominates our society as evil and dirty. Growing up in Jamaica this was the general belief and a woman's power to bind a man. Many members of both genders believe this. I want to debunk this myth. I want all women and men to celebrate women's monthly decision not to carry life, but instead to nurture the earth, themselves, existence. I had great fun writing these poems and interviewing other women to explore some of the taboos and their feelings about their menses, and also researching what has been written about this topic.

JB: In the section entitled "A Certain Time of the Month" I was struck by the fact that over 6,000 women in Puerto Rico and Haiti were, to use your terms, "guinea pigs" in "experimental biology". I wondered if you still believed that certain women's bodies retain the role of "testing sites" for various ideas and corporations?

OPA: Yes! Yes! And yes! Black women, poor women, women who are marginalised – stipulations of IMF loans to developing countries – are all connected and we are given discarded birth control pills and others, insecticides that have been taken off the markets in the metropolis as harmful to humans and infants – and are still used as testing sites; that is the hegemony of dominance.

JB: As much as I love these poems, Opal, I found that I was often confused as to who the first person narrators of many of these poems were. Was this deliberate on your part? If yes, where you trying to conflate the narrator and implicating the reader both at the same time?

OPA: We have been taught to write one way, and I am still fighting against that way, not simply out of rebellion, but because I don't think the traditional narrative structures speak to the ethos of the Caribbean, and I am still searching to find a way to conflate and combine without being accused of switching back and forth mindlessly... It's the same argument I have with the rigid tense structure – present, past and future – as so often our lives are, at any moment, rooted in all three zones. Anyway, I am/was experimenting with a narrative form that dances between first person and collective, which includes reader so that one is not merely a "reader," but one is also reading/narrating one's own story. Perhaps my reach is too ambitious and, too, I need to continue my search, my exploring of how to do this more effectively, seamlessly.

JB: One of the things that struck me while reading your poems is the demands of motherhood on your life as a writer. Do you care to comment further on this?

OPA: I am a mother to three wonderful children – well, young adults – and we are very close and raised each other, and even though they are all independent, and live in Paris, southern and northern California, respectively, I have weekly, sometimes daily conversations with all three, who will still say, "Mommy, are you listening to me?", who want my undivided attention, and we talk about everything under the sun from the intimate to the political – and it has always been like this, and then I also have a group of students from over the years, a few from the mid-Eighties who call me their mother and their children call me grandmother, and they also call and need to talk and want me to listen, and beg for advice... Yemoja sits on my head. Motherhood in all its forms has been and remains a big part of my life and does demand and infringe on my time.

JB: I have to say, I found the section "Graffiti Series" quite breathtaking. This is such a universal female experience, women talking to women, on bathroom walls. Can you explain to our readers how this series of poems came about and what you hope both women and men will get from this series of poems?

OPA: First, I have to say I have sneaked into a few men's restrooms, but the writing there did not appear as detailed and revealing as in the women's. This idea of these poems is old, well, since the Eighties when I was teaching at San Francisco State University and was swept away by the writings in the restroom, and thought about making a film, which I never did. Then I began copying some of what was written in my notebook. Later, late-Eighties, through the Nineties, while teaching at UC Berkeley, I began drafting poems based on some of the writings. I wrote a one-woman play, which I performed, and which I later expanded, based on bathroom graffiti and which is the last poetic play in the collection. As I was writing these I imagined them being performed around college campuses, like *The Vagina Monologues*. I am still hoping someone will be interested in doing a movie with the poems. I was excited to learn last year when I was invited to the University of Puerto Rico to share my work that a student there either had done or was working on her MFA thesis on bathroom graffiti.

We tend to dismiss or underestimate the need for public discourse; that everyone wants/needs to be heard, that there are things women and men can discuss publicly, anonymously, that they don't think they can privately, even with their most trusted friends. Bathroom and other graffiti sites create safe spaces for people to express their ideas without having to face the judgment, which is why the poems I included have multiple perspectives on the controversial issues.

JB: You describe the last poem in your collection as "a poetic performance piece". I think it would be better described as a tour-de-force or a pièce-de-résistance, myself. Still, I found myself wondering, what made this work a poem instead of a play?

OPA: In the past I have taught a graduate course entitled Mixed Genre, and my premise is: these different genres are imposed, artificially, and sometimes are unnecessary, and I insist that students disband and collapse these boundaries. Two of the texts I use when I teach this course are Jean Toomer's *Cane*, which I love, love, love, and which was instrumental in setting me on the writing path, and Isabel Allende's *Aphrodite*. The genesis of the play began as a series of poems that I then fused with "dialogue". It is ostensibly a prose poem in dramatic form.

JB: Finally, I know that in addition to being a writer you also have a practice of photography. Can you talk a little bit about your photographic works? What do you find, for example, your main preoccupations in photography are? Is this similar to your writing preoccupations? I also had the thought as I read your bathroom graffiti piece that photographs of what is written in women's bathrooms could make a really interesting photography project in and of itself. Any chance of this?

OPA: Let me begin by saying I did take a number of photos of the graffiti the bathrooms but now cannot find them with my moves and transitory life these last five years, consolidating, shedding and literally having stuff in three different locations... What is where, I cannot say and ownership/possession is becoming less important. Okay, back to your question. I would say I have been seriously photographing since the mid-Eighties and I still love people and faces. I have at least three books I want to do on Jamaica: one for children, entitled Our Boonoonoos Children. (I have such a vast collection of children from all over Jamaica, no permissions, but such sweet shots... One on Rastafarians, from Bingis I attended, one just of market place and people.)

Then there are several books I could do of Brazil, my three trips, and living there for three months, same of Egypt, Spain, Morocco, Cuba, and Trinidad, amazing images of children, Carnival as well as Easter Sunday, also of Haiti, which I am working on now, and have been since the 2012 earthquake, and now too St Croix. I love candid faces, gestures, landscape, and since the early Nineties, I've been experimenting with words and images and more recently, changing the texture in Photoshop. Plus, for the last three years I have been curating an annual Black History Exhibition in St Croix, which always includes photography.

I need a patron and assistance to complete these projects, and I will take a chauffeur and a housekeeper, too! I have been fortunate that my photos have been exhibited and a few published in journals, but I cannot keep up with my writing and mothering and teaching to get the photos out more, which is what I would like to do.

JOURNEYING TOWARDS INTEGRATION: NOVELIST PATRICIA POWELL TACKLES HEALING

Patricia Powell was born in Jamaica and moved with her family to the United States in 1982. She is the award winning author of four novels including *Me Dying Trial* (1993), *A Small Gathering of Bones* (1994), *The Pagoda* (1998) and *The Fullness of Everything* (2009). She is currently Associate Professor of English at Mills College in California.

❧

JB: Patricia, thank you so much for your novel, *The Fullness of Everything*. I remember Jeremy Poynting of Peepal Tree Press telling me what a fantastic novel it was and when I read it I agreed. I know that a novel has different meanings, depending upon who is reading it, but if you as the author were to give a synopsis of this novel, what would you say it is about?

PP: *The Fullness of Everything* is a novel about healing, and by that I mean restoring balance and health to situations where there is severe wounding. In our society, sexual violence is shrouded in so much silence and shame that neither the violator nor the survivor can ever speak of it, much less seek help. And we now know that whatever is never addressed doesn't simply go away but sinks into the shadow parts of our unconsciousness where it can then distort our thoughts and actions in the most horrific ways imaginable. *The Fullness of Everything* is a story about two brothers who are no longer willing to live with the secrets and lies buried within their family and who, in unearthing and bringing them to light, make room for more sharing and vulnerability and intimacy in their relationships with spouses and children, make room for forgiveness, and for new ways of living masculinity. Working hard and putting food on the table are no longer measures of what it means to be a good man. Neither is sexual prowess or the ability to control one's feelings. In this novel, masculinity also includes being the primary nurturer, the sole caregiver of the little girl who's adopted; it means being the kind and loving father to the effeminate son; it includes being the one to confront the philandering and abusive father, and to also recognise his frailties; it includes befriending and being witness to the pain and suffering of the woman who as a young girl had been sexually violated by the father and who ended up bearing his child. And perhaps most importantly, it means being attentive to one's feelings, figuring out what they mean and the ways in which they continue to determine our actions, consciously and unconsciously.

Ultimately, *The Fullness of Everything* is about the healing this family that has been destroyed by violence undergoes on many levels – mentally, physically, emotionally, spiritually – and the transformation that occurs. By the end of the novel, one gets the sense that the abuse stops here and that a new paradigm has been put in place. A form of emotional intelligence – knowing and understanding feelings so that we can direct every action in a positive way – becomes the new law of the land. And the love and respect for human lives and especially for the feminine that emerges from this new paradigm is now part of the template that infuses the bloodstream of both the past and future generations of this family.

JB: There is a spiritual practice – coning – that is referenced frequently in the novel. Can you describe this practice and what it is suppose to achieve?

PP: To open a coning is basically to open communication with a healing team of light beings or spirit allies who work on the individual on all levels – emotionally, physically, mentally, spiritually – so that health and balance can be achieved. Terrified of the cancer that's slowly attacking her body, Marie Jose [Winston's partner] has been on a desperate search for the modality that will save her life. Allopathic medicine is not enough, and she's enlisted the help of a team of spirit healers, including the devic realm (spiritual intelligence or spiritual architect that give rise to all forms), Pan (nature spirits that work with devas to help make this form possible) and the appropriate members of the white brotherhood (highly evolved masters of light) and her higher self. With no spiritual practices of his own, Winston has come to adopt some of hers and this is what has helped him to develop internal strength and power that ultimately gives him the courage to challenge his father and to challenge an outdated model of masculinity that has wrought havoc on people's lives, both men and women, and to begin to put something else in place.

A coning is prayer, meditation and spiritual and energetic healing. When one opens a coning, one opens into a co-creative conversation with the spirit realms and with one's higher self so that healing can occur on all the levels of the body. In the Christian tradition, one might enter into prayer with God or Jesus or the Virgin or the Archangel Michael or a combination. In another tradition, one might open it with Jesus or Oshun or with a beloved ancestor.

In the coning, one opens into dialogue with a medical team that's composed of the Overlighting Deva of Healing Cancer in Marie Jose's case, Pan, who is in charge of all the nature sprits involved with healing cancer on the earth plane, the appropriate members of the White Brotherhood involved in healing cancer and one's higher self. Each healing can last up to 45 minutes.

Michaelle Wright's book MAP, *Medical Assistance Program*, explains all of this beautifully.

JB: Like several other Jamaican authors, you choose to tell your story from multiple perspectives. Why was that important for you to do in this novel?

PP: I had never written a book from multiple perspectives before and so this was a new experience and it was very challenging. How to keep the stories and the characters and the voices and the perspectives separate and distinct? Where to end one story and begin the other? What is the arc for each character and how is that different for each character? These were just some of the questions I wrestled with. Not eager to try this again anytime soon and yet this novel demanded these shifting perspectives. The novel wasn't just interested in the perspective of the brother who left, but also the one who stayed. It was interested in the plight of the little girl, the outside child, the new sister who came late into their lives. And there was interest too in Rosa's mother, though the book doesn't give the mother her own voice. I was not ready to write her story – the story of a girl sexually violated by her godfather, who ends up bearing his child, felt huge and devastating and I just didn't feel capable of doing justice to that important story that so many women have known. But I certainly wanted the brothers to have to clean up their father's mess and deal with that, deal with her. In real life, I could imagine very well how those brothers could've easily dismissed her or seen her as the one who seduced their father, as it's almost always the girl's fault when rape happens. Why was she wearing that dress? Why was she talking to that boy? Why was she smiling, why was she breathing, why was she being human; it must've been her fault. Often, we blame and punish her so as to avoid being responsible for our base feelings and even baser actions. We blame and punish her so we don't have to change, the status quo can stay intact, and we can continue our pattern of being irresponsible, and undiscerning and cruel. But what would happen if more men allowed themselves to be curious about their sexual impulses? What if they didn't allow themselves to be so paralysed by their own feelings of shame? My friend who used to work in a domestic abuse shelter in The Bahamas told me the story of the man who called the hotline one night. He had been sexually abused as a boy and now that he had kids he was afraid of his feelings around them. What if more men were willing to seek out the ear of a compassionate friend who would help them find professional help?

Most importantly in this book, I wanted to write a healing scene for Rosa's mother, who was just a girl then, the night after the father rapes her. This is my favourite part of the entire book. I feel as if I was writing that scene for every little girl who's been sexually violated by the male authority figure in her life, every little girl who's been raped and cannot speak or fight back, cannot stand up for herself, cannot utter the betrayal, the crushing hurt that has just occurred. Cannot tell anyone. Every little girl who sits in that silence and that suffering and rage and humiliation and that sadness, while her body, her vagina, her anus burns and bleeds. That scene is for them. It says yes, I see you. I see you. When the tendency is for everyone else – men and women alike – to pretend not to see what just happened, not to acknowledge what just happened, not to know what happened, I want all the little girls who have been violated by adult men, who should know better, to know that I see you in your pain. Because to be witnessed and supported lets her know that her experience is valid and validation can empower her to take action when it is time. And I will bathe her and hold her and cry with her and apply salve to her wounds and let her know that the person who did that to her is no friend, no godfather, no trustworthy individual, that this person who is masquerading as family is a killer, a baby killer; he has just crushed an important piece of her spirit.

JB: Sticking to the idea of point of view and perspective, one thing I noticed here is that though they are different perspectives, there is one overall voice in the novel. Winston sounds exactly like Septimus, for example. Consequently, this made me wonder who is the overall narrator of this novel and how did you settle on this narrator?

PP: I tried to make the voices and perspectives of Winston and Septimus very different, but if they sound very alike then perhaps I have failed. Perhaps I am writing, as I have always done, after all from one perspective. But certainly it was Winston's story that drew me to the book. What does it mean to go home again after all these years of running away? Can you return and still maintain your adult self or do you become a child again, vying for attention, crying at every hurt, fighting and squabbling with your sibling, sitting in a corner and stewing in your feelings, afraid to move and to take right action? What does one do with all the memories that have been stirred again? Do you turn a blind eye, or do you begin to face the difficult things, name them one by one, and begin to dismantle them, even the parts that you hold on to for dear life, they are so much a part of your identity? What tools do you need, what level of consciousness and of heartfulness would you need to truly heal the damage in a family, a damage that didn't just begin with this generation but which might have been inherited from many generations past as family traumas so often are?

And perhaps Septimus is the part of Winston's consciousness that stayed, the part hungry and desperate for the father's love and attention and recognition. Because every boy adores his father and wants his father to adore him in return. But what if the boy adores the father but the father is critical of the boy, the way he looks, the way he is in his humanness, and the father is not very forthcoming in his love for his son, what might the boy have to do to get that love? So the part of Winston that wanted that love, stayed behind and settled for the status quo, for to challenge the father, to speak out against his improper behaviour and lose that love would be akin to death. So the promise was that he would always turn a blind eye and never develop his voice or his integrity or true independence; he would never stand for anything, not for intimacy with his son or with his wife, because growth would mean loss, and he was not willing to jeopardise his father's love.

To extend this metaphor even further, one could say that Winston's journey home is truly a soul retrieval. And I'm thinking of soul retrieval here in the way Native American shamans define it – that whenever we suffer an emotional or physical trauma, a part of the soul (essence, life force, vitality that ensures that the self continues to thrive) flees the body or disassociates from it in order to survive the experience. Although soul loss can be a useful survival mechanism, it can also leave the person incomplete, out of balance, and unable to thrive in the most important ways. Shamans believe that eventually these lost aspects of the soul must be returned home to the person for integration, and these shamans usually "journey" into the unconscious or shamanic realms to retrieve them.

Though I'm only now just entertaining this idea because of the questions, I can see how Winston's journey home is so that he can finally collect and integrate all the scattered parts of himself, the split-off aspects of his consciousness that escaped due to the challenges in that household when he was a boy. Unable to handle the challenges then, he left for thirty years refusing to look back, but during that time (unbeknownst to him) he was developing inner resources, he was putting his psychological house in order for the new parts to feel safe once they returned. Rosa, too, is part of that retrieval. She is a symbol of the vulnerable feminine self that he'd had to hide in order for his father to respect him. In Winston's worldview, true masculinity in a man is when both the masculine and feminine are in complete balance. He befriends Rosa, his former self, he falls in love with her all over again, he wants to adopt her and take her home to the US. He wants to raise her so she'll grow; he wants that aspect of himself to flourish. He cannot imagine his life as a complete man without this female aspect of himself also thriving. And I'm not thinking here that he is trans or transvestite or gay; he is a straight man who loves women, but a straight man who knows that true masculinity can never be devoid of the feminine principles of life.

JB: You have notably done away with several literary conventions in this novel, like quotation marks around speech, which I appreciate very much, this breaking of rules. But what that meant, though, was that it was hard at times to separate a character's thoughts from his actions. I am still not sure if Fiona is cheating on her husband, for example, or if it is all just in her husband's mind. Was that the effect you were going for, and, if yes, why was this important to you?

PP: When I did away with the quotations I was also just experimenting. My hope was that the delineations between thoughts and actions would still be very clear. But I see what you mean about the ways in which those distinctions can sometimes merge and become less clear. In the case of Septimus and Fiona, Fiona did cheat on her husband. But all of this is narrated from Septimus' perspective because I wanted to show how the affair not only impacted Septimus, but also invited him to grow and change in important ways that actually brought them closer together. First of all, there is his jealousy and his rage. He obsesses over the affair, replaying it again and again in his mind, the way we often do when we are jealous and knee-deep in the feelings of abandonment and despair. There are times he weeps and times he wants to smash her, his own pain so unbearable he must strike out. He never does retaliate by beating her, which would only have worsened the situation. But as he continues to replay the encounter and sit in his suffering, new realisations begin to emerge. When he compares himself to Robbie Chen, the man with whom Fiona has the affair, the man who is also the father of her two children, he also sees his own shortcomings, he sees that he's not a very affectionate man, emotions don't come easy, he is more taken with the dead than he is with the living, and that his father's love is more important than anything. Though it's a painful recognition, he comes to understand why she might want to return to Robbie; his wife is starved for affection and for intimacy; she is starved for nurturing and for care. He could've abused her, he could've left, he couldn't find any number of women uninterested in challenging him, he could've stayed emotionally withdrawn so as to punish her, but instead he stays and decides to change, decides to try and become more of the kind of man, the kind of lover who will make her happy and ultimately make himself happy. Thankfully for Septimus, he's interested in the challenge.

JB: This is a novel about men, and it takes us quite intimately and convincingly, it seems, into the world of men. Why was it important for you, as a female author, to explore such a masculine world and was this especially hard for you to do?

PP: I enjoy writing from the male perspective. In many ways it feels easier. And perhaps that's because I am female and turning that kind of gaze on myself is so much harder because I don't have the distance of gender. And there are so many other women writers who do it so skilfully and so beautifully. In this novel though, because of the themes, it seemed super important that it truly is about men and several generations of them even, so we can see the evolutionary change. This is a novel about love and about healing. It is about spirituality and parental nurturing. It is about sexual abuse. Often men are left out of these kinds of stories. They are on the periphery. Women are at the centre. In this book, I wanted the men to be at the centre, because if we are to grow and develop and change as a people, men need to develop themselves emotionally and spiritually. Healing and nurturing and loving and intimacy shouldn't just be the domain of women. It should be everybody's domain. That is true nation-building. In this book I wanted to explore what that could look like in this particular family. Here is the father who is the powerful head of household and also the sexual predator. Here is the father who is setting the standards for this family. I wanted the sons to be the healers. I wanted them to be courageous enough to confront the father, to put a stop to his actions if they can, to care for the women who have been violated and to create a new life-affirming paradigm for this family. I wanted them to be the vulnerable ones, the ones who must undergo change to keep the women they love in their lives. I wanted them to learn how to be truly loving fathers, not just providers, not just authority figures who shout out orders, but ones who truly see their effeminate sons, and love them for all of their mannish and womanish ways, love them for their two-gendered magnificence.

JB: Patricia, women never really seem to have an emerged voice in this novel. For example, I could never really say I have heard from Fiona. I am thinking that this is a deliberate strategy on your part, this silencing of many of the women in the novel, this seeing and interpreting them through male eyes, am I correct in my thinking here? If yes, can you walk us through your reasons for doing this?

PP: I don't like thinking of myself as a writer who silences the women in the novel, but it's true the women are not as emerged. So let's just say that while the women are speaking from the periphery, their actions, though slight, are as loud and frightening as the voices of those thinking, feeling men. Fiona is a businesswoman; she is financially independent, and so is Septimus in his work as a burial man. But she needs something else now in her marriage; she wants to be with a man who will meet her emotionally, a man who is nurturing and sensitive. She is done with the strong, hard-working and silent type. She wants an emotionally intelligent man, an evolved man. And the affair was the way she loudly communicated her needs. The affair could've meant the end of the marriage in some relationships, but Septimus used it differently; he heard the messages inside the clarion call of the affair once he stopped to listen and he rose to the occasion. The mother in the story is a more complicated character. Of the same generation as the father, she was more willing, it seems, to remain silent and to stay in that oppressive marriage. Still she makes a very surprising move once the father dies: she immediately remarries. Which makes me wonder: had she been seeing this man on the sly all along? All this time, had she been getting her loving and companionship elsewhere? Is this what gave her the strength to stay? And did she stay for Rosa? Rosa's mother and her healing will have to be for another book. But until Winston appeared on the scene with Rosa in tow, it seemed as if she had locked off that part of her life. Now that he shows up triggering memories, what will become of her? And what will become of Marie Jose, who is so preoccupied with her cancer and her survival and her healing, there seems to be little room for anything or anyone else? But Rosa wants family and she wants Winston to be happy. And I think eventually Rosa will get her way.

JB: The novel is very interior-looking, and there is a level of self-absorption to all the characters. I can't begin to tell how many times I counted someone saying something to the effect of "what about me and my needs?" in this novel. How do you explain this level of interiority and self-absorption in the characters?

PP: Anyone who has been in long-term therapy knows that this kind of thorough psychological investigation runs the risk of turning into self-absorption. One has to make sure they strike the right balance between turning inward in a deep and investigative manner, and using the knowledge and wisdom and pain found there to make changes in the self that then allows them to create freedom for themselves and for all beings in the world. I think that our religions have taught us to look outside of ourselves for answers. We are taught to look to the preacher, look to the Bible. We have forgotten the vast interior teeming with life force that lives inside us. We have forgotten our hearts, and how to love. Perhaps there was a time in our history when it was not okay to love. When those we loved were raped or taken away or sold or killed or maimed. Though that was a long time ago, perhaps we are still playing out that narrative – can't trust love. Perhaps we have to unlearn all of this, and a certain level of emotional investigation can help us to go back to listening to the selves that we banished underneath the house bottom so that we could survive, didn't fall apart when everything and everyone we loved and held dear was going to shit around us and being taken away. Those selves might still be crying from underneath the house bottom – what about me, what about my needs, what about me – and dying for us to welcome them home. Needs are important. We all have them, and sometimes they are manageable and sometimes they are huge and overwhelming. Not many of us got our needs met as children; our parents, through no fault of their own, were busy trying to survive and to make ends meet and to make sure we had food, we had clothes, we had education, we had our basic needs taken care of. For some of us, this can be enough; for others, not at all; some of us can turn into adults who are like hungry ghosts, we can't get filled up nowhere nohow, and we prey on those less powerful. It's important to identify needs when they emerge, to locate them and investigate them, to see what yearnings are present, to put aside guilt and shame and to take the best action. We need to take action fuelled by love and integrity. If we can't feel or don't want to, what will prevent us from being cruel and tyrannical? What will prevent us from being abusive? I don't know the psyche of people who are sexually abusive, but I would say the father in the story had a lot of feelings he couldn't understand, that the father was in a lot of pain. And as a society, we are going to have to find ways to support these men who are in terrible pain and who inflict it everywhere they go and in everything they do.

JB: Child abuse, particularly child sexual abuse, is a huge theme in this work. What's more, there seem to be no structures in place to respond to the levels of abuse meted out to children in Jamaican society. How do you account for the rage directed at mainly the female child and later the adult female body, in this novel, by men in the society? There seems to be an aberrant silencing that goes on around this issue.

PP: Having grown up in that culture, I know that rage first-hand and no, I cannot account for it except to say that there is terrible fear of the feminine. The logic here is that one rages against the thing inside them they fear most. Men are terrified of the feminine inside themselves and outside and they seek to destroy it at every turn. When I began writing the *The Fullness*, I was not only experimenting with form, I was experimenting too with the nature of the novel and of storytelling. Stories carry energy. And too often they still carry the template of our outmoded values that we still hold dear, whether we realise it or not. A story that holds on to an old value can keep us stuck in primitive and destructive patterns, which can make us ill, or they can keep us comfortable and complacent and myopic.

When I started *The Fullness* I wanted to write a new kind of story. Aware of our terrible, terrible history of slavery, and the vile punishments meted out when we resisted, and we resisted only because we were magnificent beings, we were humans, and aware too that those memories live inside us still, they live in our cells, our DNA strands, we pass them on from generation to generation. They show up differently in all of us; still the remnants are there, they continue to shape so much of the way we live, the way we love. We have to be so watchful of ourselves, so vigilant. I wanted the novel to bring about a shift in consciousness. I wanted to chronicle the atrocities, yes, but I also wanted to write the healing response; I wanted to give the character and the reader the antidote, the narrative medicine so that healing can happen. That was my intention when I started writing the book. I don't know if I was successful; the reader will have to say. But I'm desperate for new stories and new paradigms that can affect our states of mind and help us thrive. Through pet scans scientists are finding out that the brain shows different patterns of blood flow when we are happy and when we are depressed. Since the brain can regulate everything in the body, when the brain changes so does the body. What new stories can we tell to ignite joy in the brain, to change perceptions of the world, our perceptions of each other and how we can perceive our experiences?

JB: The little girl Rosa is one of the strongest characterisations I have read in a long time, even though at times I question the things that come out of her mouth. But there is no denying that she lives on long after one closes the book. Yet, like Rosa, I too am confused about her place in the family. It seems as though Rosa is a gift to her father, even though her existence came about through a great atrocity, yes?

PP: In Jamaica, we refer to someone like Rosa as the outside child. So often the outside child is the one we turn into the maid, or the one who is molested or otherwise violated, or the one who gets the hand-me-down clothes, the one who is least educated. The one who becomes the shadow, the discarded thing we want to keep apart, keep out of sight. And that was a story I wanted to change. Because everyone knows inside the shadow there is also the gift. Inside the parts of us we want to cast away, the parts we dislike, there is also a gem of creativity that will take our lives, our creations to the next level. This little girl, Rosa, is no different. She is the shadow, the other, and she is also the gift. And not just for the father is she a gift, but for Winston as well, and for Septimus. If he allows himself, Septimus can rest now; he no longer has to keep burying the dead. In some ways she is the dead sister/daughter reincarnated. She is the child Winston has always wanted. She represents the feminine/the vulnerable aspects of self that might have a chance of actually thriving in that family, where before the father made every attempt to destroy it, in himself and in his sons. She is the outside child, but her presence is the glue that holds the family together. She brings laughter and love and light where before there had only been discord. She is the connector between the generations, between the father and the sons, she is the one who brings the brothers closer, she is the visionary who brings past and present together, not just in life but in death. She lives and communicates in at least two worlds, the living and the un-living. She is a seer and a healer, and intuitively she also knows she cannot survive there in that house with her father, she needs Winston to take her away. She is a magical child, a lightning rod of sorts; all shadow material must be attended to once she is present.

JB: This novel's point of view on death is one of the most interesting I have read in a long time. To put it mildly, death does not mean the end of existence, but rather a continuation of the work that needs to be done. Yet, I often wondered, with the undead coming and going in these pages, if these undead "souls" did not cause more confusion and pain after death than they did in life? Was this the point you were trying to make here?

PP: I simply wanted to acknowledge that though people die and we bury them, if there is unresolved business, then those people, those memories of unpleasant things that were done, are very much alive in us. Unpleasant matter may be buried, too, inside us, but upon any serious investigation, we'll soon find they continue to haunt us and cripple our relationships or our work in the world, until we make some kind of peace with them. When the past is present, it is as if time has stopped, there is no past, no future, simply the now where everything is present and we are in the centre of that roiling storm. Winston had been away for 30 years, yet when he returns it's as if he'd stepped back into a time warp, a kind of frozen past, an arrested development. And his task in the book is to clear this past, to find some kind of peace or resolution with it so he can move forward in his life and in his relationships. He cannot clear the past with the tools that were used to create the past; he has to employ a new and elevated kind of consciousness. And that's where the conings come in, the meditation practices that he inherited from his European girlfriend, having no Afro-Caribbean modalities of his own to help and support him through these troubled times. In his efforts to forget, he disregarded everything related to home. And I would even go further to say that the undead running through our lives, filling us with confusion and pain, don't just refer to dead people, the undead that haunt us still are also memories, traumatic happenings that occurred early in life, the undead are those aspects of our unconscious that are not at peace and that continue to haunt us still, creating havoc until we attend to them.

JB: Finally, you have, by now, published four well-received novels, Patricia. As a last question I would like to know what you are working on now, and when might we see the next work from you?

PP: I have always wanted to write a book that was narrative medicine, a book that would bring healings to the psyche and change consciousness. *The Fullness of Everything* was the beginning of that project and my mission now is to go further with that project, to push the boundaries of the book to see what is possible. I've just completed a collection of short stories called "Come Closer". These stories came out of a period of intense meditation practice. I wrote them down, one word, one sentence at a time, till I had eight stories that transformed me on the way out and that, I believe, have the power to transform readers as well. The stories are bringing awareness to hidden aspects of our unconscious motivations. They are retrieving split-off parts of the personality due to trauma. They are showing us the choices we make to stay safe from the pain of loving and losing. They are collapsing the rigid boundaries between the masculine and feminine in ourselves and in relationships. I call these stories transmissions, but others might call them magical realism or modern ancient myths. I am sending out the manuscript as we speak and my hope is these stories will touch readers in the deepest parts of themselves for these stories are everybody's stories. The characters mirror our own hunger for alternative ways of living and loving. They mirror our own desire for new narratives and our willingness to risk all for freedom, and for connection with another and with ourselves. There is love at the heart of every story, leading us toward what we've always known: that change is possible and union is our ultimate goal.

WOMEN TAKE CENTRESTAGE AND SET THE RECORD STRAIGHT IN SHARA MCCALLUM'S POETRY

Shara McCallum is the author of five previous books of poetry: *The Water Between Us* (1999); *Song of Thieves* (2003); *The Face of Water: New and Selected Poems* (2011), *This Strange Land* (2011), and *Madwoman* (2017), which won the OCM Bocas 2018 poetry prize. She has a forthcoming collection, *No Ruined Stone* due in 2020.

She is the recipient of a Fellowship from the National Endowment for the Arts, individual artist grants from the Tennessee Arts Commission and the Barbara Deming Memorial Fund, the Agnes Lynch Starrett Poetry Prize, and an Academy of American Poets Prize, and has been a Cave Canem Fellow and a Walter E. Dakin Fellow at the Sewanee Writers' Conference.

McCallum was on the permanent faculty of the MFA program at the University of Memphis and the Stonecoast Low-Residency MFA program at the University of Southern Maine and has served as visiting faculty for the Catskill Poetry Workshop, the West Virginia Writers Workshop, the Frost Place, and the Chautauqua Writer's Center.

She lives with her family in Pennsylvania, where she is Liberal Arts Professor of English at Penn State University.

❧

JB: Shara, congratulations on your OCM Bocas Award for Caribbean Literature in Poetry win for your collection of poems, *Madwoman*. I guess that's a good place to start our discussion. When I was reading through your collection of new and selected poems, I started seeing the madwoman as a theme and trope throughout your work. When did you realise her as such, and who would you say is the madwoman?

SM: Thank you, Jacqueline. I was grateful to the judges and Bocas for that. It meant a great deal to me and especially for this book, which is the culmination of something I've been writing toward for a time, as you recognised. In retrospect, I can see I was working with the trope of the madwoman but wasn't thinking that way at first. The first two poems I wrote dealing with that figure, one from her point of view and a prose poem about her, appeared in my second book. That was published in 2003 and those poems written sometime around 2000. I thought I was done with her (or her with me) after the second book, and then she resurfaced 10 years later. This time she was far more polyvocal, her voice notably rangier, if that's a word – shifting between an array of tones and attitudes (prophetic, funny, angry, grief-stricken). I wasn't sure who she was at first, and I wrote the poems in a way to try to answer the question for myself: who is this woman I keep hearing? What conditions of her life created the fault lines in her? I considered that she might be me and so in the poem "Ten Things", for example, I went down the road of using my autobiography to situate the sites of her rupture. Everything in that poem is true. The same is the case in many of the poems where I look at her fracturing through the lens of race, immigration, sexual assault, parent-child relationships, and grief over the loss of people and places – much of it is borrowing from and building off personal experience, but it didn't end there as it never has for me. I've written for a long time with the intent of trying to unpack what various forces do to the self, the notion we all seem to have that who we are is stable and fixed. And I knew if this Madwoman I kept hearing was me, she wasn't only me. She was/is also the women in my family and the women from history and myth who interest me most – women who won't conform to what the societies and cultures they've inhabited throughout time expect or want them to be. Women who chafe against convention. *Madwoman*, as a book, is a kind of origin story of this particular version of a figure who is far from being mine alone (least of which in literary terms), and the fact that she is many-selved became how I had to engage with her. If I were going to invoke her, I knew I would have to admit all of her, even the parts that are contradictory and that frightened me most. I found my inability to pin her down or reduce her to a singular self became the truest response to the question: who is the madwoman? She is personal, cultural, mythic, historical, and political all at once and manifests in and through the various ways we understand "being" a self in the world.

JB: Folktales are very important to your work, and in your retelling and reworking of Jamaican folktales they are often infused with nostalgia for Jamaica. So, are you remembering, recouping or doing something else with the many Jamaican folktales that you utilise in your work?

SM: Yes, I'm very drawn to folktales, those of Jamaican origins in particular, but not exclusively. As a poet, I also like to work with fairy tales, biblical stories from the Judeo-Christian tradition, Greco-Roman myths, and stories from any other folk, religious, and mythological traditions that strike me. If I were a visual artist as well as writer, like you are, I think I would be a painter who dwells in the space between the real and surreal. As a poet instead, I am fascinated by the realms of magic and dream and their relationship to our waking lives and our rational minds.

But to try to answer why Jamaican folktales in particular – undoubtedly, it's in good part because I remember hearing some of them growing up, as you mention. Retelling folktales and their kin (idiomatic expressions, aphorisms) have been a way for me to thread aspects of the Jamaican oral tradition and culture I grew up with into my poems and that may be what you mean by nostalgia. That word is a loaded term and usually used with derision in regard to literature – but I freely admit to having a backward-glancing tendency as a writer, the desire to sound the past in the present. Both of the impulses you mention – to remember and to recoup – are bound up for me in the act of writing and Jamaican folktales are just one of the ways that I try to construct poems that hold onto that which has been lost or feels in danger of being lost to me. But some of the stories I've woven into poems or woven poems out of are those I am sure I am simply bringing in for the metaphoric value they carry. For as far back as my memory extends, I have a tendency to read signs. I don't have much religious faith any longer, but I still love the realm of metaphor, which is the realm of the spirit. I don't actually know how not to see the things of the world as metaphor and I don't know how to read any of the stories I love best in only a literal sense. I think of them almost immediately as allegorical, told to unlock truths that are too complex or difficult to apprehend directly. Anancy, for example, is the kind of figure who endures in the imagination because he represents many conflicting aspects of the self in one vessel – he is often selfish and greedy, so in that regard offers a cautionary tale of the baser aspects of our nature. And yet, here is this tiny creature who routinely outwits others with far more power and who often is the cause of so much that happens in the stories, good and bad. The twinness in his nature is where his appeal lies for me.

JB: Another issue that is very prominent in your work is the troubled terrain of race and racial classification both on and off the island of Jamaica. The situation within your work becomes even more intriguing because while the narrator in your work is often insisting upon her Jamaicanness and not her "foreignness" while on the island, despite her "white" skin, she often does that while speaking from within the tenets of the black protest religion of Rastafarianism. So, I will just ask you, how do you understand your racial classification and do you identify with any of the tenets of Rastafarianism?

SM: I'll begin by saying I am mixed-race, look white to most (many?) but not all people, and understand my racial classification as being black. In terms of Rasta, as you know I was raised in Twelve Tribes. More specifically, I was born in 1972 and left Jamaica in 1981 and for nearly the first decade of my life I grew up in the Twelve Tribes community in Kingston, which my parents had joined before I was born. In terms of my parents' racial classifications, my father was a light-skinned black Jamaican who identified as black. My mother is Venezuelan. She immigrated to Jamaica as a child, and her own racial background is mostly European and some Amerindian. She identifies as Venezuelan and Jamaican and as a white Hispanic. I come from parents who were "mixed" themselves and, like many mixed-race and mixed-nation peoples in the late 20th and now in the 21st centuries, they and I were asked in indirect and direct ways to "identify" ourselves from childhood and adolescence on. Prior to the late 20th century, if you were a person of mixed race, the legal and societal codes that were part and parcel of slavery and colonisation in the Americas would have more or less rendered the decision for you. The very notion of "choice" or idea of self-identifying was, until very recently, a moot one. On top of my ancestry, the politics and philosophies of Rastafari deeply impacted me and were imprinted on me as a child. While I don't practise as Rasta now (I am now Jewish), I can clearly see how the worldview it imparted endures in me. That worldview isn't one I can summarise quickly here, but I will say that in regard to race, Rastafari was a black empowerment movement as much as a spiritual path. I was being made aware, even before I could articulate it, that I had to fight against white supremacy, its systems, beliefs, and the individuals that denigrate blackness, including even those of us who are in part or whole African descended yet carry antipathy toward blackness or self-hatred in ourselves. The other force that shaped me hugely, regarding race, was migration. I think coming to the US at the age I did played as much of a role in how I eventually came to see and identify myself as black, as did being raised Rasta. I left Jamaica in 1981, when I was almost nine and that early part of my life was formative for true. But I came of age in Miami and became an adult in the United States and America has indelibly shaped me as well, especially in regard to race. The politics of race I encountered once I landed in the US cemented my views on my own racial identity/classification. Legally and otherwise, in the late 20th century when I was coming of age in the US, to be any part black was to choose to either acknowledge that you were black or to "pass". That choice, as it were, felt like a non-choice to me. It felt like being told you can either tell a truth that will cause you to continually have to explain yourself to others or you can lie. I chose and choose the former, even while I am aware of how vexed it is. But race is vexing and vexed, and the situation is far more so for the majority of black people who look black and cannot "pass". That seems obvious to me, but I need to say this every time I talk about race now. In a book of essays I'm writing at present, there are several where I focus on the very questions you are raising. Even now in my mid-forties, I am still trying to grapple with the significance of being black, from my admittedly small vantage point, in the face of shifting political, geographic, and historical meanings of blackness.

JB: Throughout your works, a lot of attention is paid to a father who goes away in several ways: emotionally, psychically into madness and physically into abandonment and ultimately death. This is a father who also beats the mother. Yet, what is interesting in reading through the works as a whole is that the father is almost always treated with tenderness and understanding, while there is deep ambivalence towards the mother-figure in your work. How do you explain this?

SM: Wow, your questions are like a scalpel, which I appreciate! My father had mental illness – schizophrenia. There is one poem in my second book where I mention that he beat my mother. As far as I know, from her retelling of that incident many years later, he was not aware of what he was doing at the time because of how sick he'd become. His abandonment of her and of his children was largely due to his illness and to his ultimate suicide. He died a couple days after I left Jamaica with my mother's parents. I found out none of this until I was around twenty, and I have few intact memories of my own of my father. Much of what I know of him is second-hand; my grandparents and mother told us he died in a car accident and I grew up believing that story. As I aged and when I later learned the truth of how he died, I began to feel his absence more keenly than this presence and to look at his life through the lens of his mental illness and suicide. My mother, in contrast, stayed in Jamaica for the first year I lived in the States with my grandparents but then joined us in the US. It was a complicated living arrangement. While I spent more time in my grandparents' care/house after she returned, I also saw her continuously, often on weekends and in summers. With my mother, I think her ongoing presence in my life while I was growing up in Miami was or felt like a continued kind of "abandonment" and is the likely reason she/the mother figure shows up differently than the father. Hers was an active presence and rife with difficulty. But there are poems I've written where I've tried to engage other sides of my relationship to each of my parents. In one of the ghazals I wrote in my third book ("Neglect"), for instance, I question whether or not in dying my father got a kind of pass and was "loved best" precisely because he wasn't there to continue to disappoint me and because his life was undeniably tragic from any way you look at it. With my mother, I also have a great deal of compassion for what she went through and I hope that comes across as much as the ambivalence you rightly note is there. I wonder if my mother may have had some kind of undiagnosed mental illness because she too would become unhinged at times – or perhaps this was a response to the stressful conditions of her life and there is no name for it exactly. My mother was nineteen years old when I was born and by twenty-four had four children under the age of five, no money, and a husband who was seriously mentally ill. By following my father and becoming a Rasta, she had also fractured an already tenuous relationship with her own mother. It's true that my mother caused damage to her children, but it's equally true that she was herself, as is often the case, a product of circumstances greater than she could surmount. In my most recent book, there is a poem where I look again at an image from my childhood that has haunted me and I try to imagine that moment in time from my mother's point of view specifically ("Mother Love, a Blues"). I hope that and other poems about my mother dwell in a space of tenderness and in the desire to understand what happened to her too.

JB: Mythological and classical works are clear points of references for you, and you enjoy telling and retelling mythological and classical stories. One of my favourite poems in this regard is "Calypso". Can you talk a little bit about what you think can be gained from telling and retelling classical works? What went into the making of the truly wonderful poem "Calypso" and what are some of the things you hope readers will get from it?

SM: Yes, absolutely. The reason I revisit and retell these stories is I think they continue to shape our world and what we believe is possible or right and because these stories have always been open to interpretation it's the job of storytellers (poets included) to reinterpret them for each new generation. I loved Greek myths from I first encountered them when I was about thirteen years old. The gods and goddesses of these tales were flawed and heroic, tragic and comic, all at once and in ways that struck a chord with me and seemed to delve into the truths of human nature. I don't care much for views of human nature that seem to believe good people don't do bad things or vice versa. That seems a too-simplistic and dogmatic view of human being. It may be that such ideology works well for religious and political movements, but I think it works far less well in life and art.

   As to "Calypso" specifically: I remember exactly when I wrote the poem. I was living in upstate New York working on my PhD and had already written several of the poems in my first book that recast folktales and fairy tales and other Greek myths (including the poem "Persephone Sets the Record Straight"). The title of that poem about Persephone and my working at the time on a suite of poems that centred on the figure of the mermaid came together in "Calypso". I just started hearing her talking to me, like a Jamaican woman standing up a verandah and chatting to her friend and recounting the story of her relationship with that "idiot boy" Odysseus, and I wrote it down. She arrived on my doorstep as a contemporary dreadlocked Jamaican mermaid, and I didn't question her right to be incarnated as such. I just ran with it. The poem is a monologue – I am fond of that mode of poetry – that gives Calypso a chance to have her say.

What do I hope readers will take away? That she's not spending her time regretting the mistakes of her youth, but that she's wiser for being self-reflective about the past. That she's fair-minded – she sees men as foolish at times about love and women's roles, but also sees how women participate in their own foolishness. That she's funny and through humour is able to offer some scathing critiques of culture and politics (she starts off critiquing the tourist industry, for example, and in the process, brings in the spectre of racial and economic privilege tied to that). That she's smart and had way more power than people generally give her credit for when the traditional versions of her story get told. Almost always in the old stories and the myths, women are the minor characters and men the heroes. So, in my poems, women take centre stage and get to be the stuff of legend. The monologues I keep writing in the voices of women of myth and history are because I keep hearing these women still trying to "set the record straight".

JB: Like so many Jamaican and Caribbean women writers, Shara, you too are fascinated by the ocean, the sea and mermaids. But in your case the fascination is deepened by an absolute preoccupation with fish and fishermen. The narrators in these poems are often at seasides naming fish and watching fishermen at work. How is this lifelong visual interest tied up to your writing about mermaids? Why do you think so many Jamaican women writers, yourself included, write about this half-woman/half-fish creature?

SM: You are the second person to point out to me in the past year that I write a good deal about fish. I was doing a public Q&A in Memphis a year ago and someone else asked me this question, of why fish in particular appear so often in my poems. I never realised I was doing it that much, so had a tough time answering at first. I suspect it is tied to my lifelong visual interest with the shore and the sea, and that my love of painting and ekphrasis as a poetic mode is stealing into my poems here. I live a good distance away from the ocean/sea now, and have for most of my adult life, but every chance I have to stand at the shoreline I do. It is a feeling of being bound and boundless that the shore and sea conjure for me. I am actually terrified of the sea and obsessed with it at the same time. I don't know if I can say much more about why I return to certain vistas like the sea or why I return to certain images like fish and fishermen or snapshots of memory. Whenever I try to answer questions about images and what I choose to look at as a poet (I look at a lot more as a person who never makes it into my poems), it starts to sound like I'm evading the question, which I don't mean to do, or may even sound recursive. I go back to certain scenes and images because they draw me back to them. As to mermaids, and why the return to that figure so often, I can't speak for all Jamaican women writers but I will tell you the story of what happened to me after I had written the suite of mermaid poems that comprise the last section of my first book as a kind of answer. I was in conversation with someone who'd read the book in draft form and she commented on how perfect the mermaid was as metaphor for many of the issues – race, migration, gender & sexuality – I was confronting in the poems. That honestly had not occurred to me in such a clarified way, which seems comical to say now: the mermaid is half of one world, half of another, never quite belonging to either. Of course once this person pointed out to me what I was doing, it immediately seemed obvious, but I had not articulated that to myself while writing the poems. This experience has happened to me so often as a writer that I have come to think I am a slow learner of my own mind's working, or I must like keeping myself in the dark while I'm writing, or I am writing ahead of my own understanding. Maybe some of all of these explanations is the case. It was certainly so while I was writing my first mermaid poems that I couldn't say what I was doing or why until after I finished them. By the way, I love Goodison's poem "On Becoming a Mermaid", in which, in a brilliant inversion of the story, a mortal woman is being morphed into a fish. I also love Akhmatova's poem that ends with the line "the mermaid in question is of course dead". And Faulkner's book *As I Lay Dying* is one of the books I read early on that made a profound impact. I was about fourteen the first time I read the novel and had no inkling of being a writer then. I was just a reader and lover of books. In the public Q&A I mentioned I did last year, one of the questions posed was about my influences. After I named Faulkner's book as an early influence, I went on to explain how, when I got to the chapter about Vardaman that contains just a single sentence, it took the top off my head. Do you know what that sentence is? "My mother is a fish." When I uttered the sentence, it was a funny moment because I and everyone in the audience had the same "a-ha" experience. I have talked about loving that novel many times in the last thirty years and I had never put the pieces together before like I did last year in a room of mostly strangers. Who can really say how we become who we become, exactly, as writers or as people?

JB: Another image that recurs time and time again in your work is hair; various textures of hair: matted, locked or curly hair. In the poem "Autobiography of my Grandmother" a narrator notes:

My mother's face uncoils;
Her hands nest in my hair –
All before I discover the sea
Between my legs ...

Thereby, tangibly linking hair to sexuality. Why this steadfast focus on hair, and different types of hair, and what does this all have to say about [burgeoning] female sexuality?

SM: Hair is bound up for me in gender and in, as you say, burgeoning female sexuality – and conversely in the loss of sexuality, as we age and our hair greys and thins and we become seen increasingly as sexless in the culture at large. Hair is also inextricable for me from race and racial identity. As a mixed-race black woman, my hair has been the phenotypical feature people pick out when they try to read race on my body (that and, to put it bluntly, my backside). When I was younger and my hair was long and full and tightly coiled, it was the part of me that was often the most sexualised and commented on as such. I had a boss in Miami – this was in the early 1990s and would be less likely to happen now I suspect – who explicitly told me I could not wear my hair out when I came to work because it looked too "suggestive" and was not "professional". He wasn't the only one. Sexuality in women of all races, but especially women of colour, is still viewed through an impossible, contradictory lens: seen as life-affirming and threatening, something to desire and fear, at once. Hair is an apt metaphor but is the tangible evidence of the cultural morass of gender and race I am troubled and fascinated by. The poem you quote from here is one of many times hair arises. Salome, Medusa, Tanglehair (a character my mother made up), and others all show up as avatars of this obsession. As a writer, I don't always know why I am obsessed by things that I return to again and again, but I trust that if I follow them they will keep leading me somewhere.

JB: Tell us a little bit about your life in Jamaica: Where were you born? What schools did you attend? How often have you returned to the island? Can you see yourself living in Jamaica again?

SM: I was born in Kingston and lived mainly there. The last schools I attended were St Margaret's Prep and Hopefield Prep. I left Jamaica when I was nearly nine, when my mother's parents, who had migrated to Miami two years before, brought me and my three younger sisters to America. I didn't go back to Jamaica at all until I was in my early twenties – partly because there was no money for many years when we first came to the US, but I think it was even more so that the response most members of my family had to our migration was to fear the past and to will a kind of amnesia. It was as if that world we'd come from was hermetically sealed off once we left and this included the memory of my father. Other than my grandfather who went back to work in Kingston selling life insurance when I turned thirteen (he actually commuted from Miami after that point up until he died), no one in my family on my mother's side who migrated to the US returned/ returns very regularly, or at all, except me. As I mentioned, I started to go back to Jamaica in my early twenties on my own, and have gone back many times now in the twenty years since. Sometimes with family and work obligations in the US and other travel commitments in the US and abroad, the time between visits has stretched out longer than I'd like. I could check my passport but my guess is that I'm there on average every two or three years. I have a sister and niece in Kingston I stay with and other extended family I see when I go, but I love the country best and especially being in the Blue Mountains and Port Antonio – so I try to get outside of Kingston, too, whenever I'm there. In the past decade or so, I've met other Jamaican writers and scholars who live in Kingston and am fed by those relationships and look forward to seeing people as much as the place now. Still, I have to admit that of all the places I've travelled (and I've been fortunate in recent years especially to get to do a good bit), nothing moves me quite like the sight of certain parts of Jamaica – the sea, yes, but also sitting in my sister's living room which has a view of the mountains and where I love to see the mist that collects on the hills in the morning or feel the breeze coming across. The sensory experiences of being in Jamaica create a particular feeling in me, I guess something we call "bittersweet": that sense of love and loss all mixed up together, and it still breaks me apart when I'm getting on the plane to go back to the United States.

As to whether I could see myself living there again, I asked myself that a lot at one point but I don't anymore. I imagine it would be a cultural adjustment as I've lived in the US for a long time and came of age there, not in Jamaica. As a Jamaican-American, I'm keenly aware of how the age of my migration contributed to making me the divided/dual nation person I am. The country you first learn to drive in is the country you learn to navigate as you become an adult. So just because I love Jamaica doesn't mean that I think I would know immediately how to manoeuvre through its cultural mores – though I will say with pride that I have driven there several times now, and even in Kingston, where the traffic is so bad sometimes I feel grateful when I reach where I set out to go! All jokes aside, though, at one time I really wanted to go back and I spent a number of years wondering if and how and when I could make that happen. But my husband, who I met when I was nearly twenty-two years old, is an American and we have been together since and have two daughters born in the US who, for better and worse, we are raising here. I honestly can't see how he or they would make the transition and they have strong attachments to the US because it is their home. Between my family and the other tangible problem of finding a job (I love teaching at university in the US), migrating back isn't something that seems likely, so I've stopped thinking about that and focus on other ways I can remain connected as a Jamaican living in the diaspora.

JB: So where, then, do you consider home?

SM: First and foremost, home is the place where my husband and children are now. Because I've moved often in my life, love to travel, and as an immigrant have been shaped by the idea that you have to be ready to go at a moment's notice, I also pride myself on being able to make many places "home", on being culturally adaptable and flexible. Still, whenever I am asked where I'm from by anyone, to the amusement of my husband and children, I always say Jamaica. I've lived much longer in the US than I did in Jamaica and in the state I live in now longer than any other single place prior (Miami is a close second), but you won't find me saying I'm from Pennsylvania. It's not because I hate it. I'll absolutely front the answer by saying I live in Pennsylvania but will qualify that by adding – but I am from Jamaica. Grammar reveals a great deal to me of how we think and feel, so I think my insistence on claiming Jamaica is significant. I've met many people over the years – non-Jamaicans and even some Jamaicans – who express their disbelief when I say I'm Jamaican and this may be part of the reason I feel the need to put it out there front and centre. I'm not readily "seen" as Jamaican, and it means something to be part of the Jamaican experience. I am well aware most of the time why someone is querying my origins, but I usually just make a joke and say something like, "No, really, I'm Jamaican." I haven't forgotten where I was born. I'm insistent about this in part because I have had to insist on not forgetting.

JB: As a writer, you seem to love the registers of Jamaican English. In particular, code-switching and the use of Jamaican patois are definitive to your writing project. Why is this so important for you?

SM: Yes, I absolutely love the registers of Jamaican English. Even if when I speak it my inflections are not as natural sounding as a Jamaican who has stayed at home or who grew up longer in Jamaica than I did, I trusted the language and never questioned my capacity to write in it from I began writing poems. Because I get the patwa question a lot, with good reason as I write in patwa often, I've had to think of why it might be so instrumental to my poetry. For many reasons, is the likely truth, but the most important one I come back to is that I simply can't say things in standard English that I can in patwa. I am not just talking about meaning but also tone and music and metaphor. Patwa is often much richer in word and sound play than standard English, and as a poet my ear is drawn to double-meanings in, and the musicality of, language. It's also the case that many of the women I hear in my mind's ear talk to me in patwa. I've never "translated" a poem from one register of English to another. The speakers of the poems I hear arrive linguistically as they do, and out of their speech I build a world for them. The voice of a poem, whether it's a dramatic speaker or a lyric one, in other words, presents itself in one idiom or another – though there are many times where I hear the range between the Englishes clearly and I try to score that span of language as well. I know there is a politics attached to our use of various Englishes and I could talk at length about that, or about what I've come to learn about language through the field of linguistics – but I have to admit that my attraction to patwa in terms of poetry has been driven by my ear and by the interest I have as a writer in bringing into language character, situation, thought, and feeling as precisely as I can – finding the "best words in the best order", as Coleridge put it. There are times I will mix up Patwa/Englishes (including not knowing which expression is American or Jamaican) and not even realise it until it's been pointed out to me by someone else. With patwa, this is likely because I stopped speaking it outside my home once I came to the US, though continued to hear it inside my house. It's also very likely because my grandmother, who was a larger-than-life influence on my poetry and person, was from Trinidad originally. That's where she spent her childhood as my mother spent hers in Venezuela (for her the language issue was even starker, being a leap from Spanish to English). I didn't realise my grandmother was mixing in Trinidadian English and idioms alongside Jamaican ones – I took them all as being Jamaican and only later discovered otherwise when I would make a "mistake". Funny related story on that count: I went to Scotland for the first time a few years back and kept hearing the word "muckle". I remarked to a friend there, "Oh, we have an expression in Jamaica: 'Every mickle mek a muckle.'" Well, you know where this is going, I'm sure. That expression is Scottish (now Jamaican too, but originates in Scotland) and three of the five words in it are Scots rather than English. I felt really foolish after I proclaimed with such certainty the origins of the phrase. Back to the point: I suppose it has always seemed natural to me to use every resource in language I have access to as a writer and patwa is a wellspring.

JB: There is a stanza in your poem "From the Book of Mothers", which goes:

> Sing a light song, Mummy.
> Twinkle, twinkle –
> No the other light song.

> This little light of mine –
> No. A different light song.

What can you tell us about this gorgeous little stanza?

SM: I can tell you exactly how the particular lines you're asking about came into being. When my children were young, I sang to them most every night. Even when I was on the road, I would call in and sing them bedtime songs. I had a repertoire that included some traditional English lullabies (like "Twinkle, Twinkle, Little Star") but also contained a mix of songs I just particularly liked singing: "This Little Light of Mine", "Cry Me a River", "The Rose", "Don't Cry for Me Argentina", "Baby Mine", and others. And my children got in the habit of making requests. My grandmother called this nightly production my "concert hour". It would go on sometimes that long, I have to admit, for their pleasure as much as my own. But sometimes I couldn't figure out the particular song they wanted and they would become really irritated with me. These lines capture one of those moments. In the poem, "From the Book of Mothers", I arranged snapshots of dialogue, other bits of language, and images from my mothering and my time with my children (as well as my time with my mother, stories of mothers of myth, etc) in collage fashion to try to get metaphorically at the complexity of motherhood and the self. I'm not sure that each individual moment or source I'm drawing from comes through, or needs to. It makes me really happy to know these lines were moving to you in some way, however you took them.

Oh, I didn't find out what the song was my daughter had wanted that time until years after, when the book finally was published and the daughter in question read the poem. She explained that the song she'd been trying to get me to sing that night was "La-la-lu", another lullaby in my regular line-up which has a couple lines that gesture toward light but don't mention it explicitly. Thus, I wasn't making the connection. The song starts: "La-la-lu, la-la-lu, oh my little star sweeper/ I'll sweep the stars for you." That's the "light song" my daughter had wanted to hear.

JB: As we get towards the end of our interview, one of the other things that I notice in your work is that you sometimes seem to be having a conversation with "history". Now your idea of history is very specific. History is a woman who is always somehow in search of herself or her voice. I am thinking here of your very powerful poem "History is a Room". History stands at the door of the room of history but she cannot enter this room. What is preventing History from entering history, would you say?

SM: The same thing that continues to prevent women from taking a proportional place in society and in the record of the human story – male dominance, hegemony, ignorance, patriarchy, prejudice, religious fundamentalism of all stripes... Do I need to go on? I like very much what Eavan Boland has said about her role as a poet – to tell the distaff (female) side of history. I want to be clear too that I want history to bend toward the female rather than only to write women into history in conventional ways. Yes, it is great that Nanny was a warrior and I love the story of Nanny and what she represents, but it can't be the only way women get to play a role in the historical record is through engaging in war. In the poem you mention, the thing that prevents the woman who speaks from entering the room is that History, with a capital H, is often gendered in a way that excludes women, through our obsession with glorifying most the stories of conquest and imperialism. I think poets have a potential civic role to play if engaging with history is part of our calling (it is mine) – to restore to History a wider and fuller perspective of the past and to offer personal dimensions. Going back to Boland, I would cite her brilliant poem "Quarantine" as achieving what I mean here. The particular poem of mine you mention was in some measure a response to a chance meeting with the historian I quote from in the epigraph, Niall Ferguson. I very briefly interacted with Ferguson at a reception prior to the lecture he gave at the university where I taught at the time. I'd decided to attend both without knowing much about him or his work because I was interested in his topic – he was delivering a lecture on the history of empire. In all fairness to the man, I still haven't read his work and I bet it's more complex than the snapshot I got of it that evening. But I found his manner in person and on stage to be insufferable – his demeanour was often condescending and the seeming thoughtlessness of his argument that "Empires aren't always everywhere bad" got under my skin. He kept repeating this stupid statement all night, even when pressed in the Q&A by students and colleagues to account for the political reality of what he was saying – what such beliefs have always and continue to lead to: genocide, slavery, apartheid, disenfranchisement, persistent social inequality. I'm sure he's incredibly smart but I detest it when people use their rhetorical skill to be provocative, when they do so knowing full well that what they are saying will mean tangible loss for those with less power and will lead others in power to feel vindicated in their misuse of it. I hate that kind of "intelligence" as much as ignorance, which is saying a lot for me right now living under Trump.

But about the poem and my approach to history in poetry: I just don't agree at all that "the study of History is the study of Empire." Or I don't agree if it signals – as such statements do – that Empire is implicitly moral and good or that its means justify its ends. I'm a pretty logical person in many regards and I appreciate roads and vaccines as much as the next person, but sometimes the pragmatic argument cannot be allowed to win over the principled one that holds up justice as the ideal we should be seeking. I'm not sure if I answered your question about history or have gone too far off course now. But I hope somewhere in this I've hit on what you were hoping to hear me ruminate on.

JB: Finally, Shara, I say to you: the island of Jamaica. And you say?

SM: The place I cannot leave, that has never left me, no matter how long I've been gone, no matter where I am in the world.

'WHITE CARIBBEAN': AN INTERVIEW WITH BIOGRAPHER MICHELA CALDERARO ON THE LIFE AND WORK OF ELIOT BLISS

Michela A. Calderaro has taught English and Postcolonial Literature in Italy and the USA for many years. She was Associate Editor of *Calabash: A Journal of Caribbean Arts and Letters*; Editor of the Ford Madox Ford Newsletter and creator of the original Ford Society Website. At present, she is member of the Editorial Board of *Il Tolomeo, A Postcolonial Studies Journal*, University of Venice (Italy). Dr Calderaro's critical works include a book on Ford Madox Ford, (*A Silent New World*, Bologna 1993); numerous articles on British, American and Anglophone Caribbean writers; and a series of interviews with major Caribbean poets. In both her critical works and interviews she tries to focus on issues of identity and memory, and the way memory of the past is processed by artists.

She has edited a collection of Creole writer Eliot Bliss's unpublished poems, *Spring Evenings in Sterling Street*. Her literary biography of Bliss, *Sheer Bliss: A Creole Journey* has been accepted for a 2020 publication by the University of West Indies Press. Her blog: www.michelacalderaro.com

❧

JB: Michela, I want to really thank you for this book, *Spring Evenings in Sterling Street*, poems by the Jamaican writer Eliot Bliss. Since you argue so forcefully in your introduction about the need to know this writer, I guess my first question is: Who is Eliot Bliss?

MC: First and foremost, I think she is an unquestionably talented writer whose books and poems shed light on a very interesting literary and geo-political period.

She was born Eileen Bliss in Kingston, in 1903, while her father, an army officer, was stationed there with the West India Regiment. She spent her childhood and adolescence between Jamaica and England – where she would be sent to study in convents. Growing up in such confined environments (even prodded by her family to marry a Kingston man) she understood she did not belong in any of them and that she must live her life somewhere else, where she could express herself without inhibitions. London seemed to be the right choice. Admittedly it was a city where homosexuality was still considered a crime, but it was also a place where she felt she could "be" what she wanted to be, and indeed she soon found herself playing a part in one of the most exciting literary scenes of the century. She was also an uncompromising writer, who would never sell out.

A telling episode lies in the discussion she had with Vita Sackville-West about cutting all references to some racist remarks made by the protagonist's mother in her novel *Luminous Isle*. The episode is reported by Eliot herself in the interview with Alexandra Pringle, which constitutes the introduction to the 1984 reprint of the book. The point I'm trying to make in my introduction is that one of the reasons *Luminous Isle's* sales did not go well, notwithstanding the support offered by Vita Sackville-West and her husband, Harold Nicolson, is that, at the time of publication, the inclusion of such remarks was not viewed as strong criticism – as indeed it was – of the island white men's attitudes but, on the contrary, as an expression of Eliot's own racism.

It is interesting to note that though she says, in the same interview, that Sackville-West was "probably" right and that she should have taken away those remarks, she never even seriously considered doing that in the reprint. She was indeed an extremely determined person. In Patricia Allan-Burns's (Bliss's companion) own words, one would do better than "cross swords" with Eliot: her eyes would freeze you on the spot. And nobody would make her change her mind. Probably she was born in the wrong century. However, her inner self, I guess, will always remain a mystery, no matter how much we search.

JB: How did you come to know of and subsequently start working on Eliot Bliss? How long have you been working on her?

MC: I read the novel *Saraband* (the second edition, published in 1986) by chance, in 1998, while browsing for books in some of my favourite second-hand bookstores in New York. My main interest at the time was Jean Rhys. I was studying the literary influences of Ford Madox Ford and Modernism on Rhys's work, and had the idea of using the semiotics of passion to analyse Rhys's work. Well, the moment I held *Saraband* in my hands the whole Rhys's project fell through. Here there was an author, a Rhys's contemporary, who was not only a friend of Rhys's, but born in the Caribbean! An author I had never heard of. It was all very exciting. Not to mention the fact that I didn't agree at all with the suggestion that her book was merely bildungsroman.

Little by little I found out that a couple of dissertations had been written about her novels, and that Evelyn O'Callaghan had mentioned Bliss's work in her book *Woman Version: Theoretical Approaches to West Indian Fiction by Women*. However, I still could not find anything about her life. I began to be very curious…

JB: Can you explain the transformation from Eileen to Eliot?

MC: She became Eliot when, after cutting her hair short, she could also finally cut the umbilical cord that had tied her to a certain class and environment. Together with cutting her hair came the decision to change her name from the very feminine Eileen to Eliot (from T.S. Eliot and George Eliot – a woman writing under a male name). Then she went on to live with her friend Susan, as they had planned while both had been studying at a Highgate convent. Susan was not lesbian, she actually married a couple of times, but Eliot was certainly taken by her, and she is very likely one of the girls in the poem "Spring Evenings in Sterling Street".

In London, she was at the centre of literary and lesbian circles. Anna Wickham introduced her to the literary salon headed by feminist activist Natalie Clifford Barney, an American writer who was openly lesbian, and through her she was introduced to the poetry of Natalie's lover, Renée Vivien.

It was not easy, and it cost her dearly. Part of her family did not understand, let alone appreciate, the change; some of her friends disappeared, neither accepting nor approving the way she was living in London. As Louie, in her *Saraband*, says, cutting her hair, she "had robbed herself of a characteristic feature of feminine abandonment", but with it she also acquired the freedom she so much needed in order to live.

JB: You report finding dozens of unpublished works by Bliss. Can you give us a sense of what you found?

MC: When I began my search for Bliss's writings, I didn't know she had written thousands of pages of poems, novels, even plays. In the beginning, I was just puzzled because I couldn't find any essays or research papers that covered her works. It was only later on, when I could read her diaries at McFarlin Library, in Tulsa, that I became aware of Bliss's extensive writings.

Patricia Allan-Burns and I found literally hundreds of poems, many loose pages with ideas for novels, the manuscript of a novel, brief notes, letters and diaries. Another manuscript of a novel was temporarily given to me for the purpose of my research by the Eliot Bliss Estate, and will be returned after I finish my work.

The poems that are published in *Spring Evenings in Sterling Street* are just a small selection of what we retrieved. All the poems we found are extremely interesting, but I had to make a choice, and it was not easy.

Also, there are still many works that are unaccounted for, more novels, poems, and practically all the plays she wrote. I hope that the publication of her poems, and this interview, will arouse interest in her works and that curators in some libraries, or private collectors, will find her manuscripts, maybe in some collections of other authors.

JB: You say of Bliss that "[b]eing white, Creole and lesbian shaped her personality and her life". How so?

MC: What she describes in her novels and poems is a period where being lesbian and poor, in addition to coming from the colonies, was seen as a disadvantage. Eliot was also extremely proud, would neither hide nor flaunt what she was. Still, we also must remember that homosexuality in England, not to mention Jamaica, was considered a crime to be severely punished. She needed to live her life the way she felt was right, but at the same time she needed to just live. Also, the European attitude towards those who returned from the colonies was not very welcoming. Creoles were often regarded as an embarrassment: sure, they were white, but they were "white Caribbean",' that is, they were born in the colonies, meaning a sort of an outcast group – unless you were fortunate enough to live in Paris, where you were likely to be seen as exotic.

Also, in my introduction I talk of "Creole's double alienation", borrowing Evelyn O'Callaghan's expression in *Woman Version*. It is a fitting definition, describing the difficulty of being stuck in the middle, of not really belonging to any group of people. Having lived in the island for generations, Creoles were considered not white enough by white aristocracy coming from Europe, and were despised by the black inhabitants who remembered very well the behaviour of slave owners.

A good example is how Tia in Rhys's *Wide Sargasso Sea* defines Antoinette as a "white cockroach". So, Eliot felt alienated from the white people of the colony, with whom she shared little and had little in common, was socially alienated from the black mountain people, with whom she was not supposed to have friendly contacts, and her homosexuality set her even further apart. So in her case the double alienation became a triple alienation.

The choice to leave was in a way the logical result of all this.

Later on Bliss kept being what she was, never compromising, accepting the fact that her choices would affect her life, and in this she was lucky to have at her side, no matter how difficult it must have been, a great personality such as Patricia Allan-Burns.

JB: I know that you are working on a biography of Bliss; how is that going?

MC: As you well know, I've been devoting many years to Eliot Bliss. The detailed search for her writings will be part of my book "Sheer Bliss", which is a sort of biography of Bliss interwoven with my own story of what began as, and still is, an obsession.

How is it going? In a word, slowly. But I'm quite happy with what I've been doing, and hope to have a final draft ready very soon – probably by the end of summer. The main difficulty has been the scarcity of details about her life – besides what she herself chose to disclose in the introduction to the second edition of *Luminous Isle*, and what Patricia told me in the course of our many encounters.

Unfortunately, the numerous letters she wrote to Anna Wickham, which could have told us a lot about her early life in London and which were kept at Anna's house, were destroyed during the war, together with many other letters and documents. But the two unpublished novels I read shed some biographical light on the post-war period, when she was confined to her small house in the country. They were obviously biographical, just like her two published novels.

In writing a biography, one is always faced with the issue of reliability. How sincere was Bliss in her interview? How much of what she reported was the actual truth? How faithful is any autobiographical narrative to reality? But this is the vital question regarding any author, not just Bliss, isn't it?

JB: You say that for Bliss, her homeland became "… a co-protagonist of her work". What do you mean by this?

MC: Jamaica is mentioned in all her works. One way or another, it seems that she cannot but talk about Jamaica, even when talking about something else. Everything orbits around her homeland. She was influenced, especially in her poems, by the colours, by the suffocating atmosphere of the island, the blinding sun, the humidity, the lusciousness and greenness of the plants, the heat. The relationships that are established between characters could only happen "there", in that land.

She dedicates whole paragraphs, pages even, to the Blue Mountains of Jamaica: Without those paragraphs there would not be any story to write. It is only because the protagonists live in Jamaica, or must leave Jamaica, or must return to Jamaica, or desired someone they were not even remotely allowed to in Jamaica, that the books had any reason to be written. Even a storm or heavy rain become a reflection of what goes on within the heart of the protagonist.

The character of Rebekkah, the black girl from the mountain – with whom Emmeline, the protagonist of *Luminous Isle*, feels "completely happy, [and] in solid harmony" – stands for the island and it is through Rebekkah that the island takes centre stage and becomes a protagonist in the personal story of Eliot and the fictional story of Emmeline. The realisation of the impossibility of a closer relationship adds a motive for choosing exile.

JB: I am curious about the fact that Bliss and her work sank into oblivion, and that very little is known about her life. This is despite the fact that she garnered considerable acclaim for at least one of her novels. I have noticed that it is not that women artists do not produce, but their works, despite whatever acclaim they may obtain during their lifetime, are often "disappeared" and these women and their works "sink into oblivion". I am curious about your views as to what is at work here. For a long time it was believed women just did not produce.

MC: Women have always produced, either transmitting their works through the oral tradition or writing – diaries, for instance. Being published was a different story. I think it was a question of market. The publishing world was in the hands of men; they would decide whom to publish. Women writers were relegated to the role of writers of children books, or of cheap romance novels. In order to be published, some would even use male pseudonyms, and certainly could not make a living out of writing.

Some would publish a novel, be considered a new voice in the literary panorama of the period, and then disappear, often because they had no means of supporting themselves with their writings, so they had to find a job to pay the bills; some never wrote a second novel; some continued to write, but left their works in the drawer. I'm not so sure that things are really that different these days. It may be easier for a woman to be acknowledged as a writer, and then published, but a woman has to work harder to keep being published; at least, this is my impression.

By the way, there's another poet who has sunk into oblivion and should be "rescued" – Patience Ross, Bliss's lover at the time of the publication of *Saraband*. She was quite a good poet herself, but you cannot find any publications of her works nor any reviews or studies.

JB: In your quite riveting introduction to Bliss's poems, Michela, you make compelling ties between Bliss's work and that of Jean Rhys. Bliss and Rhys were tackling the same subject matter. Yet Rhys has gone on to be canonised and Bliss has sunk into oblivion, how do you account for this?

MC: There are a few points to discuss here. First of all, it is my strong belief that Rhys was influenced by Bliss's *Luminous Isle*. This is a fact that, to me, is indisputable. Bliss wrote her novel some thirty years before Rhys's *Wide Sargasso Sea*, and not only was the book well-known at the time of publication, but Bliss had sent a copy to Rhys much before Rhys began writing her own novel and, finally, Rhys had exchanged letters with Bliss on the meaning of the "wide Sargasso sea". Moreover, you only have to read the opening paragraphs of the two books to recognise who influenced whom and how.

Regarding the question of oblivion and canonisation: Rhys had a real master of letters to teach her how to write and get her published: her mentor and lover, Ford Madox Ford. Ford was a great writer, an excellent editor and protector of younger writers. He actually took her in, into his own house – a thing that was not actually appreciated by his wife. He taught her how to construct a novel, how and what to cut in order to reach the perfection of the written page. And Rhys followed his lessons. Bliss never had such an editor or mentor. She had friends who tried to help her, like Anna Wickham and Vita Sackville-West, but no real mentor or editor in the publishing world.

And then of course there's the problem of going around and promoting your book, as noted by Eliot herself in the introduction to *Luminous Isle*. She was very, very poor, she didn't have fine clothes and was too proud to admit it. So, she sort of secluded herself, in London first, and in the country later. In addition to that there is the problem of the subject matter. True, it is the same subject matter, but... at the time of *Luminous Isle's* publication the Caribbean colonies were still a reality in Britain, and, as I just mentioned, some remarks in the book were considered crude and racist – whereas those remarks, and the whole book, were actually a cry for justice, a hard look at a very unpleasant reality.

Bliss's works should always be read on different levels: the personal, the historical and the political. Though these levels are fused together on the page you can clearly understand Bliss's strong criticism of a reality she had no power to change.

Also, of those women, who had "garnered acclaim" during their lifetime, as you say, very little is known because they had no influential relations. Once their books went out of print they also disappeared and nobody was interested in knowing why. I want to add, going back to your previous question about Jean Rhys, canonisation and oblivion, that even Jean Rhys was believed to be dead, her books were out of print and nobody remembered her, then she published *Wide Sargasso Sea*... and the whole thing began rolling again!

JB: You say that what is atypical of Eliot Bliss is that instead of letting her heroines live the life that she aspired to, rather it was Bliss herself who "lived the kind of life that she had dreamed of". What about her personality allowed for this?

MC: We should bear in mind that she was a writer, and she wanted to be published and appreciated. When Radclyffe Hall published *The Well of Loneliness* in 1928, the very first openly lesbian novel of the 20th century, the book was immediately banned in the UK. Being a crime, homosexuality could lead to imprisonment of those who were then defined as "invert". Eliot Bliss did not want to undergo the same ordeal; she could not afford it, she did not belong to the privileged classes, she had to earn her living. She was not hiding who she was, but in order to publish her works, she had to hide who her heroines were. Though, of course, a close reading might have unveiled the truth, luckily for her this reading was not carried through, and a certain hint of homosexuality might have been accepted as a merely girlish thing. Moreover, the fact that two girls would live together was not seen as a sign of "depravation", as it would have with two men living together.

Contrary to her heroines, whose lifestyles were "impeccable", her real life would lead her into distressing, if not altogether dangerous, situations. Only Anna Wickham who, being lesbian herself – though married – understood very well what her younger friend was going through, and would come to her rescue.

JB: The two main themes I see in the poems of Bliss are that of nostalgia for her homeland, and a preoccupation with death. The nostalgia that writers away from the Caribbean tend to have in their works is well documented. More confusing is her preoccupation with death. How do you understand this preoccupation?

MC: Though the preoccupation with death is almost a fixture in all her works (prose and poetry), it is in her poems that it is most evident. It is important to remember that she wrote and rewrote her poems throughout her life. Poems that were just sketched in the 1930s were later edited in the 1960s or even '70s or '80s, and were consequently influenced by the emotions she was experiencing at the time of these rewrites. Unfortunately, there is no way to know exactly when she edited the poems, since she would date only her first drafts.

To me this obsession seems to be twofold: On the one hand it is likely related to the death of many of her women friends. At least two should be pointed out. One was a woman whose identity has remained a mystery – the woman whose initials are AMG and to whom a selection of poems was dedicated. Unfortunately, Patricia could not help me here, because this woman belonged to the period before she met Eliot. The other woman is one of the greatest loves of her life, an American woman named Cairn, whom she met through a friend and was the reason she went at least twice to the US. In the end, however, she always came back to Patricia.

On the other hand, I think the obsession had to do with a metaphorical death: the death of her past, of her previous life. I do not wish to offer any psychoanalytical reading of her work or life, but only to point out that in order to become Eliot, Eileen had to be forsaken, buried.

JB: Finally, am I correct in reading "secrets" in Bliss's poems? For example, time and time again there is the reference to a "dangerous love" in her poems. Am I correct in thinking these "secrets" in her poems have to do with Bliss's lesbianism?

MC: You are totally right. Again, we must go back to the freedom she granted herself and the restraint she had to apply to her heroines. Her love poems might be read as dedicated to a man, at least this is what you may understand if you read them without knowing the context, which is what would happen had she published the poems in the 1930s.

Even the poem "Spring Evenings in Sterling Street" could be perceived as a description of a heterosexual relationship; it is only after you learn that she was lesbian that the poems suddenly open up a whole new scenario.

The same with two other poems – "Use Me Thou; With Beauty" and "Perfect Measure", which are extremely sensual, erotic you might say – that she dedicated to Anna Wickham, and that in my view subvert the common idea and understanding that the two of them were just friends and that Eliot regarded Anna as a mother figure. Anna might not have been in love with Eliot, but Eliot was certainly in love with Anna. Why write such poems if she were not deeply and passionately in love? Yes, she had to keep her "secrets" from the public in order to be published, otherwise her work would have been surely banned and she herself would have become an outcast. Just remember that even Anna, who was more famous and established as a poet, was not flaunting her homosexuality.

IXORA CHAIN

AN AFTERWORD WITH JACQUELINE BISHOP AND
THE INTERVIEWEES

WITH MARCIA DOUGLAS

Jacqueline Bishop and I met at the beautiful Dushanbe Teahouse in Boulder, Colorado, during the spring of 2018. There, at the foot of the Rocky Mountains, we discussed Jamaica, our writing lives and the importance of community. We also spoke about her *Jamaica Observer* pieces and the powerful interviews she has collected. Jacqueline Bishop is an interviewer par excellence and her interviews of Jamaican women writers, mostly in the *Jamaica Observer*'s *Bookends*, spanning 2003 to present, are not only entertaining but also erudite and valuable. It was during this conversation, too, that we talked about the possibility of soliciting questions from her interviewees, creating a forum for each writer to "turn the tables" and interview Jacqueline. I was pleased when, a few months later, she sent a list of the illustrious authors along with a request to solicit and assemble the questions. The Jacqueline Bishop interview project was underway.

In the conversation which follows, 16 writers (Sharon Leach, Keisha-Gaye Anderson, Opal Palmer Adisa, Shara McCallum, Millicent Graham, Velma Pollard, Tanya Shirley, Jean D'Costa, Michela Calderaro, Christine Craig, Ann-Margaret Lim, Hazel Campbell, Pamela Mordecai, Patricia Powell, Kerry Young and Lorna Goodison) engage with Jacqueline on topics varying from her work as an artist and scholar to her thoughts on culture, creativity and diaspora. I opened the dialogue with a question of my own.

MARCIA DOUGLAS: You have given so many women writers the opportunity to share their voices, Jacqueline, so I am pleased that you are bringing the interview series full circle by inviting your interviewees to now interview you. You are skilled at the art of the interview and many readers have enjoyed the conversations you have ignited. I'm curious – what inspired you to take on this project in the first place? That is, how did the series begin? And is there something that fuelled it and kept it going?

JB: Like so many things I do, Marcia, the series began without my knowing that the series had begun. Sometime back when I was a graduate student in the NYU Creative Writing Program, I started being preoccupied with who was going to publish the works of Caribbean writers, not in book form, but as a literary journal on the mainland United States. I'd had the wonderful opportunity of studying poetry with Lorna Goodison at the Caribbean Writers Summer Program at the University of Miami; that summer Earl Lovelace was teaching fiction and there was a critical component to that month-long programme, as well. I felt as if I was in heaven with writers and teachers from all over the Caribbean, but soon I began wondering who was going to publish all these wonderful voices?

At NYU, I was introduced to Kamau Braithwaite and Paule Marshall and Edward J. Sullivan (who works on Latin American and Caribbean visual art). I then went on to found *Calabash: A Journal of Caribbean Arts & Letters*, which I edited and which lasted for about 10 years. A central component of *Calabash* was conducting interviews, because I felt that interviews with Caribbean writers and visual artists in general were lacking. If interviews with writers and visual artists in the Caribbean were lacking, those with women writers and visual artists were especially lacking, and the ones I could find often did not treat the women with the kind of seriousness or rigorousness that I was after, which of course meant that they did not oftentimes accord the women the respect their work demanded. I was determined to change this. Because *Calabash* was published only once a year, and it had other components in addition to interviews, it was hard for me to do too many interviews.

A few years into doing *Calabash* I met Sharon Leach and we just clicked; we shared many of the same ideas regarding interviews and women writers. I think perhaps the first interview I did for *Bookends* was Hazel Campbell, who had published three collections of short stories, and I thought that noteworthy enough to interview her about it. That was back in 2013. Honestly, I don't know who else would have paid attention to one of our best writers who had put out three excellent short story collections.

The interviews as a series really picked up in 2015, because I realised that many women had written books, but no one was taking them seriously enough to ask them about their works. That, in a sense, is how the series got started. What has fuelled the interviews and kept them going is that, firstly, Sharon continued to make a space for the interviews in *Bookends*, and secondly, so many people seemed to appreciate them. When the women interviewed here sent back their answers, they said things like, *This interview was like a scalpel! You dig deep!* Or: *Jacqueline, it's the first time people have taken me and my work so seriously!* Hearing these things made me know that I was on the right track. And these interviews get around. Not just in the Caribbean, but outside the region as well, and they are not available online. Recently I contacted a writer's booking agent in the United Kingdom about an interview and I got ready to start explaining my case when the agent said,

"Oh no, we know all about your interviews! They've reached us here in England!" Examples like that fuelled the series and kept me going. I take enormous pleasure in thinking these women's voices and their works and words are getting out into the world.

SHARON LEACH: Jacqueline, I've said this to you before, and in response to this, you've mentioned that there is an arc to a good interview. What, exactly, is this arc that you refer to?

JB: You are a fiction writer and a screenplay writer and the editor of *Bookends*, Sharon, so you know that a good piece of writing has to cohere, and be immersive. None of the genres of creative writing says that *this* is the way that you have to start a play or a poem or a piece of fiction or *this* is the way that you have to end it, but throughout, you need to answer certain basic *who, what, where, when and how* questions for your reader or your reader will be unbearably confused. It is how you answer those questions that creates a narrative arc. I think this is more instinctive than anything else, as it is when you are writing a creative piece. You ask yourself: When do I change the momentum of this piece? What would I, as the interviewer, like to know more from this person and how would I like to know it? The context of a series adds its own challenges to a narrative arc. Jamaicans, as you and I know, are among the most discerning audiences in the world. You better come good if you are going to entertain a large Jamaican audience. I had the chance to do some work for Jamaica's 50th Independence with the Jamaican embassy in Washington, DC, and I remember someone there telling me that so many countries actually test their new products on Jamaican audiences. So you see what we are dealing with here!

With that in mind, I knew that I had to vary the ways in which the interviews were presented, the order of the questions I asked, all while building to a crescendo and getting really rich answers from the interviewees. In this regard, I think my training in oral history at Columbia University's famed oral history programme really helped a lot. But I also get the sense, honestly, that many of these women were waiting for a good, solid interview, and that, too, is what we are experiencing here: their chance to tell their story. Since they are creative writers and storytellers themselves, they too can appreciate the building of momentum in the questions, the need to slow down at times, the creation of imagery; all that culminates in a dramatic arc.

KEISHA-GAYE ANDERSON: Jacqueline, as a multi-talented artist and scholar who works across different mediums, how do you determine what mode of expression to use for your creative ideas? Which ideas become visual art, poems, or fiction? What is that process like for you?

JB: The most I can say, Keisha-Gaye, is that each medium "feels" different.

A poem does not have the feel of a fictional piece, even though once I have written or am in the process of writing a fictional piece, I notice that the poet in me steps in and begins to make word choices based on the musicality of words. So, lately, I find myself occupying, more and more, a space between fiction and poetry in my fictional pieces. This is never so with poetry, where it is all about the musicality of the words first and foremost, and then I have to see how I can find a narrative device that adheres to the musicality of the language. In other words, I know which works are poems, fiction, essays right off.

I often feel that my visual art is its own thing and quite distinct and separate from my writing life, but I just had an exhibition, "By the Rivers of Babylon", which was essentially text-based paintings. The two excellent essays in the catalogue for that exhibition, by the Italian scholar Michela Calderaro and the well-known painter Margaret Evangeline, both pointed out that here was a moment when the writer and the visual artist got fused in my work, so maybe more of that is going on than I realise. I also find the interviewer in me is raising her head, because I know that you too are a writer and a visual artist, so I want to turn this question back on you, to hear how you would answer it. I guess the long and short of my answer, then, Keisha-Gaye, is that I think of these areas as separate and distinct, but I would not at all be surprised if someone came along and showed me how they were not.

OPAL PALMER ADISA: How does your writing feed your visual arts and vice versa?

JB: My standard answer for that now, Opal, is that they live in separate rooms in an apartment. But I can see a day when this is no longer so, when they begin to be not roommates, but rather the single occupant in that apartment. Indeed, that day is already happening, albeit timidly. Recently, I was asked for a work for a collection that someone is putting together. I ended up writing something that I called a short-short story, meaning, this was something that had an imposed word count to it, and wasn't the longer short stories that I sometimes write. These short-short stories sometimes feel like poems to me. But the story that came out was interesting, because it was about a graduate student on the quest to find an enslaved woman who had been a visual artist, and I was a little amazed about this because, in looking at the enslaved woman's art forms, it was some of the very art forms that I had practised and the women in my family had also practised and that I had used extensively in an art project a few years before. I don't know if it's the same with you, Opal, but when it comes to my longer fiction pieces I often get an idea for a novel (and lately, novellas) and I write them down, and with your question I went to look and was surprised at how many future pieces I had planned that directly or indirectly were influenced by the fact that

I am, as well, a visual artist. So while, for the moment, they are roommates, the day will come when they are the sole occupant of the house.

SHARA MCCALLUM: I have a long-standing interest in the relationship between visual art and poetry, and my questions for you are in that realm. Typically, it seems to me, there are collaborations between poets and painters that result in each artist contributing to a jointly created work. Or, in traditional ekphrastic poetry, there is often no collaboration as the visual artist is either no longer alive or not involved in the process. In this mode, poets write poems in isolation that respond to a given work of art or to an artist's body of work. Since you are a practising writer who writes in various genres, as well as a practising visual artist, it seems to me ekphrasis would happen differently, not as a collaboration or response between artists that could be tracked, but perhaps as a process that is more simultaneous as the creative mind/force resides in one body. Would you speak about your work in terms of the concept of ekphrasis: does the idea of one mode of art speaking to/for another come into play for you and if so, how? What is the relationship between your different processes as a maker of objects and crafter of words? How do the various practices with which you are engaged relate to one another?

JB: Shara, for quite a long time your question stumped me, and I spent days thinking about it. That is not at all a bad thing. I rather like these meaty questions that force me to really think about what I am doing. Then one morning, when I woke up early, it occurred to me that the answer to your question might be found in my earliest published works, a small gorgeous book that I have always loved, *Writers Who Paint, Painters Who write: 3 Jamaican Artists*, which features my work, and the works of Earl McKenzie and Ralph Thompson. This beautiful little book was published by Peepal Tree Press back in 2007 and republished in 2009.

But first let's start with the poetry. At the time of my first and second poetry collections, I did not know what ekphrastic poetry was, but I see that I was voyaging into that territory all along. I think it was Tanya Shirley who mentioned ekphrastic poetry in relation to my work in a review, and I found myself really thinking about what that might mean. When I look back at my first collection *Fauna*, I find myself looking quite closely at works of art and almost trying to make poems works of visual art – "The Picture", "My Father: a Snapshot", "The Raft of the Medusa", "The Scene of Mutiny", "Yoshitoshi's Women". What is interesting to me is how intensely I was looking at visual art, but also these poems record, as well, my early frustrated attempts at making visual art, painting specifically. "The Scene of The Mutiny" is dedicated to Peter Homitzy, with whom I was then studying painting at The Arts Students League in New York. My early paintings weren't turning out as I wanted them to, and one day he said to me, something to the effect that visual artists aren't trying to represent the world as it is; they are instead trying to remake the world. That was the thing I needed to remember. He should have told me, too, that frustration is inbuilt with being a visual artist, particularly when one paints! But you can see that even then, in my earliest beginnings, outside of the visual art work that I did by myself, for myself, I was trying to somehow enjoin both forms, but as I answered Opal's question above, being a writer and a visual artist feels very separate to me.

The visual arts theme becomes more pronounced in my second collection, *Snapshots from Istanbul*, where there are poems about the artists Georgia O'Keeffe and Gauguin and poems about photography, and once again the framing of poems as photographs ("The Girl With The Haunting Green Eyes", "Snapshots from Istanbul"), which really shouldn't be so new to me at all, because Loretta Collins Klobah, I now remember, brought up something about this in an interview she conducted with me. But I see very clearly now that perhaps there was more unconscious overlap than I often think there is.

By the time I'd put on the exhibition that led to the book *Writers Who Paint, Painters Who Write*, some significant changes had happened in my life where the visual arts were concerned. For one thing, by then I had met the noted Caribbean and Latin American art historian Edward J. Sullivan, had taken his class on Caribbean art at NYU as a graduate student, and through him got a grant to spend the summer in Jamaica looking at Jamaican self-taught art. I cannot emphasise enough how earth-shattering that Edward Sullivan class and spending that summer in Jamaica were. Whereas before I knew there was something called Caribbean literature, I had no comprehension at all that there was something called Caribbean or even Jamaican art. My world has never been the same since Edward's class. But what does any of this have to do with that little book *Writers Who Paint, Painters Who Write: 3 Jamaican Artists*?

Now, when I go back and look at the essay I wrote in that book, I see that (for that book, at least) I was trying to merge the writer and the visual artist. In that book at least, both the creative writer and visual artist existed in one body and spoke with one voice. I made a coherent enough statement in the book how my art forms then were connected. It is interesting to me that these days they feel so separate, but I would not at all be surprised if some insightful critic showed me that what you asked about was indeed going on in my work. Maybe things feel this way because of my processes as a maker of objects and crafter of words. Most days, I have to make a conscious decision as to which of my projects I am going to work on, and oftentimes it is the project I have a firm deadline for, or the one I feel I have too long neglected. Consequently, I am waiting for the moment, and I hope with all my heart it will be soon, when I can consciously engage with my various practices as one and somehow relate one medium to one another, and perhaps one project to another, in a conscious, self-directed way. This will require serious funding opportunities. But for now, being a creative writer and visual artist feels quite disparate and separate to me.

MILLICENT GRAHAM: Last year at the National Gallery of Jamaica's Biennial I found myself between the proverbial rock and hard place as I stood in a space within your extraordinary installation, Jacqueline. I am relying on memory and am desperate to recall the interplay of sound and written phrases. I cannot remember it fully, but I remember a visceral response to something that was both sensory and sensual. It provoked thoughts of self and custom and identity. I remember the strange game I played standing in the in-between, moving my head from side to side, screen to screen, as the scanned fragment of words became this heady meditation. So I would like to ask: What is the creative impulse for your artwork? And how do you manage to evoke in the viewer such powerful questions of self? Is this all by design?

JB: I know exactly the pieces that you are talking about, Millicent. They are sound and video pieces from my Female Sexual Desires Project. Perhaps, I should first start by explaining what that project was all about. It occupied much of my time for the three years I was getting my MFA at the Maryland Institute College of Art, but the truth is, I'd been thinking about that project long before that. I had a simple enough premise. I believed then, and still do believe now, that it is fairly easy to access what male sexual desires are, particularly male heterosexual desires: it is used in selling cars and cigarettes, and is in songs and movies and is everywhere present around us. But when I tried to do the same with female sexual desires I drew a total blank. So I went on an odyssey of sorts to find out what constituted female sexual desires. Of course, everyone kept telling me this had been done before but, honestly, even where same-sex desire was concerned, in the visual arts I could not find anything on female sexual desires, and believe me, for years I looked and asked feminist art historians and librarians and people who should know.

I set out then to ask women about their sexual desires, and this turned out to be harder than I expected. Women did not want to share their desires for a variety of reasons, including the fact that many felt this was so personal, which I understood, but there were racial, ethnic and gender considerations as well. In short, I found that several white women did not feel that this was a project I should be telling as a woman – this was not my lane, but theirs – and women of colour, particularly black women, were really petrified of the oversexed stereotype that they felt burdened with enough already. Still I persisted. I eventually ended up developing an anonymous way of getting responses, and when the *Huffington Post* got involved, then responses started flooding in. I ended up with enough work to make several bodies of work: quilts, woven pieces, embroidery drawings, videos and audio pieces. Altogether, from conception to completion, the work took me three full years, working steadily, to make. When I had my thesis exhibition at MICA it took up several rooms and many people came to see it and it sparked many discussions.

When I was thinking about what to showcase at the Biennial in Jamaica I faced a dilemma. I was entering through the section where you had to be juried in. There is nothing particularly Caribbean or Jamaican about the Female Sexual Desires Project outside of its maker. I was speaking in the project as a woman, not as a Caribbean or black woman, but as a woman claiming a prerogative that white women had long claimed. How would that go over in a place like Jamaica? I knew that space would be a consideration; the project is big. Plus, how would I get the work to the island? I had been through that rigmarole before. So I submitted two works for consideration. One consisting of the video and audio pieces from the Female Sexual Desires Project and another that incorporated more Caribbean imagery that, interestingly enough, did not make it into the biennial.

Millicent, I was so nervous about how this work would be received in Jamaica! As you know, ours is a highly religious society – I really need to check if Jamaica is truly listed in the *Guinness World Records* as having the most churches per square mile! – but wouldn't you know it, the work was warmly received and I heard that there were always crowds around it. I was even invited talk about it on the radio. This is in keeping with the general reception of the work when it is shown. I was told women were more comfortable with the work than men were, which is very interesting, and what I also found in the United States. I was in the gallery in Maryland once when a married couple came in. They did not know I was the artist. The husband was urging the wife along, and she said to him, "Look, why don't you go and leave me? I like what I am looking at here." He got quite huffy. It was then that I looked at their matching wedding rings, and smiled. Another time, someone (I am assuming it was a mother from the conver-sation) came with a woman who had suffered some sort of sexual trauma. Again, from the discussion, the work was found to be positive and healing, even as issues of sexual trauma are represented in it. Another time, I came upon three women dressed from head to toe in black, as veiled Muslims reading and viewing the work. Of course someone – I am assuming this was a man – tried to vandalise the work, which launched an investigation. Female sexual desires were more powerful, Millicent, than even I knew they would be, though the difficulties I ran into while making the work should have alerted me. You don't know while you are making your work if you will connect with or evoke powerful emotions in viewers. In fact, you don't even know if your work will get shown at all. You're more just following your areas of interest and pursuing investigations into things you find interesting or compelling.

VELMA POLLARD: What advice can you offer new artists with multiple talents about apportioning time to each passion? You run several lives: academic, writer (in different genres), painter.

JB: Sometimes, Velma, apportioning time is very practical. You work on what you have a deadline for at the moment. Secondly, you work on what catches your fancy, what is your current darling. For some time now, this book has been my darling, so I have been spending considerable time with it over and above other things. But even then, maybe I am spending time with other areas of my life in spending time with this book because this book could be considered an academic undertaking, though it does not feel that way at all to me. It feels more like a gigantic warm embrace in which I get to sit and listen to and talk with so many women I greatly admire.

Practically speaking though, I live my life through lists and actual and self-imposed deadlines. The most important deadlines being, of course, the self-imposed ones. It seems that I am always planning in advance what I am going to do with whatever time I have. I also find that I am constantly asking myself which aspect of my creative life is being short-changed and then making room for that. Have I been writing a lot of fiction lately? Or have I completed a collection of stories lately? Then I start to feel that it's poetry's turn. That sort of thing.

The visual arts require spaces and resources so I find that I am planning a visual arts project in advance of doing it, depending on what equipment I might need. When I was doing the Female Sexual Desires Project, for example, it required an embroidery machine and quilting equipment and space – lots and lots of space – which I did not have in my apartment, so I pretty much knew that this would have to be a project that had to be completed when I was in residence at the Maryland Institute College of Art. So those are some of the considerations that go into apportioning time to each passion.

TANYA SHIRLEY: So much of your work is invested in privileging the voices of women. Do you think women are suitably represented in the arts? As female artists, do we have equal access to funding and opportunities to exhibit and share our work?

JB: Where the visual arts are concerned, women artists in Jamaica are now on par with male artists in terms of sales and so on, but even there, things are a bit more complicated than they seem. When you look closely at that situation you begin to realise that factors such as race, class and even colour are assisting the women artists who do well in the Jamaican art market and its overseas extensions. The artwork that I have chosen for the cover of this book is a good case study of what I mean by this. The work on the cover is an embroidery piece that came out of The Jamaica Women's League, which, in short, had many black lower-class women making wonderful pieces of embroidery largely for the tourist market. To date, I have not been able to find out who made this piece; there are complicated reasons for this. The more I dig into it, the more I realise that there were and are dedicated and sharp distinctions made as to who could and should be called an artist and what could and should be called art, which in fact obviated someone like the maker of this outstanding piece of work claiming it as art because of race and class and even gender distinctions. The woman who made this piece would be a "craft" worker. End of story. Not an artist. And to be frank about this, Tanya, I don't see too many trained women visual artists questioning these distinctions. What I see, instead, are trained women artists who will utilise these "craft" forms in their own work, without really looking back to and actually bringing the "craft makers" into the galleries and exhibition spaces and inviting them into the great sisterhood of artists on the island. These "craft makers" have absolutely no access to funding and exhibition opportunities. Race, colour, gender and especially class are big issues here. As women visual artists we really need to look at ourselves and what we might be perpetuating.

Things get that much more complicated if we start thinking about the situation of writers. This is where I see, unequivocally, that things are not equal in terms of gender. What is interesting to me is that if you look back at the so-called Golden Age of Caribbean writing (almost all male, incidentally), these men never seemed to have the kinds of adversarial positions that I see being taken towards women writers by so many of the male writers of our generation! I've had the chance to interview women from an earlier generation who do not speak of such an adversarial situation with the male writers. They seemed more encouraged and supported then by the men, instead of the kind of urgent ushering out the door by the male writers of their female counterparts that obtains today. This closing of ranks around a few male writers as urgently definitive of this generation of Caribbean and Jamaican writers – it is all kind of astonishing and definitely troubling.

In addition, I have seen famous white and other women writers and critics – European and American – champion the most misogynistic representations in Caribbean and specifically Jamaican male literature that they would otherwise call out, were that same misogyny being perpetrated on the bodies of white and other female characters in *their* ranks and in their countries. It makes you wonder what they even think of the black male Jamaican writers in the first place! And then these utterly misogynistic things are rewarded with all kinds of prizes! But on the island, too, we have a cadre of people calling women "harpies" and such awful misogynistic things, all in the name of privileging male voices. So, no, Tanya, when it comes to literature and publishing, at this time at least, women are not suitably represented in creative writing and I do not believe female writers have equal access to funding and opportunities to share our work. That is why I privilege women's voices.

I want to say one last thing. There are a few male writers who have reached out to me to say they too see what is going on – this business of people so eager to be kingmakers and coming up with ridiculous lists of who is important and who is not, where creative writing is concerned – and they think it wrong. So I do not want to give the impression that this is happening with *all* male writers in or from Jamaica: it is just happening with too many of them.

TANYA SHIRLEY: I am amazed by your ability to tackle several projects simultaneously; projects that often seek to enrich the lives of others. What role do you think community plays in the creation and distribution of art for Caribbean artists? Does art have a responsibility to engage with and represent a particular community?

JB: Taking the last part of your question first, about whether art has a responsibility to engage with and represent a particular community, I think this is entirely up to the artist and the goals that she sets for her work. Of course, once you create a work it goes out into the world, if you are lucky, and you lose some ownership over its interpretation, but I don't know how much I, for example, think about that when I am creating a work. In fact, I think the work creates me more often than I create it, and, indeed, I oftentimes feel like I am nothing but a conduit for the art to make its way out into the world.

After the artist has made the work, though, I do believe that they have some responsibility for this thing that they have created and, yes, I do think that they have to answer for it. For even as I am a conduit for this thing I do, I craft my work, and in doing so I am fully present, using all my faculties, and it is then that I must start asking myself some serious questions about this thing that I have created and, yes, how it represents the community of people I am writing about. I take very seriously that comment by Lorna Goodison in her interview when she recalled someone saying to her that, based on the books they'd read, the Caribbean seemed be the worst place in which to grow up as a child. That hurt mi heart so, too.

I grew up in a situation in Jamaica where I was very much nurtured by, and seemed to always be part of a community. Part of the reason that I did not know my mother well as a child was that she was very active in the 1970s in the People's National Party. She was secretary to Anthony Spaulding, and was always travelling all over Jamaica with the PNP Youth Organisation. She fully believed in the dream of a better Jamaica. Sometimes she would take me to party conferences with her in Jones Town or at the National Stadium and she took me to see Sistren plays, and all the dreams that she and the other women had for Jamaica, I guess, seeped right into me. It was a quite heady time in Jamaica, and you had the feeling that things were going to change and they were building a new, more hopeful Jamaica, largely for people like me, their children. Experiences like those shape you, they mark you, and they imbue you with a sense of responsibility to one's chosen and beloved community.

I have talked about the district of Nonsuch, where my mother and all her kin is from, a million times before and I am going to talk about it to you again, Tanya, because here, as well, I got a firm grounding in community. Honestly, there is nothing much to see or do in this small district. The first time I told Sharon Leach that only two-hundred and fifty people lived in Nonsuch she laughed me to scorn and said there were more than two-hundred and fifty people on her job! Still, Nonsuch is and was my world. As a child, there was no place I loved going to like Nonsuch. I felt so free there. There is a river running through the district and I especially love rivers! Everyone seemed to know to whom I belonged. They did not call me by my name, mind you. Rather, I was "Celeste great-grand", or "Mama Lou granddaughter". My great-grandfather was what you would call "Jamaican white", and the truth is I was fascinated with his pale limpid hair, blue eyes and freckled skin because he looked so different from everybody else I knew. He was not Nonsuch-born, not a born-ya; he'd come looking for work and met my jet-black great-grandmother, and that was that. He stayed.

Still, my great-grandfather and I would go walking in the bushes, and on Emancipation Day, he would tell me in all seriousness to look out for slaves because they always returned on that day, and then he would tell me all about the terribleness of slavery, all the while pointing out different plants and bushes and explaining their uses to me. He would tell me stories too about children that all seemed to somehow reverberate around one's responsibility to self and community. When I wrote that first collection of mine, *Fauna*, I did it far away from Jamaica; I did it in graduate school in New York, but who was that collection largely about? My great-grandmother and my great-grandfather, the island of Jamaica and the communities that I know and love there. I think criticism is a good thing, especially when it is done fairly, but you can imagine why I get so annoyed when I see destructive forces at work in Jamaica trying to tear down and mash up the place. It is because, for better or worse, I believe for artists like myself the community plays a central role in the creation of my work. It can also help with the distribution of our work. But, really, I am nothing if I am not part of a community. It is what I create out of.

JEAN D'COSTA: Was there a single reading experience that said to you, "This storytelling is electrifying, and I can tell stories too"? If so, what was the work (or the basis of the experience), and how did you unravel what you felt?

JB: When I was in first form at Holy Childhood High there was a book that was required reading, which I would never forget. I would carry those characters around with me, and over the years I would go back and visit them, though when I came to the United States I lost my treasured book which was published and available only in Jamaica. These characters were unlike any I had ever seen before. They were just like me, in the sense that they were Jamaican and they inhabited a landscape that was somewhat familiar, though also different. I ached for all that they were going through, and hoped they would find safe passage on their tumultuous journey. These characters even talked the way I talked. Let me stop calling them characters, for these children were not at all "characters" to me; they were people I knew, and there I was cheering them on.

What had happened was that these children were living in an orphanage and all the adults around them were getting sick. Worse still, the adults began dying; the children would have to fend for themselves. They would have to leave the orphanage, if they were to avoid the contagion spreading, and make a dangerous trek across the island, to a place that had previously been the home of one of the children and which had been willed to him. One scene in that book, in which the children were set upon and one child hit by a stone, his head bleeding, was seared into my consciousness. I remember telling a Jamaican friend of mine in New York about the book and him turning around and saying, "I thought I was the only one absolutely in love with that book!"

To make a long story short, the children indeed made the treacherous journey across the island and found something of a utopia waiting for them at their final destination. Oh, how happy I was! How delighted! You see, the Jamaica I lived in then, in the early 1980s, had suddenly become a very dangerous place for everyone, but more so for children. All the talk was of guns and more guns and killing on the island. The dream my mother had had for Jamaica and for her children was dying. I saw that light go out of her eyes. Migration would end up ripping my family apart, taking my mother away from me for years. But somehow, in my child's mind, if the children in that book could make it to safety, then so would I and so would our family. That is the power of great and lasting literature, especially for children.

At that time, writing a whole novel or even a short story seemed out of my reach, although I was writing my little poems. But that book was certainly electrifying. When I started writing fiction seriously, I went back and found that treasured book in Jamaica and I brought it back to New York with me. These days, I still go back to *Escape to Last Man Peak* by Jean D'Costa quite often.

JEAN D'COSTA: Have you witnessed situations and characters in life that have urged you to tell their stories, and how have you handled these missions?

JB: All the time! In fact, I just went and picked up my book *The Gymnast & Other Positions* and seven of those 10 stories were influenced by characters and situations in my life, though I don't think the people who influenced those stories would ever know this because by now the stories have been so carefully embroidered as to obscure their original source. If we look at a story like "Terra Nova", for example, that story was influenced by someone whose sister had died in the ways detailed in that story and whose mother did indeed wish her dead and who in fact became quite promiscuous. But the rest of the story is my own invention. The truth of the matter is, so many of the things that people share with me about their lives stay with me, and this story was my attempt to exorcise this story from my life, because it was indeed heavy. "Soliloquy" was similarly influenced by someone telling me about a man reading an obituary for her father, then getting in touch with her mother because of this obituary. I found the story so hilarious I had to write it and, yes, parts of it is embroidered, but that story came to me almost whole. I must say I had a great time writing it. "Effigy" came about as a result of an e-mail correspondence and is largely made up, and "Soldier" from watching television. I am the type of person who can pick out a good story in the middle of a sentence that someone is saying. Getting a good story idea, though, is just the beginning. Then there is the actual job of telling the story.

MICHELA A. CALDERARO: This is what I actually keep asking, looking for answers, and they don't come easy. Is there such a thing as a Caribbean aesthetic? That is, a play, a poem, a novel that can be defined as Caribbean? If there is, what is it that makes it Caribbean? Is it due to the work's theme? To the fact that the author is Caribbean-born? Do you believe there are certain traits that identify any artistic work as Caribbean? In view of a definition of a Caribbean aesthetic, could you share your view of "Creole" writers – that is, writers who are not fully African-Caribbean but are descendants – of European or Asian immigrants (who some argue do not belong in the Caribbean culture).

JB: Your questions admittedly, Michela, of all the questions in these interviews, kept me up the most at night and were the ones I answered last. Talk about a series of questions that I really needed to think through!

Though in some ways, they should have been the easiest because who is "fully" anything at all from the Caribbean? In any case, I will start by taking your last question first, because it is easier to tackle. The Caribbean, as we all know, is a space of energising diversity. Let everyone, as Lorna Goodison says in her interview, write them things. I think it was Walcott who said the next great Caribbean writer could very well be Chinese. Jean Rhys, after all, was white Creole and you, Michela, are doing fantastic work on another white Creole writer, this time from Jamaica: Eliot Bliss. So this Caribbean space is a really diverse, complex, complicated and interesting place that way. We all equally belong here, never mind that we all got here in very different ways.

At first I thought, well, a Caribbean aesthetic is self-consciously invoking things about the Caribbean – themes, landscape, voice, issues – and this is largely author-driven, but I am less sure now. More and more I see people questioning where, exactly, the Caribbean starts and where it ends. The boundaries of the place we seek to call the Caribbean are becoming more unbound, fluid and porous. They are turning up in places that we least expect. I run into the Caribbean all the time in expected places like London, New York City of course, and in Miami. But I was hot on the trail of Claude McKay, who was hot on the trail of the Caribbean in a place like Morocco. I honestly cannot say that when I lived in Morocco, and in all the times I have gone back there, that I've seen overt images of, let's say, Jamaica there. But, interestingly enough, McKay did.

I think then, Michela, this is where people like you come into play. People with your kind of training, who can look very closely at what it is the artist has made and sift through the seemingly obvious to see what is underneath it all, to help us to decipher codes that maybe we are not quite seeing. Maybe a Caribbean aesthetic is at times more a feeling or a notion than anything else; that nagging feeling while reading a book, for example, of something familiar. This happened to me with the work of John James Audubon, whose paintings fascinated me for years. Audubon has been credited as the father of American (meaning United States) ornithology. Just about everything I read about him privileged his upbringing in France as a child, his moving to the United States, his wandering across the United States, including the time he went to New Orleans and Louisiana, the time when his reputation was established in England, and his returning to America where he died in upstate New York. There was nothing there really to explain the familiarity that I felt towards his work, and I just put down my love of his work as my fascination with birds and my attachment to France, because of all the time I spent in Paris and Morocco.

It so happens that I recently had to be in New Orleans on another project and it was right at the time that an institution there got a folio of Audubon's bird paintings. I got in touch with the institution to see if they would allow me to look at it in real colour, and they said yes. Michela, let me tell you, I was blown away by the experience. Completely transported. Those raging Caribbean colours! This museum had a special section on Audubon and I started reading through all these old books about him and visiting the places where he lived and stayed when he was in Louisiana and New Orleans, and it all started to make sense to me. Poems started coming.

I found out that Audubon was in fact born in Haiti. I discovered an entry in which he spoke about first seeing parrots flying across the Haitian skies in all their majestic splendour, before moving to France at the start of the Haitian revolution. After his many wanderings in America, when he reached New Orleans, the place credited with him finding his artistic voice, I started wondering what happened in New Orleans to make him paint a full third of his "Birds of America" there. I believe what happened to Audubon in New Orleans is what happens to me every time I go to New Orleans, which is that I run straight into the Caribbean! Those colourful creole cottages. The bright red hibiscus flowers, green dasheen plants, condensed milk, coconut cakes called pralines, and the incessant smell of sugarcane, to say nothing of the hot tropical climate! Audubon was back in Haiti with his parrots and their blazing colours in New Orleans, as I am always back in Jamaica when I go there, and that aesthetic, I am convinced, is deeply embedded in the work of the father of American ornithology (who was an unrepentant racist, by the way, and who, interestingly enough, had so many rumours following him in New Orleans and from his days in Haiti that he himself was black!). I have yet to see someone try to unravel and speak to the Caribbean aesthetic implied and implicated in Audubon's work, but it is so there. And it was what I had been sensing for years, what I had been feeling, but I did not have a word for it, and what I'd spent so long second-guessing myself about.

So I guess what I would say is yes, there is a Caribbean aesthetic, but it may not be very obvious, and even a creator herself might not know that she is carrying it. I am convinced now that I ended up in Morocco because I had some Moroccan genes in me that I did not even know about. I found this out on a recent DNA test. We know now that trauma is passed down from one generation to another. So why not our aesthetic sense, Michela? But then, we must be wary of generalisations.

Once, an editor sent back a note about my novel *The River's Song* that said: "This story by a black woman writer has been told before!" I remember answering, "Show me where." That is something that I say in response to my work: show me where. And oftentimes that is when people realise that their assumptions about your work are not correct. Not every coming-of-age story by a black woman writer or a Caribbean woman writer, or even a Jamaican woman writer, is the same story, but we are so easily pigeonholed into a "single story". So, yes, I have had this issue come up before.

But the notion of the single story can get refracted in very interesting ways. What exactly do I mean by this? When I was in graduate school at Maryland Institute College of Art and was working on my Female Sexual Desires Project, I collected sexual desires from about one-hundred and fifty women and used these desires to make a body of work that included textile-based, audio and video work. Here again, I was being told this work had been done before, though no one could point me to where, exactly. What was interesting, though, was that I had conceptualised this project as a "we girls" project, but it was not working out that way at all. It pains me to say this, but men were initially more supportive of me than women were, and then some white women were positively hostile to me doing it. Finally, a white woman said to me, "Why are you doing this? This is our project! Why aren't you working on police brutality, which is your project?" I came to realise that anything having to do with desirability, sexuality and femininity and, of course, claiming the category of "woman" was seen as white female territory; anything racialised I could take and own. In other words, if this had been a project on Black Female Sexual Desires instead of Female Sexual Desires it would have been okay for me to do it.

That is another version of the "single story" concept that is oftentimes foisted upon writers and artists and creators who are black women and other minority groups, and we have to forever be on the lookout for such things.

CHRISTINE CRAIG: Among the many striking and haunting images from your autobiographical poems is that of your father, present but absent to his children, unseeing. Was it a conscious choice or the subconscious, acting in its secret and exciting way, that influenced you to turn this painful negative into a positive in your life? That is, a spur that drives you to be actively present, to "see" and record everything very clearly and specifically through both poetry and painting.

JB: I have to say that I have, and for a long time have had, a really good relationship with my father and with so many of the men I am related to. So I am not sure how autobiographical the poems really are of my father per se, though he would have to admit that there were areas and times in my life where and when he faltered. Not long ago, my father and I were talking, and he was looking at my life, at the writer and visual artist I've become, and he said something to the effect that, "If I could have foreseen this, I would have done more." I think, neither of my parents could have seen a life in the arts for me. I know for a fact that my father could not, and this has all come as quite a surprise, if not an outright shock to him. But truthfully, I too could not have foreseen a life for myself in the arts when I was growing up. When I was growing up, I lived with my grandmother and then my mother and my mother's side of the family, and it was only after my mother migrated that I went to live with my father. When I lived with my mother, my father helped with school fees and lunch money and such, but the bulk of my sustenance really fell on her, and I think my father really regrets this. My undergraduate years, all of that was my mother's doing. I guess one could say that it is easy for my father, now that I am adult, to forge a relationship with me, but I think that relationship was being forged long ago, and was, in fact, encouraged by the woman who is now his wife. It takes two to build and sustain a relationship and when I saw that my father wanted one, I reached across the table to make sure that there was one. It was perhaps one of the best moves that I have ever made.

This answer is a roundabout way of saying that while the poems about my father are not overtly autobiographical, I guess questions I had about him must have found their way into some of them. More often than not, though, the father that I reference in the poems was more of a spiritual father, a god figure, with me wondering how he could abandon his children, how he could let his children suffer so. It is a question I still struggle with today.

ANN-MARGARET LIM: As someone who seems to believe in the power of poetry to self-heal, at the very least, do you believe poetry can stop someone from doing something against mankind? Can poetry convince and change someone's mind, or is it only for the converted?

JB: No, no, no, Ann-Margaret, I don't believe that poetry is at all just for the converted. I believe in poetry's power – in the power of words, actually – to excite, to calm, to heal, and to transform. That is why there is a whole field called art therapy. I think poetry can cause people to stop and think and contemplate, and this is among one of poetry's many uses. One of my all-time favourite poems was introduced to me in the only workshop I had with Lorna Goodison. It was Nazim Hikmet's "Things I Didn't Know I Love". I remember falling immediately and totally in love with that poem, so much so that when I went to graduate school – where one of the requirements at the NYU Creative Writing Program, and in Sharon Old's workshop, was memorising and reciting a poem – I remember saying back that long, long poem with my eyes shut tight. I was so sure I would not remember all of it, but I did. I always return to that poem as a centring place for myself and always end up teaching it in my creative writing classes. It has the most calming effect on students, even the ones who proclaim loudly how much they hate poetry. I think that poem, among others, can stop someone from doing something hurtful against another person.

Someone said to me recently that Lorna's poem "Heartease" has gone out into the world and now occupies this place where so many people lay claim to it as a place, real or imagined, that they would like to find. A place of centring and healing. I remember reading Lorna's poem "To Us, All Flowers Are Roses" (another poem I memorised), and so much of Jamaican history and culture is imbued in it that I always feel myself changing while reading and rereading it.

When my grandmother was dying in that narrow hospital bed in Annotto Bay Hospital, the nurses and doctors said she was completely at peace singing hymns and reciting psalms from the Bible, and what are those if not praise poems? Indeed, what else takes us through our lives, my dear Ann-Margaret, but our praise songs and our poems? What else stops us from doing something, converts us or changes our minds? When I worked at UNESCO in Paris, there was a plaque that said something to the effect that, since war begins in the minds of men, this is where peace should begin also. I think poetry has a definite role to play in that regard because all actions start first and foremost in the minds of wo/men.

HAZEL CAMPBELL: Jacqueline, recently I was privileged to read some of your as-yet unpublished short stories. Your love for your homeland Jamaica is a strong part of who you are and seems to be a major influence in your writing – images, landscape, people. But yours is not romantic nostalgia. You highlight the political and social ills which have been affecting the country for some time. Why do you think this necessary?

JB: I think this is necessary because Jamaica is an incredibly complicated place. We have very real social problems that we have to deal with, and it seems to me that the elected officials, of both stripes, are overwhelmed with particularly the issues of corruption, gangs and violence. My grandmother would always lament that Jamaica never always "'tan so". That when she was growing up, Jamaica was a place where you would say in astonishment, "You know, one man kill another man a Westmoreland!" The crime and violence and murder situation on the island is baffling to even people like my father who lived through that horrendous period leading up to the 1980 election, which saw Jamaica come to the brink of civil war. And I don't think the United States and other neo-colonial powers are blameless in this at all.

But I want to point out something else. Oftentimes, complicated feelings in literature are portrayed as political and social ones, especially when it comes to writers from so-called Third World (or developing or middle-income or whatever fashionable term is being used today) countries. But love, too, and tenderness and even nostalgia can be complicated, and I wonder, why do those not get the full-on treatment they deserve? I can think of nothing more fascinating than the things people do for love, particularly when you remove romantic love from the equation. Before his downfall, that was what I found so fascinating about the work of Junot Diaz: the ways in which so many of the women he wrote about were operating out of love; love for their children; love for their country; love for each other which was not romantic or sexual. I know it is incredibly unfashionable to say this right now, because the things for which Diaz is accused are really atrocious, and I believe all the things that the women who came forward say about him. But at the same time I am still left, in his case, with female characters I know and understand. Especially his treatment of mothers and their sons who should really be doing better, but aren't. Now, to me, that is really complicated and interesting and tender and wholly believable and fully human. I aim to do something similar in my work.

PAMELA MORDECAI: In what way do you see your writing and art making a difference in the contemporary USA?

JB: This is a hard question to answer. I think, maybe you would have to ask someone who teaches my work, to get a sense of this. What I would like to think is that I am doing two things: that I am complicating the often-flattened American image of the place I come from as one of violence, an island of desire, or even a mere touristic image, to a more wholesome place full of living, breathing people. I would also like to believe I am intervening in certain unhelpful narratives about Jamaica and the larger Caribbean and saying, no, it nuh go so! When Marcia Douglas so kindly invited me to read at her university in Boulder, she said something so incredibly meaningful to me about *The Gymnast & Other Positions*, which she was teaching. She said, "This is such a teachable book because of all the genres and cross-referencing in it!" I hope I'm doing that for Jamaica, creating rich cross-references. Other times, people have sent me essays that students have written on my work, and you get a glimpse of the impact that your work is having. But it is hard to know and see clearly.

PATRICIA POWELL: Given all the writers you've spoken with and interviewed over these many years and given the state of our world right now, what are some of the themes you think we need to grapple with as Caribbean writers living at home and abroad?

JB: I still think we have to insist on telling the stories of women and girls. Now more than ever. Because there are powerful forces both within Jamaica and elsewhere seeking to silence and/or distort our stories and our voices. It is so interesting that I should get this question from you, Patricia, because I think your focus on healing, and the various pathways to healing, is one theme that we really need to examine more.

How Caribbean women and particularly Jamaican women understand

and negotiate their own sexual agency and sexual pleasure in the face of often transactional sexual exchange and such hyper-masculinity and over-zealous and over-religious policing of female sexuality and female sexual desires is another huge area waiting to be explored fully and further. Women telling erotic tales for their/our pleasure and as a sign of their/our agency and power.

The physical environment, on which so much of our identity both within and outside of the region is understood, not as tourism or what people call the tourism product, but in terms of how the people who live, work, love and die in the Caribbean islands understand and interact with the animal and plant life, with the sun, moon and stars and the ever-present blue mountains that, yes, people like Lorna Goodison and Velma Pollard have been extolling for years, needs to take centre stage in more of our works. We have really messed up beach policies on an island surrounded by the sea. In any case, the beaches are eroding and we are losing our fishes. Too many of the rivers that some of us played in as children have now been poisoned. How are we going to tackle these issues in literature?

I am also fascinated by the ways in which a writer like Marcia Douglas is using her work to question what a novel is. How do you put such a thing as a novel together? She seems to be asserting that a novel does not have to be a linear narrative at all. I find that very, very exciting.

Another area of intense excitement for me is looking at all the women who have paved a way out of no way for us women writers; specifically, the Jean D'Costas, Hazel Campbells and Christine Craigs of our world. Let me be clear here: These writers are still here, they are still writing, they are still innovating, and they could run circles around younger writers any day of the week! But younger writers have to decide how to handle the founda-tions of an incredible legacy. These are but some of the themes we have to grapple with today.

KERRY YOUNG: What have you learnt about Jamaican women and Jamaican women writers as a result of working on this book and these interviews in the last couple of years?

JB: I have learnt that Jamaica is a rich dynamic and very complicated place. There are so many Jamaicas at work in these interviews. There is always the danger that places like Jamaica are reduced to the telling of one story or become known for only one kind of violent narrative. What these interviews show us is that Jamaica is like a canvas that is given to all her writers, with certain key elements in place, but we all choose variously the ways we add to that canvas to tell our individual and various Jamaican stories. You, Kerry, for example, tell many different tales in your compulsively readable Jamaican stories, but at the root of them is the Chinese-Jamaican story refracted in a multitude of different ways, whether it is just-off-the-boat Chinese migrating to Jamaica, or mixed-race Jamaican-Chinese, or many permutations within that continuum. I honestly cannot say I know of another Jamaican writer to date who has done such a sustained and deep dive into the Chinese-Jamaican story as you have. The stories you have written into the overall Jamaican story only add to giving a better and more complete knowledge of who we are as Jamaicans, negating the "one Jamaican story" narrative.

Jamaican women are equally diverse in what they write, when they write and how they write – which is another surprising revelation in this book. For a place some would consider "small", we have produced an amazing array of world-class poets, short story writers, children's book writers and novelists. What is more, several of these writers cross genres easily and effectively, as though genres were things someone else constructed that have little or nothing to do with them. That, to me, is just amazing. Yet for all the work that Jamaican women writers have done and continue to do, they still, like so many other women writers around the world are writing against the grain of the "grand male writers' tradition", and this is something I am hoping that a book like this will help to put a dent in.

LORNA GOODISON: If someone woke you up from deep sleep in the middle of the night and asked you: "Who are you, and what is it that you do?", how would you respond?

JB: Outside of talking about being a writer and a visual artist, I think I would start talking about my relationships. I would start off first by saying I am the child of Michael and Marjorie, and that, as a child I thought my mother was the most beautiful woman in the world with her dark skin and her big Afro, and how my tall, lean, good-looking father, whom I still think of as one of the most handsome men I've ever known, for a long time set me up to have a weakness for good-looking men. I would move on to talking about my grandmother, and this memory that has always stayed with me: One day when I was a wee thing at John Mills All-Age School, I kept trying to convince my little friends that we had a foreigner at home and they would not believe me, so off we all set for my home on Penrith Road, us little jing-bang pickaninnies, probably in grades one or two. Oh, all the roads we had to cross! When my grandmother saw me, she was so startled she ordered us right back to school. I started crying, because I was shame can't be done, but then my grandmother called out to me from the top-floor window of the house and rained foreign sweeties down on us!

Then, Lorna, I would talk next about my great-grandparents in Non-such, and how a part of me has always longed for the settled, beautiful, loving relationship they had. A relationship that would go on to encompass four generations. We great-grandchildren grew up knowing that we belonged to someone. But perhaps, unconsciously, my great-grandparents taught me another lesson, for, to my child's eyes, my great-grandfather looked white, and so I learnt very early on that people who were seemingly different-looking could in fact live together and get along together and be family. This might seem very obvious in the Jamaican and Caribbean case, but not so much when one starts moving out to and living in other parts of the world. That your family could be all kinds of people. My great-grandfather allowed my great-grandmother to be. To make her patchworks and her collages and simply *be*. The other day Sharon Leach and I were on one of our marathon phone calls and she said, "Jacqueline, the men in your family are lovers, not fighters. Very tender souls. Pure cha-cha boys!" And I think this is largely true. These days when I see misogyny in the Jamaican context, and elsewhere, I am still a little befuddled by it. My great-grandfather would have us children tumbling all over him. We would go on long walks in the countryside and he would talk history to me. He was always telling me stories. He and my great grandmother planted and sold roses together. My eternal image is of him trying to calm her down because my great-grandmother could get fiery.

Outside of my family, though, I think if someone should ask me who I am and what I do, I would want to be able to say that I am a friend. Friendship means a great deal to me, as does community. The community of Nonsuch, for example, means a lot to me. I was really happy when I was able to execute a project that put the kids in the Nonsuch Primary School in conversation with kids at Kipp:Starr in Harlem, New York, with travel between both countries and communities for the children. And my various artistic communities of course mean a lot to me. Friendly rivalry can take place, criticism definitely, but not wickedness and bad-mind and definitely not misogyny.

Finally, Lorna, you might not know this, but who I am and what I do is tied up in large part with who you are and what you do. Years ago, I was your student for a summer at the University of Miami. I remember seeing you for the first time as you walked across campus. Your hair was out and you were wearing a long flowing cotton dress. I think the colour of your dress was yellow. You walked under a tree full of orange blossoms. The image is etched and so finely detailed in my mind, even though this was years and years ago. The class was full of students from all over the Caribbean; I distinctly remember Hazel Simmons-McDonald, Jennifer Rahim and Anson Gonzalez. When you got to class and after you introduced yourself and had us introduce ourselves, you pulled out pictures, and we each got one. We started writing. The poem I wrote that day was called "The Picture" and it found its way into my first collection of poems. In so many ways, I think that my way of finding my poetic voice was in and through your work. As the summer progressed, I was in enormous emotional pain. I was suffering a terrible heartbreak over a man who really was not worth it. You were kind enough to want to know what was going on. We ended up reading Nazim Hikmet's "Things I Didn't Know I Loved" and, even more movingly, "Saint Francis and the Sow" by Galway Kinnell. I had gotten into the Graduate Program in Creative Writing where Kinnell taught. In private, you told me it would be okay. I was young, and did not know it then, but you were absolutely correct. It was going to be okay.

I had no idea then who Anson Gonzalez was, and all he had done and tried to do for creative writing in Trinidad. But you did. You talked the director of the summer programme into giving him an award, in recognition for his hard and dedicated work. When it was time to hand out the award at our concluding reading, you didn't want anyone saying how you had worked over the summer to facilitate this award for Anson Gonzalez. Yes, Lorna Goodison, I am so outing you right now! I spoke with you then about starting a literary journal named *Calabash* at NYU, to publish all these writers from all over the Caribbean; you nodded in agreement. We never did leave each other's lives after that, even when we did not speak for years at a time.

What I learnt from you, Lorna, is that community matters. That it is integral to this work we do as writers, artists and creators. That we need to look out for and take care of each other. I guess my ultimate answer, then, to the question of who I am, and what it is that I do is that I am Jacqueline Bishop and I want to do the very same things that Lorna Goodison is doing.

ABOUT THE INTERVIEWERS

Jacqueline Bishop is an award-winning photographer, painter and writer born and raised in Jamaica, who now lives and works in New York City. She is the author of a novel, *The River's Song* (2007), two collections of poems, *Fauna* (2006), and *Snapshots from Istanbul* (2009), an art book, *Writers Who Paint, Painters Who Write: Three Jamaican Artists* (2007), and most recently, *The Gymnast and other Positions* (2015), a collection of short stories, essays and interviews, which won the non-fiction award in 2016 OCM Bocas Prize for Caribbean Literature.

Jacqueline Bishop has had art exhibitions in Europe, North Africa, the United States and Jamaica. She writes a monthly article exploring women and visual culture for the *Huffington Post* and does a series of interviews with artists and art professionals for the *Jamaica Observer* Arts Magazine. Jacqueline Bishop has twice been awarded Fulbright Fellowships, including a year-long grant to Morocco and again as a UNESCO/Fulbright fellow to France. She teaches in the Liberal Studies Program at New York University, and is the founding editor of *Calabash: A Journal of Caribbean Art & Letters*. She is currently researching in the UK.

Dolace McLean holds a law degree from Cornell University Law School and a Ph.D. in English, with a concentration on property law and literature, from New York University. Currently, she holds the position as Legal Counsel to the Lieutenant Governor of the United States Virgin Islands. Formerly McLean owned her own law firm specializing in appellate advocacy. An active member of the Virgin Islands academic and legal communities, Dolace is also a former faculty member of the University of the Virgin Islands where she served as an Assistant Professor of English and produced book reviews, interviews and articles dealing with Law & Caribbean Literature.

INDEX

Opal Palmer Adisa

Caribbean Passion
ISBN: 9781900715928; pp. 96; pub. 2004, £7.99
In a dialectic of oppression and resistance, childhood includes both the affirmation of parents who make her 'leap fences' and the 'jeer of strange men on the street/ that made your feet stumble'; and men are portrayed both as predators and as the objects of erotic desire. This vision of contraries is rooted in an intensely sensuous apprehension of the physical world, drawing from it rewardingly emblematic metaphors, starting points for engaging, conversational meditations on aspects of remembered experience.

I Name Me Name
ISBN: 9781845230449; pp. 160; pub. 2008; £9.99
Autobiographical prose, dramatic monologues, lyric poems, praise songs, blues and prophetic rants enact the construction of an identity, whose centre is a Rastafarian sense of 'i-ness', whose outer dimensions encompass an African Jamaican/American woman's radical consciousness of gender, race, geography, the spiritual and the sensual as the co-ordinates of a dynamic space for dialogue and connection.

Until Judgement Comes
ISBN: 9781845230425; pp. 240; pub. 2007; £8.99
The stories in this collection move the heart and the head. They concern the mystery that is men: men of beauty who are as cane stalks swaying in the breeze, men who are afraid of and despise women, men who prey on women, men who have lost themselves, men trapped in sexual and religious guilt, men who love women and men who are searching for their humanity...

Painting Away Regrets
ISBN: 9781845231521; pp. 358; pub. 2011; £12.99
Christine and Donald are two modern, urban professionals, fundamentally unsuited to one another, but bound by the one thing they have in common – sexual chemistry. Marriage and four children later, they are at a crossroads. Moving easily between the Caribbean, Africa and the USA, the novel dances between the real-life drama that unfolds between the couple, and the spiritual world of the Orishas where every human act has a spiritual ramification.

Jacqueline Bishop

Fauna
ISBN: 9781845230326; pp. 84; pub. 2006; £7.99
"To render the familiar strange and new again is the task of gifted poets. Jacqueline Bishop's poems do this in wonderful ways. She calls upon powerful sources, including world mythology, her own Jamaican ancestry and her full-woman experiences to create these fabulous, shining songs of innocence, loss, birth, rebirth, wit and wisdom. Good job Miss Jacqueline!" – Lorna Goodison

The River's Song
ISBN: 9781845230388; pp. 196; pub. 2007; £8.99
Gloria, living with her mother in a Kingston tenement yard, wins a scholarship to one of Jamaica's best girls' schools. She is the engaging narrator of both the alienating and transforming experiences of an education that takes her away from her mother, friends and the island. She conveys her consciousness of bodily change and sexual awakening; her growth of adult awareness of Jamaica's class divisions, endemic violence and the then new spectre of HIV-AIDS with a winning freshness of expression.

Snapshots from Istanbul
ISBN: 9781845231149; pp. 80; pub. 2009; £7.99
The collection has the intimacy of the confessional, but one grounded in a structure of other narratives and voices that create a counterpoint of dialogue in which the lyric 'I' is only one point of reference. Poems explore the lives of the exiled Roman poet Ovid, and the journeying painter Gauguin, as well as revealing and sometimes painful sojourn in Morocco. Between such differing reasons for departure, Bishop locates her own explorations of where home might be. Like Gauguin, Bishop is driven by the need to discover one's necessity and do it; but as a woman she wonders about those abandoned by such quests.

The Gymnast and Other Positions
ISBN: 9781845233150; pp. 206; pub. 2015; £12.99
Beginning with the promptings of the erotic title story, Jacqueline Bishop saw the hybrid format of this book, with its mix of short stories, essays and interviews, as a way to explore where she had arrived at in a career that encompassed being published as a novelist, poet, critic and exhibited as an artist. How did these sundry positions connect together? What aspects of both conscious intention and unconscious, interior motivations did they reveal? Winner of the 2016 OCM Bocas Prize for Non Fiction.

Hazel Campbell, *Jamaica on My Mind*
ISBN: 9781845234409; pp. 346; pub. 2019; £14.99
These are stories shaped by an artist who never tells the reader what to think, but it is clear enough that here is a radical vision of Caribbean possibility combined with a sharp awareness of how reality so often falls short. Observant of the inequalities of Jamaican society, her writing is neither sentimental nor judgemental over the way her characters so often make the wrong choices. In the space between desire and outcomes, there is often the deepest and most painful kind of comedy. "Jacob Bubbles", a double narrative criss-crossing the days of slavery with the years of political and armed gang warfare between rival communities implicitly asks, in all seriousness, which of her two Jacobs is most free. This collection brings together stories from *The Rag Doll and Other Stories*, *Women's Tongue* and *Singerman*, and eight new stories.

Christine Craig, *All Things Bright & Quadrille for Tigers*
ISBN: 9781845231729; pp. 160; pub. 2010; £9.99
This double collection exemplifies sharp observation, disarming honesty about human complexities, and a sophisticated sense of landscape and space. These are poems about Jamaica that express an undoubted but often troubled and

uncertain love for the island and a pride in how its creative power spreads beyond its shores. Offering a compelling immersion into what can best be described as Caribbean metaphysical poetics, this collection contains an indigenous secular spirituality that obscures the divide between the spiritual and the sensual.

Marcia Douglas

Electricty Comes to Cocoa Bottom
ISBN: 9781900715287; pp. 80; pub. 1999; £7.99
This collection takes the reader on a journey of light, from the flicker of the firefly in rural Jamaica, through the half-moonlight of the limbo of exile in the USA to the point of arrival and reconnection imaged by the eight-pointed star. It is also a journey of the voice, traversing back and forth across the Atlantic and across continents, pushing its way through word censors and voice mufflers and ending in tongues of fire. A Poetry Book Society recommendation, its selector commented on the "intent but relaxed concentration which ushers the reader into the life of a poem and makes the event... seem for a while like the centre of things. This is a rich and very welcome book."

Notes from a Writer's Book of Cures and Spells
ISBN: 9781845230166; pp. 200; pub. 2005; £9.99
"Writing is a cover for necromancy", Carmen Innocencia accuses her creator, Flamingo Tongue, a young Jamaican writer. Carmen is not the only one of Flamingo's creations to confront her author, for her characters and their tragic, heartening stories come vividly alive, perhaps too alive, and just to make sure she can control them, Flamingo makes doll figures of them, but even then... As Carmen's accusation suggests, this is a novel set at the cross-roads between the living and the dead – a cemetery literally becomes the refuge of the orphaned children at the narrative's centre. This a world where election-time violence, dreams, spirit possession and women who become snails are equally real.

The Marvellous Equations of the Dread: a Novel in Bass Riddim
ISBN: 9781845233327; pp. 285; pub. 2016; £9.99
Bob Marley is dead. The Emperor Haile Selassie has been brutally murdered. The Kingston gangs are at war, and the people have lost all trust in self-serving politicians. It is hard to imagine worse times. Marcia Douglas tells the twin stories of Jamaica's nihilistic violence and its wondrously creative humanity and does truthful justice to both. The novel spans the Kingston ghettoes, the Emperor's palace in Addis Ababa and Zion; the stories of the deaf Leenah who writes a powerful woman version of events; the relationship between Fall-down (street madman and fallen angel) and Delroy the orphaned street-boy, and the meetings in the clock tower at Half Way Tree between Bob Marley, Marcus Garvey and the island's dead. Once, an enslaved boy was hung from the silk cotton tree in 1766; the novel sets out to retrieve the word at the tip of his tongue.

Millicent A.A. Graham

The Damp in Things
ISBN: 9781845230838; pp. 58; pub. 2009; £7.99
These are poems about family, love, spirituality, fear and desire, where

the dampness of things is equally about the humid sensuality of the island, andt Graham's belief in fecundity, fertility and the unruliness of the imagination. Her sense of irony, and instinct for freshness in image constantly surprise. Graham knows the tradition of Caribbean poetry, and is deeply aware of the value of both homage and resistance. The result is a wonderfully executed balancing act that ultimately suggests a newness of sensibility and imagination.

The Way Home
ISBN: 9781845232344; pp. 56; pub 2014; £8.99
There are comforts – the landscape, the flora and fauna, the food, festivals, country Sundays and moments of tenderness – and there are the disquiets – the bullying, the violence, the fearfulness of childhood, the failure of memory, the losses. In these intimate poems, Millicent Graham further marks out a distinct poetic territory for herself with an immediately recognizable voice, an assured handling of language and a daring richness of image. These are quirky, haunting, profoundly intelligent poems; with their allusions to popular culture, classic literature, myth and folklore, they resist any easy categorization.

Sharon Leach, *Love It When You Come, Hate It When You Go*
ISBN: 9781845232368; pp. 162; pub. 2014; £8.99
These stories occupy new territory in Caribbean writing. Their characters are neither the rural folk, the sufferers of the urban ghetto, or the old prosperous brown and white middle class of the hills rising above the city, but the black urban salariat of the unstable lands in between, of the new housing developments. These are people struggling for their place in the world, eager for entry into the middle class but always anxious that their hold on security is precarious. Characters pay lip service to the pieties of family life, but discover they are no less spaces of risk, vulnerability and abuse. Sharon Leach brings a cool, unsentimental eye to her characters' misjudgements and self-deceptions without losing sight of their humanity. She writes about sex, its joys, disappointments and degradations with a frankness little matched in existing Caribbean writing.

Ann-Margaret Lim
The Festival of Wild Orchid
ISBN: 9781845232016; pp. 80; pub. 2012; £8.99
Poems of pungent phrase and arresting image respond frankly to the poverty, sharp social divisions, endemic violence and misogyny that blight Jamaican lives. Written in both standard Caribbean English and Jamaican patois, the poems reveal an engaging poetic persona, bold and questioning, who sees her world with wit and insight. The shaping of that persona is explored in poems that reflect on a Chinese and African Jamaican heritage and on experiences good and bad.

Kingston Buttercup
ISBN: 9781845233303; pp. 72; pub. 2016; £8.99
A fresh, honest, and tenderly-fierce perspective comes through in highly readable lyric poems that explore a range of locales, from the sea bottom, the underside of bridges, the riverbeds, the Taíno hills, the cane fields, the Kingston cityscape and the Jamaican countryside. She draws from complex subject matter: plantation diaries, slave narratives, and the poet's own family's multi-generational, entwined

stories from China, West Africa, Venezuela, Puerto Rico, and Jamaica. Lim writes about life as a woman, daughter and mother with empathy, great love and the sometimes urgent, cleansing fire.

Shara McCallum
The Face of Water: New & Selected Poems
ISBN: 9781845231866; pp. 140; pub. 2011; £9.99
Poems reflect a Jamaican childhood in a Rastafarian home filled with reckless idealism, the potential for emotional pathology, and a grounding in folk traditions, and explore what it means to emerge from such a space and enter a new world of American landscapes and values. These are poems of deft craft with a sense of music caught in graceful lines. Poems transform the most painful and sometimes mundane details of life into works of terrible and satisfying beauty.

Madwoman
ISBN: 9781845233396; pp. 72; pub. 2017; £8.99
"Shara McCallum is like a great marathoner traversing myth, mind, and memory. Her work steers us through the heart of troubled landscapes, as well as the landscapes of the troubled heart. 'In the country where she lives which is no country, the madwoman maps desire's coordinates onto her body,' she writes in this wise, fiery new collection. There are no other poets writing with McCallum's beautiful intensities of form and feeling." —Terrance Hayes

Velma Pollard
And Caret Bay Again, New and Selected Poems
ISBN: 9781845232092; pp. 190; pub. 2013; £10.99
Since her first published collection in 1988, but as an established poet long before then, Velma Pollard has been an essential voice of Jamaica and the Caribbean. In this selection from four previous collections and a substantial set of new poems, we see the signal qualities of her work – its mature reflectiveness, quiet integrity, its ability to reach to the heart of Caribbean tragedies, both political and personal, without sentimentality, stridency or loss of hope.

Considering Woman I & II
ISBN: 9781845231699; pp. 160; pub. 2010; £8.99
In 1989, Velma Pollard's *Considering Woman* – short stories, fables and memoir – announced an important publishing debut. Twenty years later, a second collection, *Considering Woman II*, various and rich in its own right, was brought into dialogue with the republishing of the earlier pieces in a single volume. If the later stories no longer feel the need to reflect on the process and reception of women's writing (which the earlier collection does very wittily), across all the work is an acutely sensitive consciousness of the consequences of the passage of time.

Patricia Powell
The Fullness of Everything
ISBN: 9781845231132; pp. 232; pub. 2009; £8.99
When Winston receives a telegram informing him of his father's imminent death, his return to Jamaica is very reluctant. Twenty-five years in the USA

without contact with his family has allowed resentments to mature and trap him in the traumas of his childhood. When he discovers he has a half-sister no one has told him about, his fury knows no bounds. But it is Rosa, his father's outside child, who in the end offers Winston some focus for his feelings. Told through the perspectives of Winston and his estranged brother, Septimus, the novel becomes the story of their attempts to heal the breach between them. Seamlessly combining an intense psychological realism with magical elements that are no surprise to her characters, the novel has much to say about the power of forgiveness and the possibility of transcending hurt.

Olive Senior
The Pain Tree
ISBN: 9781845233488; pp. 184; pub. 2017; £9.99
These stories are wide-ranging in scope, time period, theme, locale, and voice. There is – along with her characteristic "conversational voice" – reverence, wit and wisdom, satire, humour, and even farce. The stories range in time from around the second world war to the present and the terror of gang warfare in the city. Like her earlier stories, Jamaica is the setting, but the range of characters presented are universally recognisable as people in crisis or on the cusp of transformation. Perhaps more directly than in earlier collections, Olive Senior reveals a radically critical moral and social vision.

Tanya Shirley
She Who Sleeps with Bones
ISBN: 9781845230876; pp. 76; pub. 2009; £7.99
The hauntings of memory lead to eloquently shaped epiphanies that turn what appear on the surface to be simple and tidy stories into profound meditations on the human condition. Shirley acts as a witness to the lives of those around her, yet she is a biased witness, one who has become so enmeshed in the lives of her 'characters' that gradually we become convinced that she has erased the lines that would allow us to distinguish her from the people who enter her work. The collection is anchored by a series of spiritual poems that beautifully enact the mysteries of inner sight and clairvoyance of a poet who is a reluctant seer, who comes from a family of seers.

The Merchant of Feathers
ISBN: 9781845232337; pp. 72; pub. 2014; £8.99
This second collection of poems confirms why Tanya Shirley is so much in demand for readings, presenting a poetic persona of a woman who is "sometimes dangling from high wires/ but always out in the open". So that whilst there is no one who so wittily skewers the misogynistic, she is also honest about the complicity of women in their own acts of submission, of how "I danced flat-footed in your dense air". There is joy in the energy and delights of the body but also a keen awareness of ageing and the body's derelictions. If there is one overarching vision it is that love is "larger than the space we live in", a love represented by the "merchant of feathers… now a woman/ selling softness in these hard times", or the mother who tends the battered face of her son, the victim of a homophobic beating.

YOU CAN ORDER DIRECT FROM WWW.PEEPALTREEPRESS.COM